POSSUMS
& BIRD DOGS

PETER NOLAN

POSSUMS
& BIRD DOGS

**AUSTRALIAN ARMY AVIATION'S
161 RECONNAISSANCE FLIGHT
IN SOUTH VIETNAM**

ALLEN&UNWIN

First published in 2006

Copyright © Peter Nolan 2006

All rights reserved. No part of this book may be reproduced or transmitted in any form or by any means, electronic or mechanical, including photocopying, recording or by any information storage and retrieval system, without prior permission in writing from the publisher. The *Australian Copyright Act 1968* (the Act) allows a maximum of one chapter or 10% of this book, whichever is the greater, to be photocopied by any educational institution for its educational purposes provided that the educational institution (or body that administers it) has given a remuneration notice to Copyright Agency Limited (CAL) under the Act.

Allen & Unwin
83 Alexander Street
Crows Nest NSW 2065
Australia
Phone: (61 2) 8425 0100
Fax: (61 2) 9906 2218
Email: info@allenandunwin.com
Web: www.allenandunwin.com

National Library of Australia
Cataloguing-in-Publication entry:

Nolan, Peter Edward, 1940– .
    Possums and bird dogs : Australian Army Aviation's 161
    Reconnaissance Flight in South Vietnam.

    ISBN 1 74114 635 6 (pbk.).
    ISBN 1 74175 042 3 (limited edition HB)

    1. Australia. Army Aviation Corp. Reconnaissance flight,
    161 – History. 2. Vietnamese Conflict, 1961–1975 –
    Personal narratives, Australian. 3. Vietnamese Conflict,
    1961–1975 – Aerial operations, Australian. I. Australia.
    Army Aviation Corp. Reconnaissance flight, 161. II. Title.

959.7043394

Maps by Winifred Mumford
Typeset in 12/14 pt Adobe Garamond by Midland Typesetters, Australia
Printed by CMO Image Printing, Singapore

10 9 8 7 6 5 4 3 2 1

*This book is dedicated to the Australians and
New Zealanders of 161 Reconnaissance Flight, especially
those who did not return or did not grow old*

Contents

Foreword by Brigadier Bill Mellor — ix
List of maps — xiii
Preface — xv
Prologue — xvii

Part 1: Deployment to Bien Hoa 1965–66
1   161 Recce Flight: Formation and deployment — 3
2   Bien Hoa: Fitting in — 10
3   Learning the ropes: October 1965–May 1966 — 20

Part 2: Joining the Task Force
4   The 1st Australian Task Force — 39
5   Vung Tau: May 1966–March 1967 — 52
6   Relocation to Nui Dat — 67
7   Nui Dat: March–December 1967 — 85

Part 3: The Tet Offensive
8   The Tet and Second General Offensives: January–July 1968 — 105
9   The aftermath: August 1968–February 1969 — 126

Part 4: Pacification: March 1969–September 1971

10	Pacification: March–December 1969	139
11	Maintaining the effort: January–December 1970	158
12	The final challenge: January–September 1971	175
13	The end phase: August 1971–March 1972	193

Epilogue		203
Appendix 1: 161 Reconnaissance Flight/161 (Independent)		
Reconnaissance Flight: Nominal Roll 1965–72		204
Appendix 2: Honours and awards		211
Glossary of terms and acronyms		216
Notes		221
Bibliography		231
Index		233

Foreword

Ambrose Bierce, in his bitingly satirical book, *The Devil's Dictionary*, defines history as 'an account mostly false, of events mostly unimportant, which are brought about by rulers mostly knaves, and soldiers mostly fools'. It is a cynical view, quite devoid of any understanding of the role of the reader in determining the success or otherwise of a historical account. No doubt there are many well-regarded histories of knavish rulers and foolish soldiers, but those that are inaccurate or irrelevant do not survive for long.

There are many accounts of the Australian involvement in the Vietnam War, ranging from analyses of the strategic direction of the war through to the detailed examination of a single battle. On return from South Vietnam, each battalion that served there produced an account of the tour, which has served as a contemporary record of the people, places and events that contributed to the Vietnam experience. Other units and organisations have done the same, sometimes following the passage of many years, and the gaining of much perspective. In nearly all of these accounts, the service and achievements of the small Army Aviation contingent that supported the various units has been at least acknowledged and more often lauded. While this has provided a thin and disjointed view of Army Aviation in Vietnam, nowhere has there been a complete account of the Vietnam experience of 161 (Independent) Reconnaissance Flight. This has left a deficiency in the coverage of the Vietnam War and a gap in the development of the Australian Army's aviation capability that has grown more pronounced as the years have passed.

Army Aviation, with its fledgling capability, was not even a recognised branch of the Army when the first Army and Air Force personnel of 161 Recce Flight arrived at Bien Hoa in 1965. That it became officially established as a corps, alongside the Infantry, Artillery, Armour and others, just three years later is due in no small part to the energy and service of that group and the others that followed. The growth of the Australian Army Aviation Corps and the aeronautical elements of the Royal Australian Electrical and Mechanical Engineers since then has been extraordinary and it has all been built on the solid foundation of the operational successes of the Possums of 161 Recce Flight.

For those who joined Army Aviation shortly after the withdrawal of the Flight from South Vietnam, the lack of a written account of what was done, by whom, and how, was largely inconsequential. The instructors, the technicians, the supply personnel and commanders had all served with the Possums, and most would willingly pass on their wisdom and experience to those eager to learn. There was no doubt envy on the part of the recipients, and perhaps a little disdain from a very few of those who had met the challenges of Vietnam for those who hadn't. But the lessons from the first time that the Australian Army had fielded a unit of light helicopters and fixed wing aircraft in an operational setting were there to be learned. The Mess bars and the Diggers' boozers were as much a part of the training regime as the cockpit and the classroom.

As time passed, however, there were fewer and fewer captains and corporals to whom the new pilots and technicians could turn to find out what it was really like. For a very long time, mapping surveys of neighbouring countries provided the only opportunities to get overseas on an operation, and the only people who shot at Army aircraft were frightened tribesmen and angry farmers—both with comforting inaccuracy. The opportunity to gain from the experience of others diminished and was replaced by the requirement to learn only through doctrine. But doctrine without the leaven of history is flat and arid, and the learning is correspondingly limited.

From this perspective alone, the value of this book cannot be overstated. It paints a comprehensive and detailed picture of the service of 161 in Vietnam and does so using the broader canvas of the operations of the Australian Task Force. It shows how the soldiers and airmen of the Flight developed and adapted to the new and changing environment, and handled the challenges and stresses of war. It portrays the camaraderie and the tensions that come with operational service, but with added perspective that only distance can provide.

This is not a text-book history, but a textual history. War diary entries and anecdotes rest comfortably side by side; the former providing the veracity, the latter providing the colour and atmosphere. It makes for an excellent balance. Peter Nolan is to be commended for his perseverance, his patience and his entertaining and informative product. Some may take the Bierce approach and quibble with the accuracy of this or that; some may challenge the relevance of bits and pieces; but no one who reads *Possums and Bird Dogs* will hold to the view that the leaders of 161 (Independent) Recce Flight were knaves and the soldiers and airmen were fools.

W.J.A. Mellor, DSC, AM
Brigadier (Ret)
Brookfield, Queensland
27 November 2005

Maps

1. Map 2.1: 173 Brigade base area and Australian unit locations — 12
2. Map 3.1: Third Corps Tactical Zone — 21
3. Map 3.2: Phuoc Tuy province — 33
4. Map 4.1: Initial 1ATF tactical area of responsibility, June 1966 — 43
5. Map 6.1: Australian task force base, Nui Dat, 1967 — 69
6. Map 8.1: 1ATF deployment on Operation *Coburg*, January 1968 — 107
7. Map 8.2: 1ATF deployment on Operation *Toan Thang 1*, April–June 1968 — 114

Preface

As the first Australian Army Aviation unit to be deployed on active service, 161 Reconnaissance Flight made an important contribution to Australian operations during the conflict in South Vietnam. In the longer term, its success was vital to the ongoing development of Army Aviation's role and capabilities. The Flight's history assumes added significance when viewed in this light. The men who flew its aircraft using the Possum call sign went on to become leaders in Army Aviation. Similarly, the task force officers who flew with them during battalion operations later occupied very senior posts in the Australian Defence Force. They had first-hand experience of the vital role that versatile aircraft, used with initiative, could play in the prosecution of the ground war. With their support, Army Aviation has not looked back. Among its current flying units is a later version of 161 Reconnaissance Flight that continues to perform with distinction in areas where units of the Australian Defence Force are sent in pursuit of military and humanitarian objectives.

My aim in compiling this history was to ensure that 161's story was recorded while opportunities remained to obtain oral histories. We have already lost many of our colleagues. The passing of my good friend Lieutenant Colonel (Retired) Tom Guivarra in 2004 was a reminder that time is precious. He was one of a kind who is sadly missed wherever

Army aviators gather. The memories of the veterans I interviewed complemented the unit history collected over many years by Warrant Officer (Retired) Len Avery for the 161 Recce Association. Len's records and technical knowledge were invaluable. His dedication was recognised by the award of a Medal of the Order of Australia (OAM) in the Australia Day 2006 honours list. He is the real historian behind this project and must be acknowledged as such. The official histories so ably written by Ian McNeill and Ashley Ekins also assisted greatly in the development of a framework to place 161's role in the context of the complex and diverse operations undertaken in South Vietnam.

My foremost concern was to provide an accurate historical record that encompassed the various locations from which the Flight operated; the diversity of operational tasks undertaken; the introduction of new aircraft types and capabilities; and 161's relationships with other units and forces. I have tried to avoid a dry recitation of operations and events by telling much of the story through the voices of the pilots and the men who supported the sustained, intensive flying effort required.

I extend heartfelt thanks to all who contributed to this project. It began with my wife Robyn showing war historian Gary McKay some whimsical drivel I had written about my tour with 161. Gary put it to me that there was a large gap in the military record that I should help to fill. Robyn, a clinical psychologist who has treated many veterans with war-related disorders, urged me to accept the challenge. She also contributed valuable technical support, using her computing skills to good effect in the restoration and preservation of written and photographic records. Gary has been a great mentor. As the author of several similar histories, his advice on content and research made instant sense to me.

Thanks also to Ian Bowring of Allen & Unwin, who granted my plea for a few thousand extra words, and to the Possums of 161 who agreed to be interviewed. To those I missed, and to the many whose stories are not told, I apologise. Sadly, all of the people and events of seven years cannot be covered in any one book of reasonable size. Those who do have a voice speak for all of you. Their stories show clearly that the success of 161 was founded in a 'whatever it takes' attitude shared by all elements of the Flight. Whether rogues or heroes, you delivered the goods with style. Thank you all for the humour as well as the professionalism. I am proud to have served with you.

Prologue

The story of Army Aviation begins before the days of the First World War, a conflict in which Army pilots flew their vulnerable little aeroplanes in dizzying duels with their opponents and lived and died according to a code of chivalry unseen in later wars. The aeroplane's potential as a weapon of war was not then fully appreciated, but it was already apparent that an observer could see much further, and in much more detail, from the basket of a tethered balloon. The cockpit of an aircraft was an even better vantage point as it could be moved as required to extend the view or to gain a sharper focus. In this way, airborne visual reconnaissance techniques were born.

Technological advances brought new capabilities. Airborne radio communications enabled reconnaissance pilots to provide immediate information on the movements of enemy forces to commanders on the ground. They could observe the impact of artillery shells and quickly bring the big guns on to target. The advent of airborne photography permitted hard evidence to be provided to sceptical command staff. A hundred and one uses were soon found for aircraft in support of tactical, liaison and logistic support operations, and the introduction of light observation helicopters in the early 1950s marked the beginning of a new era. A helicopter could operate from a small landing zone instead of the airstrip required by its fixed wing counterpart. Larger helicopters enabled pilots to insert troops, resupply them and evacuate the wounded. The need for paratroops was thus reduced. Still to come were the armed fixed and rotary winged aircraft that could provide close air support for the troops on the ground as well as being the eyes and ears of the battlefield. Military aviation had come to stay, with the United States leading the charge in terms of technology and new battlefield doctrine.

A vital testing ground for the new US Army Aviation capabilities was the war in Vietnam. Australian Army Aviation, expanded in 1960 to provide better and more varied support for troops in the field, earned its spurs there as well.

Australian Army Aviation: A brief history

The Australian Flying Corps was manned by Army pilots during the First World War. The Royal Australian Air Force (RAAF) was founded in 1921 and the Australian Army's links with aviation became tenuous as the RAAF assumed responsibility for flying machines of all types. However, a continuing association with British Army Aviation provided a source of training and experience to maintain a core of Army flying expertise. Australian Army pilots served with UK forces in Korea, with Captain Bryan Luscombe the first Australian Army pilot to be killed in action. They also flew in the Far East with British forces.

In Australia, from 1951 to 1960, Army pilots flew Austers of 16 Air Observation Post (AOP) Flight, supported by RAAF and Army flying instructors and RAAF maintenance staff. Another small flying unit, 1 Army Aviation Company, was formed at Sydney's Bankstown airport in mid-1957 to support Army operations including Survey Corps tasks, Citizens' Military Force exercises and reconnaissance for the School of Military Engineering. The unit had no aircraft, so pilots hired whatever they could in the locality they were tasked for.

One of its foundation members, then Sergeant Bevan Smith, recalled this adventurous period:

> We hired the aircraft from aero clubs, private owners, crop dusters—anywhere we could get them. We hired them where it was most cost effective; for example when operating in the south of Western Australia we would hire in Perth. When working in the Kimberley we sometimes hired

in Adelaide. Unfortunately, the only aircraft we could hire there was a Cessna 180 crop duster which was full of chemical residue and most unpleasant to fly in turbulent conditions as the cockpit became a cloud of foul smelling dust. Its call sign was Romeo Alpha Tango, which was appropriate. It was a mess and became known as 'The Rampant Rodent'. We once received a signal from Staff Sergeant Charlie Miller in Normanton saying, 'Lost engine on take off.' This was literally true. The engine mounts had rusted through and the engine drooped down into the cowl. Fortunately, he was not yet airborne and could abort the take-off.[1]

Better things were to come. On 1 December 1960, the formation of 16 Army Light Aircraft Squadron (16 ALA) established a significant operational and training capability. Equipped with Cessna 180 fixed wing aeroplanes and Bell Sioux G2A helicopters, the squadron could eventually deploy aircraft in support of single service, joint and combined operations. There was still a strong RAAF presence in both aircrew and maintenance roles, but fitters and turners and vehicle mechanics from the Corps of Royal Australian Electrical and Mechanical Engineers (RAEME) were being trained as airframe and engine fitters. Instrument, radio and electrical tradesmen joined them to enable the Army to service its own aircraft. On the flying side, Army fixed wing pilots underwent instructor training and gained instructional experience with the Royal Air Force Central Flying School and the UK Army Air Corps. Their rotary wing counterparts were trained at the US Army Aviation Centre at Fort Rucker in Alabama. On their return to Australia, the new Army qualified flying instructors (QFIs) began to fill instructional and command roles in which they trained Army graduates of the RAAF's Basic Flying Training School at Point Cook, Victoria, to fly Army aircraft. Within a few years, 16 ALA would be self-sufficient.

The RAAF's operational and technical oversight of Australian Army aviation was reflected in a directive which defined precisely the scope and limitations of the latter:

> The roles of Army Aviation are:
> 1   Command and control.
> 2   Artillery observation.
> 3   Liaison and communication duties.
> 4   Air dispatch letter services, message dropping and photo delivery.
> 5   Battlefield surveillance, including reconnaissance to supplement that carried out by the Navy and Air Force.

6. Cable laying and carrying of equipment to establish radio relay stations.
7. As a supplementary role, support of survey operations by the deployment and maintenance of field survey teams and the carriage of airborne survey equipment within the capacity of Army aircraft to meet the basic roles and with air transport support being provided by the Air Force.
8. Additional tasks normally performed by Navy and Air Force aircraft but which may be undertaken by Army aircraft, within the capacity of the aircraft to meet the basic roles, including:
    i photography;
    ii casualty evacuation; and
    iii limited urgent carriage of freight and personnel.[2]

These guidelines were reflected in the use of Army aircraft from the early 1960s. RAAF oversight of Army flying and maintenance operations continued during the Vietnam era. This circumstance created friction at times. The progressive ideas and practices of Army operators were not appreciated by conservative senior RAAF officers whose approach to operations reflected their experience of conventional warfare rather than the counterinsurgency doctrine which was the basis for Army operations in South Vietnam.

Vietnam: The seeds of conflict

The background to the conflict in South Vietnam is a story in two parts. The colonisation of Vietnam by France is a long and colourful saga that reached its climax after the Second World War. In 1946, the Revolutionary League for the Independence of Vietnam led by Ho Chi Minh rose against the French. The uprising triggered the First Indochina War which culminated in the bloody defeat of the French at Dien Bien Phu in May 1954. Despite this victory, Vietnam was far from being a unified nation rejoicing in its freedom from a colonial master. There was already an established rivalry between the political forces of the north and south of Vietnam that threatened the outbreak of civil war. A Geneva Conference was convened in May 1954 to seek a solution. Vietnam was temporarily partitioned into North and South at the 17th parallel, with the aim of having a national election by 1956 aimed at unification under one government. Ho Chi Minh quickly took formal control of North Vietnam. In the South, Ngo Dinh Diem was installed as prime minister under the emperor Bao Dai, but it wasn't long before Bao Dai was ousted in 1955 and Diem, as its first president, announced the formation of the Republic of Vietnam. The national elections planned to unify Vietnam did not eventuate. Instead, the stage was set for further hostilities.

The broader backdrop to the conflict was the Cold War. Following the Second World War, the West was fearful of the spread of Marxist-Leninist influence. Mao Tse Tung's victory against the Nationalist forces of Chiang Kai-Shek in China fuelled the perception of communism as a threat to Western interests. The United States responded with a foreign policy of containment of further attempts to expand communist influence in Asia. The Korean War was conducted along these lines and reached its impasse in 1953. At the same time, the Americans were propping up the French in Vietnam against the communist-supported forces of Ho Chi Minh. The ousting of the French and the subsequent partition of Vietnam along Cold War lines was sufficient to ensure continuing American support for Diem's regime in the South. The Domino Theory of incremental communist expansion through the subjugation of smaller nations became the rationale for the ever-increasing involvement of the United States in Indochina.

In 1957, Viet Cong[3] guerillas, their officers trained by North Vietnamese communists, commenced operations in South Vietnam against officials and institutions of President Diem's government. Their numbers included fighters hardened by previous conflicts with Japan during the Second World War and France in the First Indochina War. The Viet Cong were opposed by the Army of the Republic of South Vietnam (ARVN), backed by American aid and military advisors.

In March 1959, Ho Chi Minh declared a 'people's war' to unite all of Vietnam, thus triggering the Second Indochina War. Within months, the construction of the vital Ho Chi Minh trail began. Used to funnel a stream of North Vietnam Army soldiers and equipment into South Vietnam, the trail became a 2400-kilometre network of jungle trails and mountain passes along Vietnam's western border and through eastern regions of Laos and Cambodia.

The broader political scene continued to develop along established Cold War lines. In January 1961, Soviet President Nikita Kruschev pledged support for wars of national liberation worldwide. Ho Chi

Minh was greatly encouraged in his aim of unifying Vietnam as a communist state. In February 1962, the United States Military Assistance Command for Vietnam was established to support the gradual escalation of American military involvement in Vietnam. By the end of 1964, American military advisors there numbered 23 000. At the same time an estimated 170 000 Viet Cong and North Vietnamese Army soldiers had begun waging coordinated attacks against ARVN troops in the Saigon area.

By early 1965, it was evident that the South Vietnamese forces were not coping. It was time for the United States to commit to the introduction of its own combat forces or to withdraw. It chose the former course with the aim of forcing a political settlement between North and South Vietnam. The first US combat troops to arrive in Vietnam, a force of 3500 marines, landed in March 1965 to defend the American air base at Da Nang. By the end of 1965, more than 180 000 US troops had been committed.

Australia's involvement began in July 1962 with the commitment of the Australian Army Training Team Vietnam (AATTV) to work with South Vietnamese forces. Militarily, Australia was in a cleft stick. Its forces were thin on the ground and there was still a commitment to a presence in Malaysia following the Malayan Emergency and the confrontation with Indonesia in the early 1960s. Britain had announced its policy of withdrawing forces east of Suez, and had in any case been replaced by the United States as Australia's primary ally following the Second World War. The Australian Government, long fearful of isolation in the context of the threat from the 'red hordes' of Asia, wanted to show its powerful friend that it was willing and able to offer support in South Vietnam. However, it would take time and conscription to build the necessary capability and there was a great deal of vacillation about the structure and strength of a military commitment. As an initial measure, the First Battalion, the Royal Australian Regiment (1RAR) was sent in June 1965 to join the US 173rd Airborne Brigade (Separate) at Bien Hoa air base near Saigon. In July 1965, the Australian Government committed support units, including an aviation element, to enhance the contribution made by 1RAR. This provided breathing space to develop a more substantial capability. In 1966, it increased its commitment to brigade level with the establishment of the 1st Australian Task Force (1ATF) at Nui Dat in Phuoc Tuy province.

So it was that 161 Reconnaissance (Recce) Flight was raised at Amberley for deployment to South Vietnam. Four Army aircraft with 51 flying and support personnel arrived at Bien Hoa in September 1965 for operations in support of 1RAR. The Flight was expanded in 1966 and renamed 161 (Independent) Recce Flight. It operated in South Vietnam until 1972.

This is 161's story.

Part 1

Deployment to Bien Hoa 1965–66

1

161 Recce Flight:
Formation and deployment

Captain Paul Lipscombe was a happy man. It was a clear midwinter day in July 1965 at RAAF Base Amberley in southeast Queensland. The base was host to 16 Army Light Aircraft Squadron (16 ALA), in which Paul served as an instructor pilot on Cessna 180 fixed wing aircraft. Paul's Commanding Officer, Lieutenant Colonel Bill Slocombe, had just told him that he was to raise and command 161 Recce Flight on operations in South Vietnam. The Flight would be the first Australian Army Aviation unit to be deployed on active service. As Officer Commanding (OC),[1] he would hold the rank of major. He would now put into practice the flying and leadership skills acquired during eleven years of training and experience since graduating from the Army's Officer Cadet School at Portsea, Victoria, in June 1954.

Paul was surprised at his selection as the first OC. The long association between Army Aviation's Air Observation Post role and the Royal Australian Artillery Corps (the 'Gunners') meant that most Army pilots had been drawn from that Corps. The Gunners now filled the senior ranks in Army Aviation. Paul, who had been assigned to the Royal Australian Army Service Corps (RAASC) on graduation from officer training, had expected them to choose one of their own to command the Flight in Vietnam. However, his experience fitted him well for the post. He learned to fly while serving in Tasmania as a platoon commander in 18 National Service Battalion. Later, he gained his UK commercial licence while on secondment to the British Army in Malaya in 1958–59. When the Australian Army called for applications for pilot training to support its expansion of aviation capabilities, Paul was ready. He was reasonably experienced and was endorsed on single and twin-engined aircraft, including the Cessna 180 which had been chosen as the Army's fixed wing aircraft. He was selected for training and in due course received his Australian Army wings. In 1961, he completed instructor training at the RAF Central Flying School before gaining experience as a staff instructor on Provost and Gnat aircraft. He was then assigned to the Army Air Corps in Britain as an instructor before moving on to flying duties at Kuching in Borneo. During the Indonesian confrontation with Malaysia, he served as the aviation officer for the British Army's 1 Commando Brigade on operations in Borneo before returning to Kuching to command 17 Flight, 656 Squadron. He then spent several months as a check pilot with the British Army flight in Hong Kong before returning to Amberley as a qualified flying instructor (QFI) to train Australian Army pilots. His familiarity with operations in the Southeast Asian environment was perhaps a factor in his selection as OC.

Preparations for deployment

The formation of 161 Recce Flight in July anticipated the Australian Government's announcement on 17 August 1965 that it was sending support units to join 1RAR at Bien Hoa in South Vietnam. Paul Lipscombe's elation at being chosen to command 161 was tempered by the fact that he had just two months to raise the unit and to have it ready for departure in September. His mind was already racing as he left his CO's office. It wasn't just a simple matter of getting hold of another couple of gung-ho pilots and heading off to join the grunts (infantry soldiers) already at war. There were formal and complex matters of planning to be undertaken: the Flight's establishment, training, operational procedures, maintenance facilities, personnel, transport, spares and many more issues had to be addressed with haste.

161 Recce Flight was allocated four aircraft: two Bell 47G-3B1 Sioux light observation helicopters and two Cessna 180 fixed wing aircraft. Apart from Paul and his Administrative Officer, Lieutenant John Purvis, there would be six officer pilots and 43 Other Ranks (ORs) including maintenance fitters, clerks, cooks, drivers, storemen, signallers—all of the elements needed to make up the small, largely self-sufficient unit that 161 had to be. The Flight was unusual in that it operated both fixed and rotary wing aircraft. Further, the aircraft maintenance workshops element included a number of Air Force tradesmen to supervise and carry out maintenance duties while more fitters and mechanics from the Royal Australian Electrical and Mechanical Engineers (RAEME) were being trained for this role.

The pilots, except for Paul's helicopter section commander Captain Bevan Smith, were relatively inexperienced and none had flown on active service. There was no time to complete the usually mandatory Battle Efficiency courses at the Jungle Training Centre at Canungra in Queensland. Paul and his officers were instead busily addressing pre-deployment training needs and developing their own Standard Operating Procedures (SOPs), based on their limited knowledge of the operational environment in South Vietnam. Forty years later, he remembers well the scramble to get ready:

> We had to draw up an Establishment Table for approval within the manpower limitation imposed—so we had to consult who and what we thought suitable regarding the capabilities we needed. When the Establishment Table was approved, we then had to write an Equipment Table. That wasn't easy to do because it was an unusual organisation; an unusual task as far as we could ascertain. It was going to be virtually unsupported in country. So John Stein [the Quartermaster of 16 ALA] and I spent a lot of time at the Ordnance Depot in Brisbane going through the shelves. The spares assessment task aside, there was a heck of a lot of work going on with the technical side. An Army HQ team had gone to Vietnam to assess what aircraft spares support was available under the US/Australia Logistics Agreement. The only comparable fixed wing aircraft operated by the Americans was the Bird Dog,[2] which didn't offer much in terms of compatibility. Details like avionics[3] and instruments servicing requirements were looked at. So many things couldn't be done until the team came back from Vietnam to say what was available there. It was frantic. A lieutenant colonel engineer came in to supervise the design of two maintenance vehicles [short wheelbase Land Rovers] which eventually became millstones around our necks. The technical side couldn't equip them properly because they didn't know

the range of test equipment that they'd need to work in with the US servicing facilities available over there. So it was very difficult for them. Then there were all of the medical and personal equipment requirements. We finished up with tons of general and technical stores. The two maintenance vehicles were so heavily laden that when it was time to embark they were driven to the Hamilton wharf in Brisbane in four-wheel drive. Regarding my personal preparations, I wasn't helicopter qualified, so in between other things I went solo in a Sioux and that was about it. Oh yes, one other thing. I got married thirteen days before we left.[4]

All too soon, it was time to go. On 13 September, a farewell parade at Amberley was reviewed by the General Officer Commanding Northern Command, Major General T.F. Cape. The Flight's aircraft and personnel were transported to Vietnam on the Royal Australian Navy troopship HMAS *Sydney*, a former aircraft carrier. Lieutenant John Purvis and Warrant Officer Class 2[5] Owen Scafe went ahead by air to Bien Hoa Air Base, 20 kilometres northeast of Saigon, to help prepare for the arrival of the main body. Ready or not, 161 Recce Flight, with a complement of just 51 and carrying the hopes of Australian Army Aviation, was about to spread its wings in a combat zone. No one expected that it would remain in that environment for almost seven years.

Voyage to Vung Tau

HMAS *Sydney* sailed from Brisbane on 14 September 1965 for the port of Vung Tau on the southeast coast of South Vietnam. Vung Tau was the gateway to 161 Recce Flight's destination of Bien Hoa air base. The men of 161 looked forward to the new experience of a fourteen-day voyage with the Royal Australian Navy. Few had any idea of what to expect after their arrival. The voyage itself was a respite period after the intensive pre-deployment activity, and they enjoyed it as such.

The trip promised to be interesting. The Navy was steeped in fine old traditions. There was the Equator to be crossed and real Navy scran (food) to be enjoyed at mealtimes. Sleeping alone in a hammock would be in sharp contrast to the bedroom pleasures left behind. One of the Flight's more colourful characters was RAAF Leading Aircraftman Jim 'Gun Dog' Crook, an affable engine fitter. He remembered the tropical voyage well:

It was a wonderful trip, but pretty damned hot and our first task every day was to tie up and stow the hammocks. The mess decks were very small so we ate in a larger kitchen area. We were taught a bit about the country we were going to and, to keep us out of mischief, we had chores to do like cleaning the toilets and showers. That was fair enough as we all used the facilities. We spent our spare time, for the first few days in particular, finding our way around the ship. There was always one place we found at the end of the day. At five o'clock we'd line up with our ration cards and two shillings. They'd punch the card and take your two bob and give you a big, icy can of beer. There was only one non-drinker in our crowd and everyone was lined up to try to get his can of beer. I managed it twice in the two weeks so that was all right.

The whole trip north, right through to Subic Bay, was great and very scenic, and from there the Yanks escorted us through to Vung Tau. It was the education of a lifetime for me. I've always been quite pleased that I was lucky enough to go on that trip. A particular highlight was the short arm inspection. The Navy had a thing about checking their troops for obvious signs of venereal disease so the Army got on the bandwagon. We had this parade and we're all standing in line with our shorts down around our bloody ankles and there's this Regimental Sergeant Major and this little Army officer, about a 20-year-old Second Lieutenant, walking along looking at everyone's yorick. Blacky [Leading Aircraftman John Black] was on my left, and as this officer gets past the bloke on my right Blacky says, 'He'll be cockeyed before he's finished.' And this little prick turns around and gets up me. I just said, 'Yes, sir. No, sir.' When he'd gone I said to Blacky, 'You bastard!!' He said, 'That's all right. What are mates for?'[6]

Meanwhile, OC Paul Lipscombe was having his own problems. The Navy Board in its collective wisdom had decided that, on arrival at Vung Tau, the Flight's Cessnas should be flown off the *Sydney* to the airfield there. Perhaps they thought it would be good for public relations. Paul was not impressed:

It was totally impracticable, but we couldn't convince them. We could have put the wings on the Cessnas and of course we could have flown them off, but not before the ship was unloaded to clear the flight deck. The ship would be at anchor then and the temperature and lack of wind would prevent us from launching. So we'd have to wait until she sailed again and then she couldn't return if we had problems because her place in the harbour would be taken. In those days, there'd be 50 to 80 ships off Vung Tau.[7]

Fortunately, the *Sydney*'s Captain disregarded the Navy Board's directives and the Americans used helicopters to unload the Cessnas.

Unfortunately, the logistics system had worked so efficiently that while the dismantled Cessnas were being lifted off the tradesmen who would reassemble them had been swept into American C-130 Hercules transports and flown to Bien Hoa. Flight Sergeant Lloyd Larney, the RAAF fitter in charge of maintenance, had to backload a team to put the Cessnas back together so they could be flown to Bien Hoa. This was duly done and it was during the flight that 161 suffered its first battle damage. Lieutenant Don Ettridge was en route from Vung Tau to Bien Hoa when he flew over the Nui Thi Vais, a range of hills in Phuoc Tuy province. As a result of not yet being fully combat-conscious, he probably cleared them by only a few hundred feet and got a hole in the elevator for his trouble.

Leading Aircraftman Jim 'Gun Dog' Crook recalled the arrival at Vung Tau with amusement:

> Our own landing was the usual Army thing of hurrying to be ready an hour early and then waiting. Then, with all our webbing and crap hanging off us, we had to go down the side of the ship into an Australian Army DUKW.[8] There were rubber dinghies circling the ship with grappling hooks to secure the underwater area. From the DUKW we transferred into a Yank Landing Ship Tank [LST]. I managed to end up with both legs in the water trying to get from one to the other with all the bloody gear on. It was only fear that got me across in the end. Then, when we reached the shore, this young Army officer who must have watched too many Marine movies got involved. When they dropped the ramp from the LST onto the beach, all the public relations people were there with the cameras running and this young Army guy is yelling, 'Come on, run! This is a beachhead landing.' He got a lot of responses and the first word was always 'Get'. Then when we got ashore it immediately pissed down with rain. They loaded us into trucks and drove us to the airfield and flew us up to Bien Hoa. We flew back to Vung Tau and finally fixed the Cessnas a few days later and then Blacky and I flew up to Bien Hoa with the pilots. It was pretty uncomfortable because we'd all had hepatitis shots in our backsides earlier that day.[9]

Captain Bevan Smith and Lieutenant Holger von Meunchhausen (yes, he was sometimes called the Red Baron) flew the two Sioux helicopters off the *Sydney* to the airfield at Vung Tau. After the necessary compass swings[10] were carried out they were to fly the choppers to Bien Hoa the following day, 29 September. Bevan recalled that day's events clearly:

> Holger and I went to the Vung Tau Operations section thinking we'd submit our flight plan to Bien Hoa. That wasn't necessary, but I was told my first job was to nominate a call sign for 161 aircraft. Individual aircraft call signs were not used in the theatre of operations. Instead, unit call signs were assigned, and each pilot had a numerical suffix to the unit call sign. The Operations Officer's exact words were, 'It has to be a unique Australian animal starting with P.' I suggested 'Platypus' but that was already in use by 1RAR. After several minutes of deliberation, I said, 'I don't know. The only thing I can suggest is Possum.' 'That will do,' was the reply. So 'Possum' became 161's call sign. That was the last time I spoke to an air traffic controller while I was in Vietnam.
>
> Holger and I departed Vung Tau as Possum 1 and Possum 2. Now, we had Plessey UHF[11] radios. They were crystal tuned and we didn't have the required crystals. Holger and I could talk to each other on the Plesseys and to Vung Tau on VHF[12], but we couldn't talk to Bien Hoa tower. I decided that we should overfly the airfield at 3000 feet, knowing that they would be expecting two Sioux helicopters and have us on radar. Unfortunately, I had picked the jet circuit height. As soon as we had crossed the runway, we were looking down the intake of an F-100 fighter jet. Fortunately, he missed us. We found out later that the correct approach procedure for a helicopter was to cross at zero feet at the runway threshold. Anyway, we located our unit area and landed safely.[13]

This was pretty scary stuff which highlighted a dangerous oversight in communications planning. The UHF radios hastily installed before the Flight's departure could not be readily re-tuned to cope with frequent changes to operating frequencies to meet US communications security requirements. The arrival at Bien Hoa would have been spectacular but less than impressive if an American fighter had taken out a Sioux on the approach. Fortunately, disaster was avoided and the Flight's personnel began the tasks of establishing camp and setting up for operations and maintenance.

Bien Hoa, originally a French military post on the northern outskirts of Bien Hoa city, was by 1965 a huge air base. It was home to United States Air Force strike and ground attack aircraft, the US Army 173rd Airborne Brigade and a host of support units including large numbers of UH-1B Iroquois helicopters for insertion of troops into the field. To the newly arrived Army and RAAF personnel of 161, it was unprecedented in terms of facilities and the intensity of operations. Somewhere here, on the outskirts of this oversized air base, the Possums would be allocated space to build their first home.

2

Bien Hoa:
Fitting in

On arrival at Bien Hoa, 161's personnel found temporary accommodation amongst 1RAR's forward company positions. These were on the 173rd Brigade perimeter, responsible for security and positioned on the most likely line of attack on the Brigade. Three weeks of October were taken up with orientation briefings and flights for the pilots, administration, interacting with 1RAR and finding a permanent location for the Flight's living and working areas. At this time, the Siouxs were parked at the back of the battalion, while the Cessnas operated from a secure compound on the airfield which housed the classified, special operations American aircraft: the high flying U-2 spy aircraft, the C-47 gunships and the C-130 Hercules transports which carried the Ryan drones.[1] It was an incongruous setting for the little Cessnas, but it enabled 161's maintenance fitters to make friends with the American specialist technicians and learn about their maintenance and supply systems. Transport was the real problem as it was several kilometres from the rest of the Flight and few vehicles were available. It was not a good place to be without adequate transport. However, the Cessnas operated from the secure area throughout the Flight's stay at Bien Hoa because there was no other suitable place.

Establishing a permanent camp

During the last week in October, the Flight was allocated a permanent area for its camp, the Sioux flight line and maintenance facilities. OC Paul Lipscombe described the Flight's new location and defences:

> Our allocated area was on the south-eastern boundary of the 173rd Brigade area, alongside the final approach to the main runway. From our location the perimeter went up to Brigade Headquarters, and next to us was the Radio Research Unit.[2] On our southern flank and around the bend in the perimeter was the D/16 Cavalry,[3] then our own 105 Battery, Royal Australian Artillery and next to it an American infantry battalion. Beyond that was 1RAR and another American infantry battalion closed up to the perimeter of the airfield.
>
> We were responsible for the defence of our own section of the perimeter, which fronted on to an old French minefield in the undershoot area. When we went out on operations we had to leave people back, because our responsibility for local defence didn't decrease while we were deployed. We had forward weapon pits inside the wire which we manned at night. As well, D/16 Cav next door provided two M-113 Armoured Personnel Carriers (APCs) with .50 calibre machine guns on and one 90mm self-propelled anti-tank gun loaded with an anti-personnel flechette round. At last light they came to our part of the perimeter and then at first light they'd buzz off back next door. So that was very helpful and we had pretty good local defence.[4]

Flight Sergeant Lloyd Larney remembered that the site preparation was rough, but by using the Flight's own resources and bartering for other needs the Possums made the best of their new location.

> It had all been thorn bush and creepers. The Yanks bulldozed it and we moved in on the bare dirt. They dug a few big drains for when the monsoon hit and that was it. Luckily, the OC was a pretty crafty bloke. The crates they'd put the Cessna mainplanes in for the trip up, good tongue and groove flooring boards, were used as flooring in the tents at Bien Hoa. And he had brought heaps of corrugated iron, crates and crates of it. We bartered it for concrete and anything else we needed. He had a pretty good idea of what was needed for the whole camp set-up.
>
> We operated the helicopters from the side of the strip, not far from the runway threshold. Our tent lines were quite close by. The noise levels were very high. You can just imagine the aircraft traffic in and out of Bien Hoa. They had the Phantoms and F-100s there and when they were on the

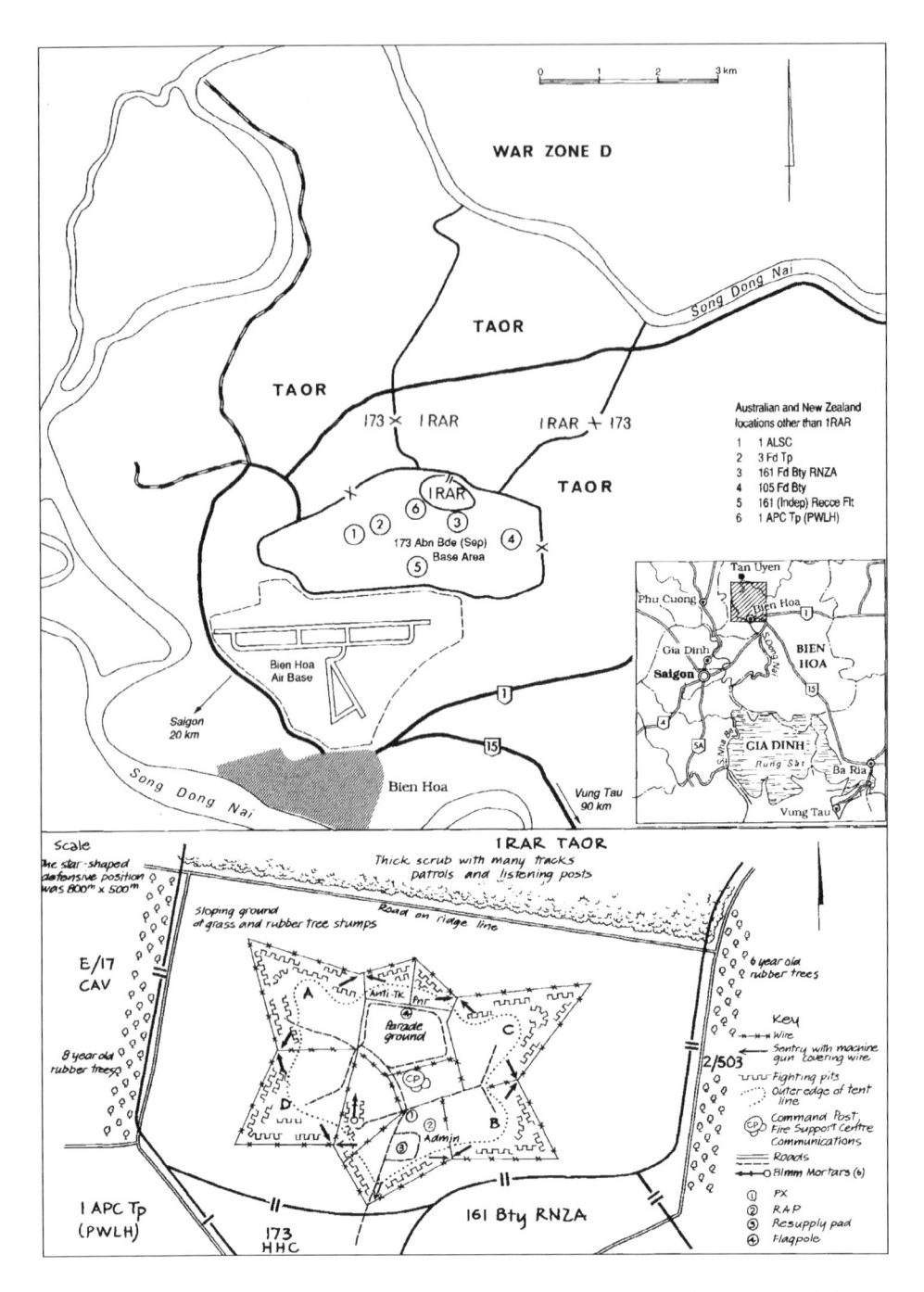

2.1 173 Brigade base area and Australian unit locations. Based on a sketch by Brigadier J. Essex–Clark, Retd.

offensive, four would take off every fifteen minutes around the clock. When they went off with the afterburners on, you might as well switch everything off. You couldn't hear a bloody thing. Then there were the big transport aircraft—C-130s, C-141s and C-123s. And when the troops went out on operations you'd see a hundred choppers in the air all at once taking a full battalion out. It looked very impressive.

We were lucky in setting up that we had some great tradesmen. I remember in particular Owen Reynolds, an electrician. He was RAEME, an excellent bloke. We had a 5 KVA generator running 24 hours a day for our power. It supplied the whole camp; lights, refrigeration, the lot. It threw a couple of bits on the armature one day. Owen said, 'We can fix it if I can have someone to give me a hand.' I volunteered and we started it up about 2 o'clock in the morning after working through the night. Another time it blew a head gasket and we worked through another night to fix it. I don't think anyone ever thanked him enough for doing the job. He was a really fantastic bloke. He was good at everything—sandbagging the vehicles, laying the barbed wire when we did the perimeter. He just seemed to know exactly what was required.[5]

From the viewpoint of the troops and their home comforts, Jim 'Gun Dog' Crook described setting up camp:

We could choose our tent site within the allocated area. So Dick Humphrey, Ralph Thorp, Blacky and I selected a site right up in the top corner. Some unkind people said we were reprobates and just wanted to get away from everybody else. It wasn't true. Ralph wasn't a reprobate. Anyway, we got settled in, and when we got wooden floors and could raise the tents and stretch them out, it was quite comfortable. We had sandbags right around, of course. It wasn't great but at least we lived in fairly comfortable tents and got three meals a day. We even had some home comforts. Blacky dug a big hole and put in a wooden box lined with insulation to make it an Esky. Now, every third night you were on guard duty, either walking between the tent lines or down in the pit. On the other two nights, you'd hook into the beer until the boozer shut at 9.30 p.m. Then we'd congregate in the top tent, where Blacky's Esky ensured there were cold drinks to be had. Paul Lipscombe would do the rounds now and again. He told me years later: 'You blokes have no idea how much I heard up there.' He never came in for a drink.

Other things weren't so easy. It was very slushy on the edge of our area, between us and the rice paddies. As part of our defences we had to put in this concertina barbed wire entanglement around our part of the perimeter. We were directed by some infantry guy: 'Let's get these RAAF blokes to carry out this shitty work, driving star pickets in and stretching this wire around.' Some of the guys were not happy. For me, it was part and parcel of the job. When it's night time and you're alone there overlooking the rice paddies and you've got all that concertina barbed wire out in front, it's a good feeling.[6]

RAAF–Army relations

Issues of discipline and morale arose between Army and RAAF personnel during the early period of 161's deployment. These are described in the official history[7] and are not discussed at length here. In brief, it appears that there were two problems. First, it was a most demanding time for all members of the Flight. They worked and flew under stressful conditions in an unfamiliar setting while at the same time trying to build adequate maintenance and living areas. Although under-resourced they had to produce the required results by whatever means. Finally, they were responsible for setting up and maintaining defences in their area of the perimeter. It is not surprising that, in these circumstances, there were clashes of priorities, procedures and personalities which fostered resentment instead of being shrugged off as irritants that inevitably arose on active service. As well, there was no RAAF officer with the Flight to whom the RAAF members could address their grievances. Some of the men therefore felt isolated and vulnerable to mistreatment by Army personnel. Others felt uncomfortable because they were less well trained than their Army counterparts in the use of weapons and operational procedures but were expected to measure up in the Army way as 'soldiers first and tradesmen second'.

The second problem was that, although the RAAF maintenance personnel were under the functional command of 161's OC at Bien Hoa, they were placed on the posted strength of the RAAF Transport Flight Vietnam at Vung Tau for the purposes of administration, pay and discipline. This arrangement was unsatisfactory for the obvious reason that the geographical separation of the two units made access to RAAF staff in Vung Tau most difficult.

Several breaches of discipline did ensue and these were referred to the RAAF commander of the Transport Flight at Vung Tau. Given the difficulties involved in establishing the facts of particular cases, outcomes were not always conducive to restoring good relations. Concerns arising from this unsatisfactory situation were eventually addressed when, in April 1966, Flying Officer Don Tidd, a RAAF engineer from 16 ALA, was assigned to 161 for two months and was placed in charge of the maintenance element. This helped to settle the working environment. Tidd returned to Australia after the Flight moved to Vung Tau in May 1966. He expressed the view to the Chief of Air Staff that the move to Vung Tau would be beneficial for the men concerned.[8] Disciplinary issues would be more easily dealt with and the RAAF tradesmen would no longer be frustrated by their inability to access their administrative support elements. Tidd was correct and there were few problems after the move.

Despite these initial difficulties experienced at Bien Hoa, Paul Lipscombe saw disciplinary issues and personality clashes as minor irritants and stressed the more important aspects of good teamwork and dedication to the task that all ranks in the workshop element displayed:

> I have to say that I was just so impressed by the blokes; both Air Force and Army, and all of the trade senior NCO's were Air Force at that stage. We never doubted their abilities. Flight Sergeant Lloyd Larney and the sergeants were just top-notch. Everyone just bogged in together and worked their butts off. And all of the tradesmen, if they didn't have something to do they got in and helped others.[9]

Maintenance and spares facilities

The Flight's maintenance facilities at Bien Hoa were built from scratch. The Australian Engineers put up a big marquee as a makeshift hangar, plus a Kingstrand hut (a large, prefabricated metal structure) for workshops. More Kingstrands were built later on; one for the officers and one for the troops as a recreation and beer hut. The troops were heavily involved in improvement work, helping to lay concrete for the floor of the maintenance hangar and building or acquiring other items to enhance the basics they were given. Gradually, the Flight achieved a more comfortable living and working situation.

From the outset, the provision of technical spares to keep 161's aircraft in the air was a challenge. Sergeant Laurie Dawber was in charge of technical spares when the Flight was deployed to Bien Hoa.

The pre-deployment assessment of spares requirements had been necessarily hurried and was based only on an estimate of flying hours and conditions in Vietnam. Many items of equipment and spares were scarce and expensive, and their use attracted the attention of ordnance staff tasked to establish more realistic usage rates and spares scalings in light of the actual experience at Bien Hoa. These officers expected 161 to implement a stringent recording system to obtain accurate data. Laurie thus occupied a particularly hot seat. He outlined his problems:

> With Phantoms regularly on finals behind the Cessnas, they literally landed at cruising speed and turned off the runway quickly to avoid being run over. Then they would have to taxi for a couple of miles. The tyres were soon showing bald spots and we'd somehow neglected to bring spares. We had our first priority requisition for tyres only a month after arrival. This brought the spiders out of the woodwork. The Ordnance Liaison Officer from Saigon turned up to see what sort of 'incompetent dill' would leave Australia without spare tyres. He found my stores tent unattended as both myself and my Corporal, George Avern, were away on other tasks. On my return, I got a blast for not operating an 'Ordnance Stores Section Accounting System'. I quickly showed him the written authorisation from the bean counters at Victoria Barracks in Brisbane which laid down the stores procedures for 161. I was told that I was to adopt 'Ordnance Stock Cards' immediately and that I'd be reported for 'unlawful procedures'. I told him I'd have to have it in writing. I was then in deep shit. He fronted me to the OC. I repeated my refusal to change and from that day I was not on Major Lipscombe's popularity list.
>
> Anyway, I set up a system that worked, and that was the most important thing. John Rawlings, the RAEME tool store corporal, shared a sleeping tent with me next to the stores tent, the workshop and the helipad for the Siouxs. So we lived right on the job and were available at night if anything was needed. I became an expert at hitching a ride to Tan Son Nhut and Long Binh where the US Army had a huge maintenance and stores set-up. I got to know my way around and was able to scrounge radio parts and other useful things. For example, I 'borrowed' an Artificial Horizon [flight instrument] for a few weeks until we got one from Australia and that saved us from sidelining an aircraft. We had other problems. Some of the high octane fuel was a bit iffy and sometimes a Sioux would have fouled plugs after only four or five hours. Our usage rate for plugs was questioned by 1 Base Ordnance Depot back in Australia and we had to put in a report through the operational and technical empires to shut them up. As I was the only Army sergeant on the workshop side, we had to work together as a team and be flexible. We bent most of the rules and ignored the rest, but we got the job done.[10]

Coping with the new environment: Unit morale

A morale-sapping development for all ranks was the deliberate delay in mail services from Australia attributed to trade union action in protest against Australia's involvement in Vietnam. Jim Crook recalled the mood of the men:

> Everyone was nearly at each others' throats because we weren't getting mail. It was all because of these union bastards holding up our mail, and refusing to load the cargo ship *Jeparit* with our supplies. Luckily, the OC kept us busy when we were off duty, cleaning up the debris left by the bulldozers when they cleared our camp area. He told Lloyd Larney, and Lloyd passed it on to me later, that he didn't care what we thought about him. He said, 'While there's a mail stoppage and these poor buggers aren't getting any mail, they can bleat about me instead of getting at each other's throats.' I thought, 'That's a couple of good marks for you, Paul.'
>
> We found a lot to laugh at as well. As I said, we had the tents raised up to maximum height with the flaps strung out on star pickets to keep the place a bit cool. But in the entrance, you had to have your poncho strung up because of the rain driving in. And this day it's the OC's inspection and here's this poncho hanging down like a nappy full of shit. The boss has his look around and goes to move out. The Admin Officer, Lieutenant Purvis, runs in front of him saying, 'Hang on, Sir! I'll just lift this up.' And he lifts it up just as the OC is walking out and it all pours down Lipscombe's back. The OC says, 'Thank you, Mr Purvis.' And there's Purvis trying to apologise, and us four in the tent trying not to burst out laughing.[11]

It must be said that Lieutenant Purvis did his best to provide other, less embarrassing diversions and hobbies to keep up morale during breaks from duty. It was a difficult task. Staying occupied is most important to the soldier on active service, but so is the challenge of bending the rules. It is very difficult to confine the troops to their lines if there are local diversions to be experienced. Australian soldiers have a fine tradition of exploiting whatever opportunities exist for the advancement of international relations by way of cultural exchange. It happened that, not far from the Australian lines at Bien Hoa, there was a village of sorts. Lloyd Larney did not go there himself, but remembers that many did:

> From the D/16 Armoured mob next to us, a heap of the blokes used to go down to the village. It was down the hill from where we were, down and

across a bit of a swamp. In between there was an asylum for the mentally ill. The troops would go at night, through the grounds of the asylum, and into the village where there were cathouses and you could get on the grog or whatever. There were guards on the gates to the asylum grounds which were the only access to the village. And these crafty bastards from 161 would take the guards a carton of cigarettes and whatever to let them through. I remember our Army cook 'Honk'—that was all he said if someone in the meal queue spoke to him; he'd just reply 'Honk'. Now, when the D/16 guys went out on ops those left behind came to eat with us. So they got to know Honk and he'd be creeping along in the dark and the blokes in the guard tower would challenge him and he'd say 'Honk'. So they'd say 'Pass, Honk!' They got to know others, of course, so it was easy enough to get down into the village. Then the military police [MP] would raid the place. The troops would hear them come in and the word would be passed: 'MP, MP!' So they'd clear off back through the asylum. The MPs would chase them but the guards at the gate wouldn't let them through.[12]

It was this pursuit of enhanced cultural relations that led to 161's first significant injury. Corporal Len Humphreys, a RAAF engine fitter and one of the 'characters' of the unit, was repatriated following a shooting incident which left him with a leg injury. Several accounts of this incident leave the author with no doubt that Len's premature departure was the fault of the overzealous American MPs.

Individual efforts contributed to the maintenance of morale. 161 had its usual unsung heroes. The clerks, the medic, the Q Store's (Quartermaster's Store) Lance Corporal Ron 'Father' Coombs and the cooks did their best to provide for the daily needs of the Flight. And while no one expects haute cuisine on active service, food is important to the soldier. Some of the American rations provided, like creamed chipped beef and dill pickles, were not palatable to the Australians but the Vietnamese in the Bien Hoa markets would take them in exchange for fresh fish and vegetables. Cooks Smithy (Corporal Charles Smith) and Honk (Private Cecil Crook) conducted many successful sorties which much improved both diet and morale. Their cookhouse was four posts with a few sheets of iron across the top and there was wire netting around it with sisal kraft paper around the bottom half. Inside, when the Flight got its generator set going, there was a refrigerator, a diesel-fuelled stove and a table for a servery. With a bit of help from the tradesmen and the two batmen (officers' servants), they did a great job.

Late 1965 gave way to Christmas and the challenges to come in 1966. Uncertain of their long-term future, 161's members of all ranks continued to refine their operational and support procedures. Spare time was put to good use in making the little area near the runway threshold at Bien Hoa a more comfortable place to work and live. It became their home, albeit a temporary one.

3

Learning the ropes:
October 1965 – May 1966

At Bien Hoa, 161 Recce Flight came under command of 1RAR with other support units to form the 1RAR Group. The battalion's operations with the US 173rd Brigade had been a sensitive issue since its arrival in June 1965. Its role had been limited to close-in operations concerning the security of the Bien Hoa air base and the surrounding area. This restriction meant that 1RAR could not participate with other battalions of the 173rd Brigade in search-and-destroy operations distant from Bien Hoa. The Australian Defence authorities' concern was that the battalion might be drawn into situations in which US tactics might entail heavier losses than could be afforded by Australia's relatively small force.[1] Negotiations led to a relaxation of guidelines in late September and 1RAR was permitted to take part in operations across the whole of the Third Corps Tactical Zone (CTZ).[2] By the end of October, the Battalion had been well and truly tested in operations at Ben Cat and in the enemy stronghold of the 'Iron Triangle' to the north of Saigon. There were casualties but 1RAR had honed its skills in difficult conditions.

161 Recce Flight operational constraints

During October the learning curve was steep as the pilots contemplated the scope of the missions before them. Apart from the many

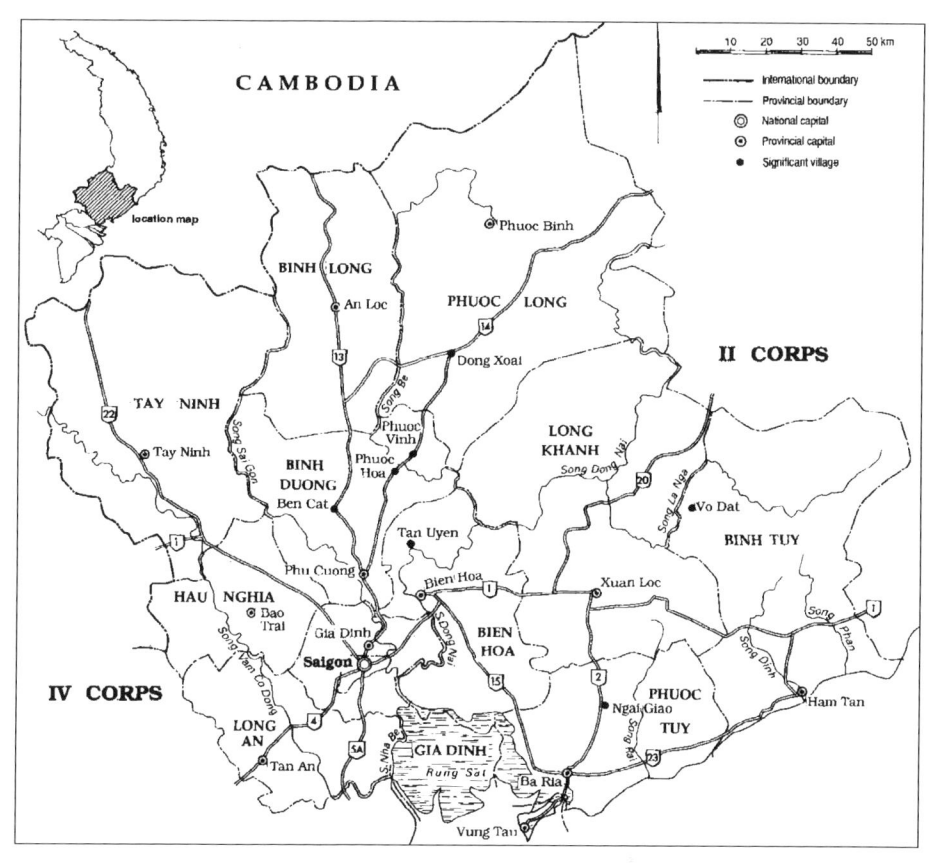

3.1 Third Corps Tactical Zone.

unknowns faced in that respect, they were conscious of the limitations imposed by their aircraft and the operating environment.

The Flight's aircraft were the Cessna 180, an observation and liaison aircraft, and the Bell 47G-3B1 Sioux light observation helicopter (OH-13 to the Americans). The Cessna was powered by a 230hp Continental engine and could carry up to four people at a cruising speed of 120 knots, while the Sioux had three seats (the third seldom used) and its 270hp turbocharged Lycoming engine enabled it to clatter along at about 60 knots. The Cessna's endurance was 3.5 hours while the Sioux could remain airborne for 2.5 hours. This meant that a Sioux in direct support of a battalion in the field would routinely have to refuel twice or three times a day.

These aircraft were barely adequate for 161's role. For much of the year, the high temperatures and humidity in South Vietnam limited the performance of the aircraft during take-off and landing in particular. In high 'density altitude' conditions, the key performance factors of engine power, propellor or rotor thrust performance and lift generated are all adversely affected. At 'all up weight' the difference between power required for take-off and the power available was relatively small for both the Sioux and the Cessna in even ideal conditions. Density altitude was thus a factor of critical importance when planning a sortie which involved carrying passengers or freight. In the conduct of operations on short strips and in tight landing zones (LZs), it was all too easy to 'not quite make it' if load limits were not strictly observed. It was therefore necessary to strike a balance between payload and performance. In the prevailing conditions, it was vital that reasonably conservative guidelines be set. It was decided that the Cessna 180 could carry its pilot and his personal equipment plus two passengers or 400 pounds (182 kilograms), while the Sioux was limited to the pilot plus one passenger or 200 pounds (91 kilograms).[3] In the case of the Sioux, a pilot was pleased to leave a heavyset commander behind and take his rat-thin intelligence officer instead.

UHF Communications remained a problem. The modern communications equipment fitted to American aircraft was easily tuned to new frequencies, but the Australians could not keep up with the changes. Without compatible UHF sets, 161's pilots had to fly around the battlefield with VHF-FM communications only (for contact with ground forces) and take their chances in the crowded skies. They could not talk with air traffic control or with US aircraft. Eventually, suitable ARC-51BX UHF radios were 'acquired' from the Americans and the pilots could operate with greater safety and flexibility. That they achieved most of their operational objectives in the early days without adequate communications is remarkable, and is testimony to the skills of pilots John Guild, Holger von Muenchhausen, Bevan Smith, Neville Pinkham, Don Ettridge, Don Cockerell and Paul Lipscombe.

Mission techniques and procedures

The routine tasks required of the Flight were visual reconnaissance (VR); direct support (DS) of battalion operations; air observation post

(AOP) in support of artillery shoots; and convoy escort, liaison and courier services. Some trial electronic surveillance operations were conducted, but this type of intelligence gathering did not become a regular function until a year or so later.[4]

Routine VR missions flown by both Cessna and Sioux entailed a careful, low-level search of relatively small areas (eight to twelve map squares) in a sortie of about two hours' duration. The aim was to detect and report on enemy activity in specific areas or to conduct a progressive, repetitive search of the tactical area of responsibility (TAOR)[5] to provide ongoing intelligence. Other VR tasks, such as reconnaissance of intended operational areas before inserting troops, were carried out during direct support of forces in the field. Command or intelligence staff would be carried to permit them to gain first-hand knowledge of the environment in which their troops would be operating. VR techniques were refined and extended during the Flight's later operations in support of the 1st Australian Task Force (1ATF) at Nui Dat, and are discussed further in that context.

The second major task was direct support of infantry forces deployed in the field on specific operations. Sioux aircraft were used as they could operate from small, rough landing zones (LZs) in densely forested or swampy areas as well as open ground. In a typical day's operations, a DS aircraft usually flew numerous sorties for the purposes of VR, command and control, liaison, resupply and evacuation of sick or wounded personnel from areas inaccessible to larger aircraft. Other tasks were assigned at the discretion of the battalion commander. If requested tasks were outside the aircraft's capabilities or would risk the aircraft and lives unnecessarily, the pilot had the discretion to refuse the task. It was his responsibility alone to assess whether the task was achievable. For all tasks accepted, it was also the pilot's responsibility to determine the best way to carry them out. Exercising these responsibilities called for firmness and tact, as the pilots were usually under the direction of officers of senior rank who were not accustomed to debating their orders with junior officers.

There were many other tasks. Air observation post sorties were allocated to either Cessna or Sioux aircraft. For scheduled firing by artillery batteries, the shoot was normally conducted by an artillery officer carried in the aircraft. If artillery fire was called for during an operation to engage a target of opportunity, the pilot would direct the shoot.

Convoy cover tasks required the pilot to carry out a route reconnaissance ahead and on the flanks of the convoy looking for obstacles, signs of enemy movement and possible ambush sites. Psychological warfare operations (leaflet dropping and voice broadcast) could be undertaken, although voice broadcast operations required the fitment of amplifier and speaker packages to generate the volume necessary for projection from a safe operating altitude.

Under the general headings of courier services and administrative support, 161 carried out a multiplicity of tasks including document runs, area familiarisation for incoming officers and passenger runs for liaison or onwards travel purposes. The Cessna was the obvious choice for courier work over longer distances because of its higher payload and cruising speed.

Commencing operations

The Flight's first operational sortie was a reconnaissance for 1RAR on 22 October in preparation for a battalion search-and-destroy operation to the northeast of Bien Hoa. The battalion's area of operations was 38 square kilometres, mostly within the Viet Cong base area known as 'War Zone D'.[6] A DS aircraft was provided from 23 to 26 October.

OC Paul Lipscombe was quick to note that 161's primary responsibility to 1RAR did not rule out support by the Flight to other elements of the brigade:

> We covered a lot of space even then. For example, we went up to Tay Ninh and other places where 1RAR never went. The other thing was that the 173rd Brigade had come from Okinawa, where it had an Aviation Platoon equipped with Beaver aircraft. The Beavers were left behind because they would be of little use at Bien Hoa, so the 173rd had a Brigade Aviation Officer but no aircraft. When we arrived with our Siouxs and Cessnas, they couldn't believe their luck. The brigade Tactical Operations Centre used to task us and Brigadier General Williamson, as brigade commander, was very very interested in what we did. Eventually, the Americans were allocated six OH-13S helicopters [US Army designation for the Sioux] but they didn't have any pilots qualified on type and the aircraft didn't arrive with dual

control kits for instructional purposes. The OH-13S was very similar to our G-3B1s except that it was narrower. It had the old G2A canopy. And my blokes couldn't believe it because they'd do 80 knots instead of the 60 knots cruising speed of the G3B-1. We hit upon a great plot. We borrowed their OH-13S aircraft for operations and I gave the Brigade Bevan Smith and our G-3B1s with the duals and he did the pilot conversions. We earned brownie points like you wouldn't believe and that sort of cooperation continued. When they eventually farewelled us it was with great regret.[7]

Captain Bevan Smith, the rotary wing section commander, described the early operational scene and gave some insights into the learning curve faced by the pilots:

The brigade had its integral aviation platoon plus a company of the 82nd Aviation Battalion attached. They had more than 100 Hueys[8] and we arrived with two Siouxs and two Cessnas. The Cessnas were the only fixed wing aircraft within the brigade group. 1RAR used them for liaison flights to Saigon. They were also used for leaflet drops and as a broadcast platform. Not long after we became operational I took the Brigade Deputy Commander on a recce in the Sioux. He said that it was the greatest recon aircraft he had ever used, and from then on I took him on a regular basis. I was also flying Hueys whenever there wasn't a lot of work for our aircraft. We had three helicopter pilots and two helicopters. Holger von Muenchhausen and John Guild would alternate on tasks. Fortunately, I had done the Huey course while in the States.

One important task for the Sioux was a nightly courier run between Brigade HQ and the US 1st Division HQ. So with the recces for the brigade and the Australian units the workload for the Sioux pilots rapidly increased. It was a steep learning curve. We had never visualised anything along the lines of the American doctrine. All of our training was based on procedures encountered in conventional war, like Second World War operations. However, while we had not trained specifically for the American type of counterinsurgency operation, our training did allow us to adapt quickly to the situation. But it was still a learning period for the whole time I was in Vietnam, as it should have been. Flying both Hueys and the Sioux, I gained a wealth of experience.[9]

It was during this learning stage that refinements to standard operating procedures became necessary in light of experience gained. Bevan recalled one such occasion:

We had guidelines, but it was impossible to cover every situation that might arise. For example, one of our pilots was operating at night from a fire support base to a location a couple of hundred metres from the target. There was an urgent requirement for an ammunition resupply. The artillery battery was firing in support of the troops who needed the ammo. The pilot had a choice. Does he fly 20 feet above the trees or try to climb and descend under the trajectory, both dangerous options? It was impossible to calculate the trajectory all the way. He could calculate the maximum height of the round using time of flight, but not the profile. So he went in low. Unfortunately, our OC could not see this and wanted me to carpet the pilot for flying low. He felt that nobody should fly below 500 feet, which is the suicide height as far as recce pilots are concerned.[10]

With experience, these and other operational issues were resolved to the benefit of all concerned. From this beginning, 161 was involved in support of all 1RAR operations as well as the tasks allocated by the brigade. Major Lipscombe was keenly aware that 161's performance would be watched closely as it was breaking new ground. He was not unduly worried as he felt that the Flight was coping well:

> Tasking for operations was okay. With just the four aircraft we'd have to say things like, 'We'll do that now, or we can do it at 11 o'clock.' But apart from that, we had no problems. We were quite flexible in our approach. There's no doubt that we were being watched closely, but there was no real pressure. We disregarded anything like that. The other thing too was that I left the bulk of the flying to the others. There were so many day-to-day, hour-to-hour things going on that I couldn't afford to be away for a day at a time.[11]

Throughout the remainder of 1965 and into 1966, the Flight continued its support role. Notable operations were *Hump* (5–9 November) and *New Life* (21 November–16 December). Operation *Hump* was a brigade level search-and-destroy operation in the Viet Cong base area War Zone D with 1RAR as one of two manoeuvre elements. The opposing Viet Cong forces were the Q762 Main Force Regiment and the D800 Main Force Battalion. For the first time Viet Cong main force units 'stood their ground in front of the brigade'.[12] In the ensuing battle the American forces claimed an overwhelming victory, but their assessment was not supported by Australian observations.[13] The Australian forces' approach to the assessment of enemy casualties was typically more conservative than that of the Americans. This was important when planning follow-up operations.

New Life was a much longer operation conducted some 80 kilometres to the northeast of Bien Hoa in Binh Tuy province. It aimed to restore government control over an area dominated by the Viet Cong and deny their forces access to the area's large rice harvest. The distance from Bien Hoa necessitated the forward deployment of 161's aircraft and maintenance crew to an airfield at the town of Vo Dat through which US forces (including 1RAR) and an ARVN division were funnelled to their respective operating areas. The Brigade maintenance area, including the 161 detachment, was established there. The Sioux helicopters were thus immediately and continuously available to the battalion for command and control, liaison and VR sorties. The Australian forces again learned much and performed with distinction during *New Life*. However, their elation was short-lived as the enemy returned soon after the operation was completed and wreaked a terrible revenge on the villagers who had cooperated with the allied forces.

Jim 'Gun Dog' Crook spent three weeks at Vo Dat and had vivid memories of both his trip there by Land Rover and life at the airstrip:

> The Charlies [enemy soldiers] had attempted to knock a bridge out, but they weren't successful. Now, when you can see aircraft coming in and dropping bloody napalm you think, 'Shit, that's close.' When we arrived, the whole joint was still smoking from where they'd beaten shit out of it the previous day. We all lived in this one big tent. The priorities were the weapon pit out front and maintaining our aircraft. Nobody had to use a cattle prod to get us to dig in and we spent every spare minute at it. We set up traps around our area as well; sharpened stakes and trip wires between the trees attached to beer cans filled with stones. Further out in front, Owen Scafe, our Operations Warrant Officer, set up another trip wire. So we felt pretty secure.
>
> We had Yanks either side of us and they were trigger-happy bastards. Every day at midday they changed the password, which was always numbers. On guard duty you'd go in each direction until you met a Yank. He'd say 'Halt. Six.' And if you didn't come back with 'Nine' you were in trouble. I dreaded the nights I had to walk from one to the other. I used to try to swap, to get into the pit where it was safer. We had an M-60. One night I'm in there and a bloody flare went off. All hell broke loose on either side. I'm watching out in front with the glasses but there's nothing. Eventually the flare died out and so did the shooting. I think a dog must have tripped it. But these bloody Yanks must have fired a thousand rounds out there. I dialled through to our command post and Bob Hart answered. I said, 'Possum Pit. All okay here; a bit of noise, but not coming from us.' He said, 'How many did you fire off?' I said, 'I didn't even push the safety

off. There was no bloody need.' Paul Lipscombe came up to me next day and said, 'You had an interesting night. I heard you when you rang ops.' I had no idea there was a line to the bugger's tent as well.

A real highlight for me was the kids up there. We used to take the tanker down to the water point to fill up, and they'd be there. There was one little girl in particular. I used to pinch a few chocolate biscuits out of our Yank ration packs for her. Now, the Red Cross used to send up gear. One time it was a big can of boiled lollies. We saved most of them for the kids. I took them down and all these women and kids were there and Coombsy took a photo of it. I wish I had a copy; these little kids, and all these lollies. Thinking about my own kids, and seeing the little ones up there, I thought 'They're kids wherever they are.' For me, it was just a great morale booster to see the looks on their faces.[14]

The learning curve continues

For the Australian fliers, it was one new experience after another. Captain Bevan Smith, with his fellow chopper pilots John Guild and Holger von Muenchhausen, found himself doing innovative things in unusual circumstances. Bevan recalled one such mission which almost went badly wrong for him:

> While it was not a daily event, it wasn't unusual for the helicopters to take ground fire. We weren't always aware of it unless we saw the muzzle flashes or a round came through the cockpit. On one occasion I was briefed to fly to a grid reference as requested by a ground party, and when I arrived at the designated spot all I could see was acres of thick jungle canopy. I thought I must be in the wrong place. The ground party threw smoke but I couldn't see it. The sergeant on the ground told me that he had me in sight and to fly in a particular direction, which I did for at least 500 metres. He still claimed to be able to see me, which I thought was impossible considering the distance I had travelled from the original grid reference and the thick canopy. Again I requested smoke and this time I saw red smoke billowing out of a clear area about 400 metres from my position. I called red and he confirmed. I flew to the area and started my descent, to be greeted by dozens of muzzle flashes.
>
> This was one of the rare occasions when the VC picked the same colour as the friendlies. If they hadn't started shooting so early they would have got me. I pulled pitch and headed over them. At that moment I received a call from the New Zealand artillery requesting my position. They said they had a target at my location. I advised them that they certainly did and that I was leaving the area.[15]

By this time Bevan's fuel was running low. He refuelled and set off again for the original grid reference, calling for smoke as he arrived. He saw a faint sign of violet smoke wafting through the canopy about 150 metres from the grid reference and the ground party confirmed violet. There was no apparent way in but the sergeant on the ground said he could talk Bevan down. He decided to give it a try:

> He was better than any controller I had ever experienced on a regular ground control approach. He had me fly over a bomb crater, then talked me down and through the trees for what seemed a mile, but was probably about 150 metres. By this time the sortie had taken over two hours, I had fallen into a trap and I had made the most hazardous approach of my career. So I was more than surprised when I found out the purpose of the mission was to collect empty jerry cans. I now had to get out of this hole. I had to back out and the sergeant again did a great job. After I had backed up for about 50 metres I found a spot where I could turn around. This relieved a lot of the pressure and I returned the jerry cans to HQ. After this task I always triple-checked when smoke was used to identify a landing area.[16]

As noted, Bevan gained much experience on Hueys at Bien Hoa. Not all of the flying was on typical Huey tasks, such as airmobile assaults. He recalled one of the more unusual tasks:

> The most useful innovation was a situation where I had been flying Huey loads of perforated steel planking [PSP],[17] trying to get one of our APCs out of a swamp. Each load gained only a few metres and it was going to take hours. I suggested that we hook a cable to the APC instead to take some of the weight with the helicopter. The idea worked and he was out of the swamp in minutes. I know that the bigger Chinook helicopters were later used in this manner, but I'm sure that this was the first attempt at getting an APC out of trouble using a helicopter.[18]

Early January 1966 saw the Flight operating in support of Operation *Crimp*, 1RAR's third and last foray into another province, and one in which it achieved distinction by penetrating an enemy headquarters tunnel complex at Cu Chi.[19] Routine operations continued during February and March in the Bien Hoa area, in support of brigade and 1RAR Group operations, and the pilots gained experience and confidence as they became more familiar with their missions and the operating environment.

Unforeseen operational hazards

The hazards of everyday flying operations from Bien Hoa were challenge enough for 161's aviators, but there was more than the enemy to face. Possum Master Paul Lipscombe recalled other incidents which kept life interesting:

> A squadron of American C-123s, call sign Ranch Hand, used to run around four abreast at 200 feet above ground level spraying their defoliant. And Bevan Smith, I think it was Bevan, was up in War Zone C or D and came bumbling over a hill and was met by four Ranch Hands and a cloud of Agent Orange which absolutely soaked him because he had the doors off. He got back to Bien Hoa and had all this oily stuff all over the aircraft. They cleaned as much off as they could, but the next morning we had to get a new cockpit bubble because it was all crazed. That was a pretty horrendous occasion.
>
> Another day at Tan Son Nhut I was number 23 cleared for take-off on the cross strip we used before they put in the parallel runway. Anything from an empty C-130 down used to take off to the north on that little cross strip. Four pairs of F-105s took off to the southwest on the main strip and all 23 of us were lined up. There was a C-123, C-130s, Bird Dogs, single Otters, and I was on the tail end. And the tower said, 'Numbers 1 to 23 cleared for take-off!' I mean, just think of the wake turbulence from an empty Herc.
>
> My worst flying experience in South Vietnam was during a night dual check with Neville Pinkham at Bien Hoa. We were cleared for take-off and a Vietnamese Air Force C-47 had taxied to the other end to take off in the opposite direction. We started rolling and got the tail up and Neville was just about to lift off when, coming towards us, we see these red and green lights and over the top went this Gooney Bird[20] and you could see the hot exhausts just there. He'd misunderstood his air traffic instructions. It was very fright-making. We had to have a beer when we eventually got back.
>
> There was also the story about the USAF pilot who was joining overhead Bien Hoa on a TACAN[21] approach—at about 14 000 feet they used to join—and his navigator looked out and there formating on their wingtip was an eight-inch shell. It was just a coincidence in time and velocity. We had eight-inch guns around there and they could put shells up to eighteen or 20 000 feet. It was surprising that there were so few aeroplanes shot down by friendly ground fire. There were huge numbers of artillery and mortar rounds being fired around the place and nine times out of ten we didn't know their location. I can only recall one aircraft—I think it was a US Army Caribou—being shot down by friendly artillery fire somewhere down in the Delta. That's absolutely amazing.[22]

Behind the operations

As OC, Paul Lipscombe was pleased with the flying effort and the results achieved given the Flight's very limited resources. There were many issues to be addressed on a day-by-day basis relating to operations, maintenance and manning. The Flight's heavily laden Land Rover maintenance vehicles were not suitable for deployment into the field, so if a maintenance crew was to be taken on operations, men and equipment usually had to be flown. It was also difficult to deploy in sufficient strength because the Flight still had to provide scarce manpower for local defence in its sector. Then there were equipment and spares issues. The OC was unstinting in his praise of the ground crew but found the combination of official and unofficial spares systems somewhat unnerving:

> For example, the maintenance guys would go over and change a radio. Now, the American system didn't account for them by serial number. You handed one in and you got another one. After Vietnam, it took years for the RAAF Support Command and Army to try to sort out radios and I don't think they ever did. Lifed components were another issue. The Americans didn't have a 'time between overhauls' period like we do. You'd take an alternator over there and you'd get a repaired one. It had a green tag on it to say it was serviceable, but it might have done thousands of hours. You didn't know, and that was a worry for the technical blokes. But then they started to get a bit flexible too and they'd run checks on exchanged items back in our own little workshop to make sure that they were okay.
>
> There were some funny things. The American logistics system was so ginormous that, once it got cranked up, it was hard to stop. For example, we put an indent in on the aviation stores centre at Long Binh for six aircraft batteries. A few days later, outside the Quartermaster's tent, there appeared this American semi-trailer with 60 batteries. They were worth $600 each, a lot of money then. And they wouldn't take them back. There was no point in persisting. The batteries consisted of a whole bunch of 2.5 volt cells. So every soldier in 1RAR and 161 had his own little fluoro light in his weapon pit until the cells went flat. You got used to these little things.[23]

Operation Abilene

On 8 March 1966 the Australian Government announced an increase in its commitment to a brigade-level task force. To prepare the way for the establishment of the task force in its intended location in Phuoc Tuy province, Operation *Abilene* was mounted from 30 March to 14 April. 1RAR was detached from the 173rd Brigade under operational command of the US 1st Infantry Division to secure the Courtenay and Binh Ba areas along Route 2 in the north of Phuoc Tuy. The aim was to secure these areas for the establishment of logistics bases in support of search-and-destroy operations against 274 and 275 VC Regiments, the primary enemy forces known to be in Phuoc Tuy. The operation's principal aim was not achieved as there were only limited engagements.[24] It did however add significantly to the Allied forces' knowledge of the situation in the province.

Abilene also brought 161 Recce Flight's first aircrew casualty. Captain Bevan Smith was severely wounded and was later medevaced[25] to Australia. He provided a graphic description of the incident:

> This was a very large op. I was supporting 1RAR and had Sergeant Clem Ebner (ops) and Airman Keith Bell (maintenance) with me. We had spent the previous night at the Courtenay rubber plantation to the north of Nui Dat. On the morning of 2 April I was flying the CO, Lieutenant Colonel Alec Preece, south on a recce along the route the troops were taking. The country to the left of the road was mainly rubber plantations, while to the right it was scrub and jungle. I asked the colonel how he wanted to conduct the flight and he elected low level, a wise move as the reason for low flying on VRs is to restrict the time the enemy has to take aim if he spots you. Our track was to the right of the road from Courtenay south to Binh Ba. We were on the treetops and had a good view through the rubber trees. I was too intent on looking into the rubber plantation across the road. I thought that I had spotted movement, and when I looked ahead again we were just leaving the tree line along Binh Ba airfield. If I had realised we were so close I would have moved over the rubber to bypass the strip. However, as it would take only about fifteen seconds to cross I carried on. Unfortunately, the Viet Cong had set up an ambush on the side of the road in the trees at the end of the airfield, directly on my flight path.
>
> My rule was to never turn away from an enemy position once I spotted muzzle flashes as in doing so the turning helicopter becomes an almost stationary target. When I saw the flashes, my first thought was to carry on as normal. Then I thought 'I can't get the CO shot' so I broke my rule and turned away to keep him out of the line of fire. At that point a round entered through the firewall parallel to the collective and took out the knuckles of my left hand. I immediately realised my mistake, and if that round had have been a couple of inches to the right we would both be

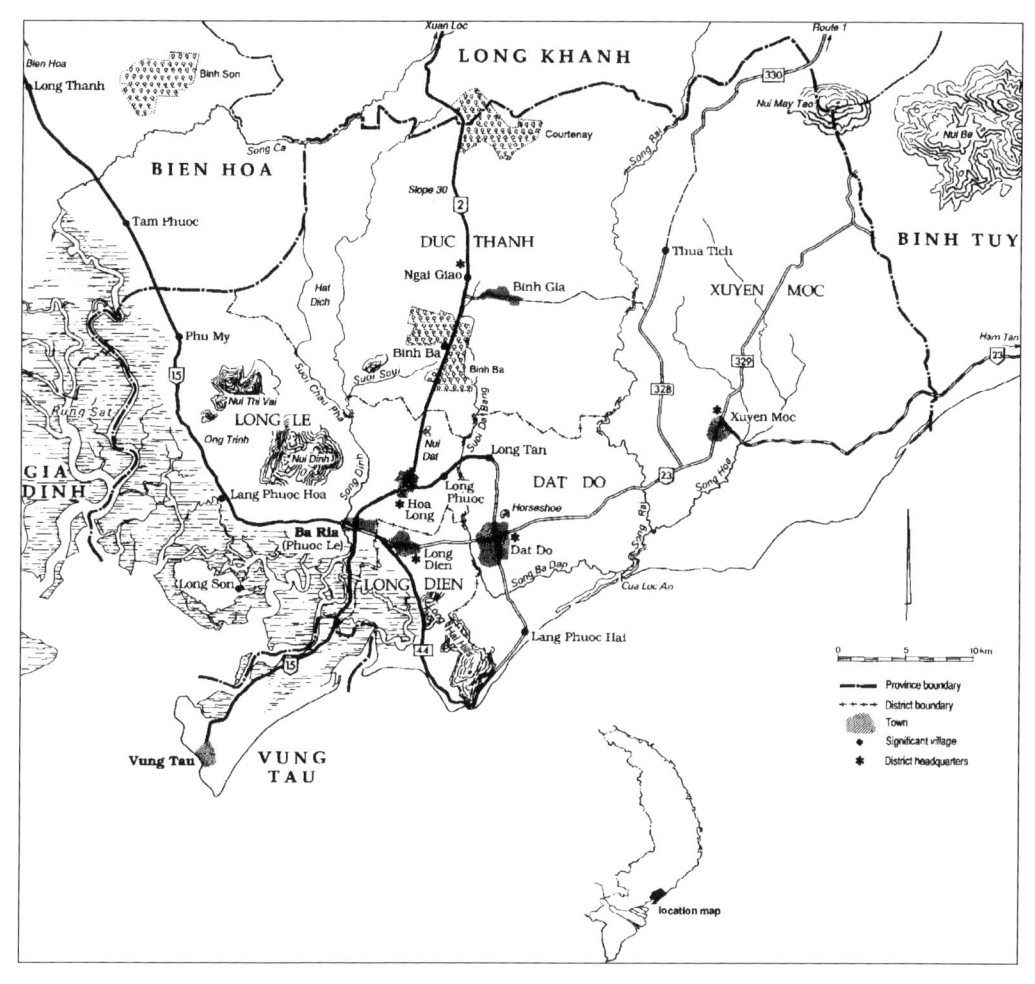

3.2 Phuoc Tuy province.

dead. My next thought was how in the hell was I going to fly without a hand to control the throttle or collective pitch. I said, 'Shit, I've been hit.' I had intended this to be on intercom only to let the CO know of our predicament, but inadvertently pressed both the intercom and transmit buttons on the cyclic. In retrospect this was a good thing. The CO was to do all the transmissions using a foot-operated button on the floor, but in the event he failed to advise anybody of the ambush or of our predicament. Fortunately, the battalion second in command [2IC], Major John Essex-Clark, was with the APC troop nearby. He heard the transmission, moved immediately and demolished the ambush.[26]

Bevan's thoughts were racing. Could he fly the Sioux with one hand? His immediate impulse was to get it on the ground. He considered autorotating into a clearing on the other side of the airfield, but realised that he couldn't close the throttle or use the collective to stop the descent. By this time the Sioux was back over the trees and he continued to assess his options:

> More rational thoughts were starting. I realised I could control the collective with my wrist. The throttle was a different matter. The tacho showed the RPM low but still well in the green, but I decided to rectify the situation. If under normal flying conditions you move the cyclic more than two or three inches in any direction you are over-controlling. I locked the cyclic with my knees and said to the CO, 'I need to adjust the throttle; hold the cyclic but for God's sake don't move it.' We were still on the treetops. The minute my right hand left the cyclic he tried to move it to his side of the cockpit. This almost inverted us into the trees. I snatched the cyclic back and recovered control. It wasn't a nice situation to be in, but it was imperative to maintain self-control and to do what had to be done.
>
> I headed for an ARVN compound I had noted on our way to Binh Ba as it appeared to be the closest secure place to land. On arrival I had to set up an approach, which entailed lowering the collective and making a relatively large throttle adjustment. As we approached the compound I explained the landing procedure to the colonel. He would have to hold the cyclic again and once I had started the approach, I would have very little control because any movement of the collective requires a throttle correction. For that reason we could have a heavy landing and, in my condition, anything might have happened. I asked him to turn off the ignition switches immediately we touched the ground. We were fortunate I had set up the approach perfectly and we finished at a three-foot hover. I lowered the collective with my wrist and breathed a sigh of relief. I was shocked when he then asked, 'Now which switches do you want me to turn off?'[27]

The ARVN troops at the compound offered the wounded pilot a morphine shot. They had a rusty old tin containing a not-so-sterile-looking needle, so Bevan declined the offer. A Huey with the battalion medical officer on board was quickly on the scene. The doctor administered morphine and dressed his hand, leaving the flying glove on. Like Bevan, he thought that the fingers would probably come off with the glove. Bevan was evacuated first to Courtenay, where he briefed Ebner and Bell on the incident and told them to check for damage and secure the aircraft. Unfortunately, he had lost a lot of blood in the cockpit. This pooled in the bubble and cooked in the sun before Holger von Muenchhausen flew it out. He told Bevan later it was putrid. There was just no way of cleaning it out on the scene.

Bevan was flown to the 93rd Evacuation Hospital at Bien Hoa where his fingers were attached with stainless steel pins through the fingers into his wrist. He was then evacuated to Australia where, despite the permanent impairment to his hand, he eventually returned to flying. He was surprised that when he first returned, little official interest was shown in his experience as the first pilot to return from South Vietnam. He thought that much could have been learned.

The winds of change

The months at Bien Hoa since 161's deployment had passed quickly. Suddenly, it was early May 1966 and the time had come for the Flight to move from Bien Hoa to Phuoc Tuy province to become part of the new task force. From 1 April the Flight was renamed 161 (Independent) Reconnaissance Flight. In Australia, preparations were already under way for its expansion in line with the government's commitment to upgrade the war effort to a task force. It was also time for some of 161's troops to go home and for replacements to arrive. On 1 May, three RAAF (Sergeant Otago, Corporal Patterson, Leading Aircraftman Wood) and eight Army personnel (Sergeant Ellis, Corporal Elson, Craftsman Willis, Corporal Byng, Craftsman Bennett, Corporal Jordan, Craftsman Hodgkinson, Corporal Bean) marched in. On 5 May, RAAF members Flight Sergeant Larney, Sergeant Higginbottom, Corporals Thorp, Black, Wilson, Crook, Humphrey, Menear and Leading Aircraftman Bell returned to Australia. Some of the reprobates were gone; others had arrived to maintain the continuity of larrikinism. The move to the Flight's second location, the quaint coastal resort of Vung Tau, was imminent. It was there that the Australian task force would assemble prior to the move to its permanent location at Nui Dat.

Part 2

Joining the Task Force

4

The 1st Australian Task Force

The 1st Australian Task Force (1ATF) built on the forces already in country by adding a second infantry battalion, a Special Air Service (SAS) squadron, combat and logistic support units and a squadron of eight Iroquois utility helicopters. Brigadier Owen Jackson was named as Commander, 1ATF. Overall command of the Australian forces would be exercised from Headquarters Australian Forces Vietnam in Saigon by Major General K. Mackay. Operational control of the Australian task force was vested in the American commander of II Field Force Vietnam, who commanded the US formations in the III Corps area which included the Australian task force location in Phuoc Tuy province.

The American commander could assign the task force a Tactical Area of Operational Responsibility (TAOR) in Phuoc Tuy province as well as requiring it to conduct operations anywhere in the South Vietnamese Army Corps II and III Tactical Zones as agreed by the Australian commander and the commander of the US Military Assistance Command Vietnam (USMACV), General Westmoreland. In simple terms, the Australians would have a good deal of autonomy within their own area of responsibility but could be called upon, after consultation, to move outside their boundaries in support of Allied operations. The task force was not expected to operate in isolation.

US operational support would be provided subject to availability and could include Army aviation, armour, artillery, air transport and close air support. Logistic and administrative support would also be provided.[1]

Nui Dat, in central Phuoc Tuy province, was selected as the base location for the task force. The main logistics elements would be grouped 30 kilometres away at the port of Vung Tau as 1 Australian Logistics Support Group (1ALSG). The RAAF Caribou and Iroquois squadrons would also be based at Vung Tau, which in addition to its port facilities had an airstrip suitable for resupply by RAAF C-130 Hercules aircraft.

The province

The Australian forces in Phuoc Tuy found themselves in a distinctive area to the southeast of the capital, Saigon. The province was bordered by the South China Sea and the Vung Tau Special Zone, and extended north to the neighbouring provinces of Long Khanh and Bien Hoa. To the east was Binh Tuy province, marked in its north by the bulk of the Nui May Tao mountain stronghold. To the west loomed the Nui Dinh and Nui Thi Vai chain of high hills, and beyond them was the vast area of marsh and mangroves known as the Rung Sat. In the south, the rugged Long Hai hills marched to the sea to the east of Vung Tau. There were no similar high areas in the centre of the province, just a scattering of small, low hills like Nui Dat itself.

Much of the province, other than the populated areas in the south, was covered in forest, ranging from low scrub and bamboo thickets to thick jungle and taller, more open forests. The large rubber plantations of Binh Ba and Courtenay had been established to the north of Nui Dat by the French. The eastern half of the province was bisected from north to south by the Song (River) Rai as it ran to the coast to the east of the Long Hais.

Phuoc Tuy measured approximately 60 kilometres from east to west and 40 kilometres from south to north. Its population of more than 100 000 was located mainly in the southern rice-growing area. Its climate was hot and wet during the summer monsoon season from

The GOC, Northern Command, Maj Gen T.F. Cape, DSO MBE, reviews
161 Recce Flight's farewell parade, RAAF Base Amberley, 13 September 1966.
L-R LAC Keith Bell, Cpl Mick Wilson, Unknown, Maj Gen Cape,
Maj Paul Lipscombe, Lt Col Bill Slocombe.
Photograph courtesy 161 Association.

Members of the Flight on 'welcome' parade in Saigon, October 1965.
Photograph: Joe Pukallus.

Fitters replacing main rotor blades, Sioux flight line, Bien Hoa, 1965.
Photograph: Keith Bell.

FSgt Lloyd Larney mixing cement; 161 lines, Bien Hoa, 1965.
Photograph: John Nickols.

Aerial view of 161 Recce Flt lines at Bien Hoa, 1965.
Photograph: Keith Bell.

Pilots Lt Holger von Muenchhausen, Capt Bevan Smith, Lt John Guild, Maj Paul Lipscombe (seated), Bien Hoa, 1966.
Photograph courtesy 161 Association.

RAAF members departing Tan Son Nhut for Australia, 5 May 1966.
L-R Ralph Thorp, Jim Crook, Lloyd Larney, John Black, Mick Wilson,
Peter Menear, Allan Higginbottom.
Photograph: Keith Bell.

Cessna servicing at Vung Tau. L-R Felix Mitchell, Keith Kerr and another RAAF fitter.
Photograph: Jack Jewell.

Second Lieutenants Tom Guivarra, Bob Askew, Colin Scott and Rob Rich, Vung Tau, 1966.
Photograph: Tom Guivarra.

Capt Neville Pinkham and Lt John Guild, Vung Tau, 1966.
Photograph: Laurie Doyle.

161 lines (centre left foreground), 1 ALSG area, Back Beach, Vung Tau, 1966.
Photograph: Rex Willis.

Flight line with workshops at rear, Vung Tau, 1966.
Photograph: Dick Knight.

161 (Indep) Recce Flight Pilots, Vung Tau, 1966. L–R back row: 2Lt Bob Askew, 2Lt Blair Weaver, 2Lt Colin Scott, 2Lt Ross Goldspink, 2Lt Adam Fritsch. Middle row: 2Lt Mike Meehan, 2Lt Chic Barron, 2Lt Tom Guivarra, Capt John Wright, 2Lt Vic Salmon, Capt Jim Campbell. Front row: Capt Dick Knight, Maj Laurie Doyle, Capt Mike Webster.
Photograph: Laurie Doyle.

Unmanned aerial vehicle and troops Geoff Pike, Felix Mitchell, Alan Sherman and unidentified onlooker, Vung Tau, 1966.
Photograph: Rex Willis.

Sioux flight line, Vung Tau, 1966–67.
Photograph: Rex Willis.

Bledisloe Cup, Vung Tau style.
Photograph: Rex Willis.

May to October and more temperate and dry for the remainder of the year. The major roads were Route 15, from Vung Tau to Bien Hoa province and Saigon; Route 2 from the provincial capital, Baria, north past Nui Dat to the big rubber plantations and into Long Khanh province; Route 23 east from Baria to the central eastern outpost of Xuyen Moc; and Route 44 branching south from Route 23 towards the coast near the Long Hais. These roads and smaller, local networks were vital to the movement of people and for commercial activity. They were also important to the Viet Cong. To the pilots of 161 Recce Flight, they would become as familiar as the streets in their home towns.

The enemy

From 1959 to 1965, the Viet Cong established a dominant presence in Phuoc Tuy. The enemy forces confronting 1ATF comprised 274 and 275 Main Force Regiments manned by regular soldiers, a provincial mobile force (D445 battalion) manned by guerillas recruited within the province, and local guerilla units manned by villagers on a part-time basis to perform minor functions such as liaison and tax-gathering, and ad hoc tasks such as road blockages.[2]

The main force regiments, which were augmented by regular soldiers of the North Vietnamese Army (NVA) as the war progressed, operated from the sparsely inhabited, jungle-covered northern half of the province. By 1965, they had well-established bases at Hat Dich in the northwest and Thua Tich in the northeast from which their influence had spread southwards.[3] The villages of Long Tan and Long Phuoc near the intended task force site of Nui Dat had been taken over by the Viet Cong. From these villages, pressure could be exerted on the nearby Vietnamese Long Le District Headquarters at Hoa Long.[4] From another stronghold in the Long Hai hills to the southeast, the Viet Cong exerted their influence over the villages of the south central rice-growing region and thus gained access to the rice harvest to feed their forces.

In June 1966, then, the newly arrived 1ATF faced an enemy force that was well established in Phuoc Tuy province on all three levels of its operations. Its bases in mountain strongholds and other locations were relatively inaccessible due to large surrounding areas of jungle, swamp or coastal marsh. The enemy units were thus very difficult to locate and attack. They had well-established supply lines, by land through the highlands to the north and by sea via the long coastal fringe. In short, the province was ideal for the enemy's purposes of insurgency against the South Vietnamese authorities and operations against the South Vietnamese and Australian forces.

Nui Dat: Selection and establishment

Nui Dat was chosen as an open, central and defendable position close enough to the provincial capital, Baria, to facilitate ongoing liaison with the Vietnamese provincial authorities. The area could accommodate the infantry battalions, their support units and an airfield. There was securable road access via Routes 2 and 15 to the logistic support group at Vung Tau. The central location facilitated deployment of forces on operations throughout the province. Importantly, the necessary establishment of a large, secure zone around the task force entailed the relocation of the citizens of only two villages, Long Tan and Long Phuoc.

During April–June 1966, 1ATF was established at Vung Tau prior to occupying its permanent base. The Fifth Battalion (5RAR) arrived at Vung Tau in May and was joined in early June by the Sixth (6RAR). The occupation of Nui Dat was a three-stage operation comprising the resettlement of the 4000 inhabitants of Long Tan and Long Phuoc; the deployment of the 173rd Airborne Brigade and 5RAR to secure the task force base area; and, finally, the move of the main body of the task force from Vung Tau to Nui Dat.

In late May, 5RAR linked up with 173rd Brigade forces to secure the area. During the clearance of Long Phuoc, US and South Vietnamese troops encountered fierce resistance from the Viet Cong D445 battalion but were successful in relocating the villagers.[5] On 5 June, Headquarters 1ATF took command at Nui Dat with 5RAR responsible for the defence of the new area. Nine days later 6RAR was moved forward from Vung Tau to help face the possible threat of large-scale enemy attack. These final moves in the occupation of Nui Dat

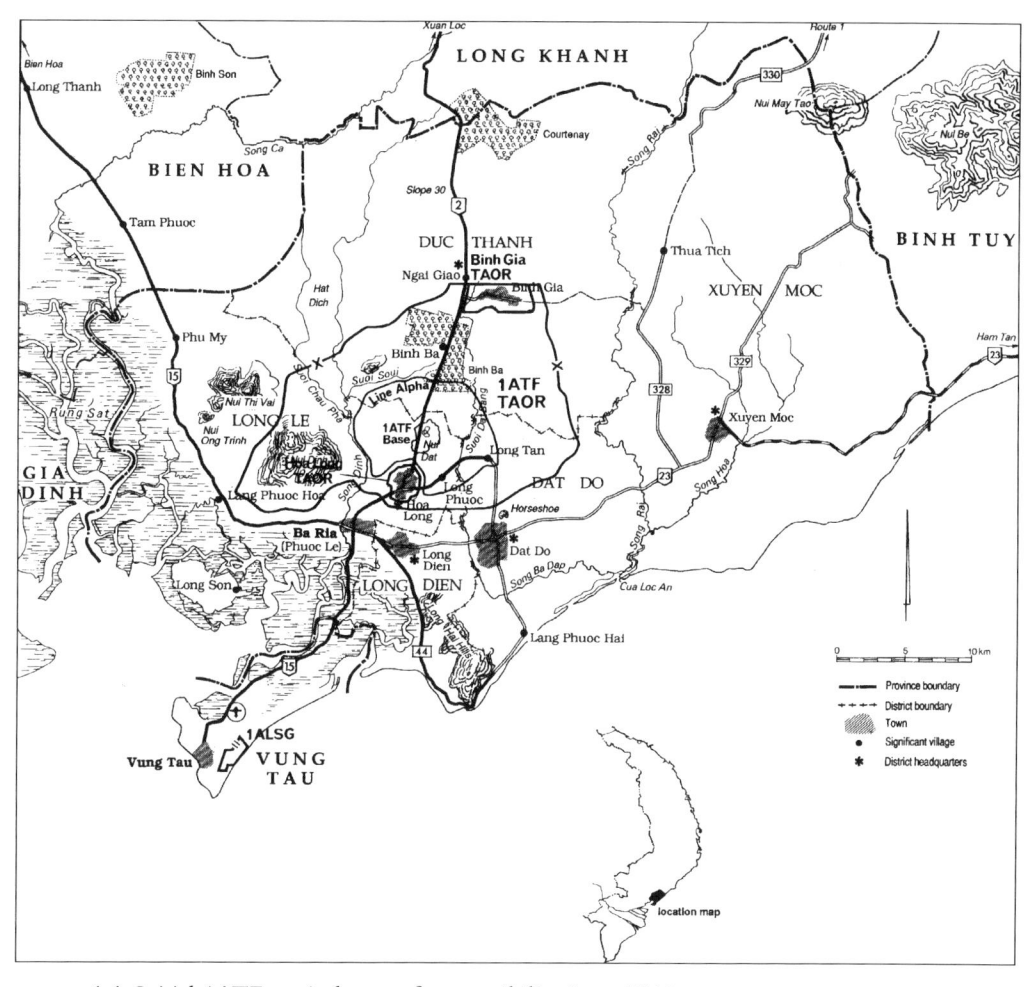

4.1 Initial 1ATF tactical area of responsibility, June 1966.

were hampered by the onset of the monsoon, which turned the area into a sea of red mud.

The limit of the area cleared of local inhabitants was known as Line Alpha. Its clearance permitted fire in defence of the base without endangering civilians. It also prevented the establishment of local facilities outside of the base to provide 'services' to the Australian soldiers as was commonly the case with American bases. This was important from the security viewpoint as well as minimising distractions from operations. The early focus was on completing the clearance out to line Alpha with SAS reconnaissance patrols venturing further out to gather intelligence on enemy movements.

Operation Enoggera

Operation *Enoggera* was conducted from 21 June to 5 July to demolish the remains of Long Phuoc. After its inhabitants had been relocated, the Viet Cong had continued to use the village as a base from which to mortar the task force area.[6] Throughout *Enoggera*, 161 Recce Flight provided an aircraft to the operating battalion, 6RAR, 'for command and control and a variety of observer and liaison tasks including air spotter for the artillery'.[7]

Long Phuoc was a large, heavily fortified village. Its extensive tunnel system had provided a secure base for battalion level operations by the Viet Cong. Its destruction was necessary for the security of the task force area. Nevertheless, it was very sad for the villagers whose home it had been and quite depressing for the soldiers of 6RAR and their support units who had to level the formerly prosperous settlement.

Enoggera completed the initial phase of the occupation of Nui Dat and paved the way for future operations against the enemy beyond Line Alpha. The aim was now to extend the controlled area further out into the TAOR. This phase was well suited to 161 Recce Flight's capabilities and skills. A dispersed and concealed enemy had to be found before he could be attacked. Detection of his movements provided an insight into his plans. A bird's eye view of a proposed area of operations helped battalion commanders to plan their operations. VR sorties checked the province's roads daily for sabotage. Meeting all of these requirements called for the versatility and flexibility offered by the Possums.

Unfortunately, the Flight was unable to join the task force at Nui Dat immediately because it lacked an airfield for the Cessnas. The Siouxs could of course operate from Nui Dat, and did so during the day. It was not practicable to split the Flight into two elements, so it remained intact at Vung Tau until the airfield at Nui Dat was completed. This meant an extra move with all of the attendant difficulties of setting up operations, maintenance and living areas. Further, the Flight had to do this without any break in operations in support of the task force.

Relocation to Vung Tau

At RAAF Base Amberley in Queensland, Captains Dick Knight and Mike Webster were engaged in preparations to bring new aircraft and personnel to upgrade the renamed 161 (Independent) Recce Flight. In late May, the group departed on HMAS *Sydney* to join the Flight at Vung Tau following its move from Bien Hoa on 13 May.

At Vung Tau, Major Paul Lipscombe was not impressed with the site chosen for 161's temporary home. He and his troops had just spent months establishing the unit at Bien Hoa and making it into a reasonably liveable place. He had not envisaged setting up camp again in the even more inhospitable area of the Vung Tau peninsula known as Back Beach.

> It was an absolutely horrendous place. It was just sand dunes, a series of about six rolling sand dunes. To the west, right across the peninsula, was open ground cleared by the US Army and the Vietnamese. The perimeter of that area was much further north. Now, we could have gone over there but the powers decided instead to put us on the beach. It was a poorly chosen site and that's really all I can say. Even with the assistance of an entire US engineer battalion it took weeks to prepare the area for 1ALSG, the logistics support group. And another thing—they put the transport company [5 Company, RAASC] in the middle, in a bowl. It was surrounded by high sand dunes and had no drainage. In those days, the transport company was responsible for fuel storage. There was a little problem attached to that. We had placed an order for 60 44-gallon drums of 80/87 octane Avgas for the Cessnas. Somehow an extra nought was added and 600 drums arrived. Anyway, Duncan Glendinning, the OC of 5 Company, turned up and said, 'I have a small problem. I've just received 600 drums of 80/87 Avgas from Singapore. I haven't got room in my compound to store it.' Nevertheless he did, and then we had these torrential monsoon rains. And poor old Duncan came galloping down and said, 'What am I going to do with these 600 drums of Avgas floating around in here?' It was all over the place.
>
> While we were there we moved twice. We were about to get more people and aircraft. We were responsible for our own security. We still had to meet our operational tasks, and it was a shambles just trying to get

organised. Fortunately, I was soon to have Dick Knight as 2IC and Mike Webster as Admin Officer to help.[8]

The reinforcements arrived on 7 June. The four extra Sioux aircraft and one Cessna increased 161's complement to nine aircraft. The additional personnel brought the unit strength to 15 officers and 78 ORs. Captain Dick Knight recorded his impressions:

> Living on Back Beach, operating from Vung Tau airfield and working for 1ATF in Phuoc Tuy province had its difficulties. Not the least of these was a command and control issue. Headquarters 1ALSG made it very difficult for us and withheld support despite having us under their administrative command. Paul Lipscombe sorted some of the problems out with the help of the commander in Saigon, General Mackay. But some difficulties remained; we were to receive no basic services or assistance in the nine months we were there.
>
> The Sergeants' Mess resolved the first problem: the sand dunes in our allocated area just south of the Composite Ordnance Depot. They invited a US Army Spec 3[9] for a beer after work. He returned for more beer for several nights, bringing his bulldozer with him. So much for the dunes. Our next problem was also solved by the US Army and had a nautical flavour. Our Messes had no flooring and there was little prospect of getting any through the system. A late night delivery of 'dunnage' [timber used for packing cargo in ships' holds] onto the adjacent beach sorted that one out. The Composite Ordnance Depot was always sympathetic to our problems and helped us with power. We had a 5 KVA generator which was inadequate for our refrigeration needs and an icemaker which had apparently been 'acquired' by a detachment from 176 Air Dispatch Company, our other neighbours. We had at long last received our entitlement of refrigerators to replace the small one salvaged from the dump at Bien Hoa. After a temporary fix we finished up with a Ford V8 25 KVA machine which was lovingly cared for by RAEME fitter Daryl Jenkins. Finally, with the aid of the engineers, we replaced our crude 'flaming fury' deep trench latrines with a superior model using bomb containers from the airfield. The Sappers implanted the containers, poured a concrete floor and enclosed it all.[10]

The troops weren't impressed with their new home either. Craftsman Paul Lidster, an airframe fitter, arrived shortly after for the first of his three tours with 161. He described life at the new camp:

> The camp hadn't been fully established as the Flight had just arrived from Bien Hoa, so we spent many hours filling sandbags. After a while you got

to hate the sand. It got into everything—soap, toothpaste, the lot. It was very fine sand, not at all like ours. The operational area was on the airfield about fifteen minutes away. It was usual when leaving for the airfield early in the morning to walk out between the sandbags at the front entrance and come back that night to find three feet of sand there. You'd have to dig your way back in. If there was nothing too pressing out at the workshop area some of us would stay back at the camp to work on improvements to the boozer and the showers and things like that. It was very basic, of course, because everything was under canvas. You were either filling sandbags or trying to keep the sand out of the place.[11]

Engine fitter Craftsman Felix Sylvester Mitchell (yes, his mum really wanted a cat) recalled his arrival at Vung Tau:

I'm thinking that this is supposed to be a lovely little Asian resort. Bullshit. I was whisked off to Back Beach where I looked around and was not excited. The best news I got was that there were no mess duties as the Vietnamese girls looked after that. Mama-san and Baby-san they were called. The concrete kitchen floor was originally laid on top of the sand but now the sand had encroached and it was about two feet above the floor and the only job you got was to go down with a shovel and try to clear some of the sand away. Eric Lindgren and Rex Willis used to run the 'canteen', for want of a better word. The initiation was to drink a can of Swan before you were able to drink anything else. And you couldn't drink it because it had been on the docks in Singapore for about three months and the cans were rusty and the beer was like piss gone bad. It was a rough time because you weren't allowed out of the area for the first six weeks. You had to 'acclimatise' and get over your inevitable attack of the Vung Tau trots [diarrhoea]. So I'm in the boozer [affectionately known to the troops as 'Club Proletariat'] a couple of days later and I haven't had the trots so I think I'm in front and I have a look at this Swan lager. There was just no way in the world I could drink it. I still remember sitting there with this beer open and I thought 'Whoops! I've got to go to the toilet.' A minute later I thought, 'No. I'll just go and have a shower.' They told me at the hospital the bug would pass through me in seven days and it did. We put the carton of Swan away for the next poor, silly bugger who was due to arrive.[12]

Maintenance and operations facilities

Out on the airfield, the facilities were also rudimentary. The 161 flight line was on the side of a taxiway. The maintenance and stores sections were housed in large tents and there were the two Land Rovers fitted with basic servicing facilities for the 'queer' trades (radio, instruments and electrical). Unlike the airframe and engine 'black' trades, where RAAF sergeants were still the senior tradesmen, the queer trades were supervised by three very competent RAEME sergeants in Stuart Wools-Cobb, Peter Bootes and Jack Ellis respectively.

There was also an operations tent where Possum Control was located. Sergeant Jack Jewell worked there for several months before moving to Nui Dat:

> Our job was to brief pilots and provide a communications link for 161 ops. We had no contact with the Yanks; we only talked to our own aircraft. We were a liaison point between the aircraft and the unit. We were responsible for looking after the briefing material, maps and other intelligence so that we could brief the pilots on things like known enemy positions and changes to US communications codes. We ran it 24 hours a day because we had pilots up at night as well. Now, I had done signals before but not a lot. They had a signals sergeant come in and there was me and two Diggers. We did a Signals course. Just before Christmas 1966 we moved up to Nui Dat. Warrant Officer Col Campbell had set up Kangaroo Control by that time.[13]

Maintenance fitters arriving from Australia after the move from Bien Hoa found the working conditions challenging. Craftsman Felix Mitchell offered his impressions:

> It was the first time I'd seen anything as rough. Amberley was great; lots of wide open spaces, concrete pads. And suddenly we're in Vietnam working on duckboards and sand; working in tents, scrounging whatever we could. The basics were there, but it was very primitive. I think, really, that the more complicated work that we did on the aircraft at the time—like putting Sioux blades together and trying to balance them—that called for persistence and ingenuity and I think it just demonstrated the attitude and skills of the Australian serviceman. I mean, the big tent where you tried to align and balance rotor blades had to be free of any draughts. I remember Rex Willis and his gang in there with his bubbles and bits and pieces and they'd yell 'Don't move! Don't move!' and the rest of us would be getting more tent flies or whatever to rig up windbreaks outside. Meanwhile, it's as hot as buggery inside the tent where they're trying to do this delicate work. I used to look back on it years later when I was working for Bell Helicopters with all of their facilities and sophisticated gear. I'd wonder how we managed to do just as well in Vietnam with almost nothing.[14]

As always, the maintenance crews found that refuelling without tanker facilities of their own was a problem to be overcome. Craftsman Paul Lidster recalled that this problem was addressed in the true spirit of US–Australian cooperation:

> We used to fly as required around the clock. Refuelling got to be a bugbear with the Yanks because we'd be requesting a tanker from the Motor Pool at all hours of the night. One day this Yank came up to us and said, 'Goddam you Aussies, I can't get any sleep when I'm on shift. Why don't you get your own tanker?' We said, 'How do we do that?' He said, 'Get your ass to the Motor Pool and sign for one.' So this RAAF fitter, Harry 'The Mouth' Wood, goes down and signs for this tanker and two or three thousand gallons of fuel for the choppers. We parked it in our area and we'd just take it down to the Motor Pool and get it refilled now and again. One day, a fair while later, the OC came out of the command post and put us all on parade. This was in the middle of the morning, so we wondered what was happening. He says, 'Look, I've just had a call from the Motor Pool. I don't care who he is, but I want Corporal Ned Kelly to go down and re-sign for our refuelling tanker.' Then he dismissed the parade and that was that.[15]

Thus it was that 161 Recce Flight settled down to its new, if unpopular, home at Vung Tau. It was to be an eventful and demanding period before the move to Nui Dat the following year. The new 2IC, Dick Knight, was concerned about the workshop personnel, who were working longer and longer hours as the flying rate continued to increase and operations throughout the night as well as the day became routine. He described their working conditions as 'atrocious'. However, there was little to be done other than to give individuals a break whenever possible. Dick decided that an occasional 'swan'—a trip with no apparent operational purpose—was needed to break the routine. Accordingly, he arranged with a contact at the nearby Cat Lo US Navy base for a couple of 161 personnel to go on a day river patrol. He went for a trial run with Sergeant Peter Timmins, arriving at dawn with a picnic lunch for a day on the water. They went on board one of two river patrol boats tasked to conduct stop-and-search inspections of craft heading up the river towards Saigon. Their craft came under fire several times during the morning and, while they were hove to for lunch, one of a passing convoy of cargo ships blew up and sank in the channel. 'Suddenly a couple of F-100s and a light fire team appeared from nowhere and blew holes in the greenery,' recalled Dick. 'Peter and I quickly agreed that perhaps this could not be classed as a recreational activity.'[16]

The following week, one of the patrol boats was lost in a firefight in the same area. So much for the relaxing 'swan' idea, but there's always another way. Some time later a quick challenge to the New Zealand Artillery battery to meet the Possum Flight on the rugby field brought an equally quick response. The Possums came off second best, but the ensuing party was enjoyed by all.

There was an alternative for those who craved the bright lights and cultural exchange. One could 'do the town' in Vung Tau, with its bars and eateries, and transport was available to get back before curfew. For those hardy souls who were persuaded by the local lovelies to carouse on through the night, it was possible to have mates cover for them by faking the roll call when the truck returned. The Lotharios would make their way back at dawn by devious means and enter the unit lines via the beachfront in various stages of undress. 'The water's great this morning' would be their feeble attempt to pretend to have gone for an early morning dip in the South China Sea.

Dick Knight was not impressed with the food, which was sourced mainly from the Americans and was not to Aussie tastes. Delicacies like weenies, powdered potatoes and eggs, dill pickles and pre-masticated steaks were not always snapped up but were not wasted. The excess could be traded. There was an American civil engineering unit at the airfield whose employees had to find their own accommodation and food. A simple exchange was agreed. One of their vehicles would call monthly into the 161 lines to pick up the unwanted delicacies. In return, a 161 vehicle would visit their depot. Dick described their store as 'like an Aladdin's Cave, full of goodies, particularly for our projected move to Nui Dat . . . nails, timber, plywood, cement, wire, fittings—all were to be useful.'[17] Dick was a great planner, and much appreciated for his sterling work as 2IC.

As 1967 beckoned, planning for the move to Nui Dat became more detailed. Captain Mike Webster and several troops stayed with 5RAR at Nui Dat for long periods to oversee the preparation of 161's new home by the Engineers. The hangar took shape, complete with concrete floor. The Possums looked forward with increasing impatience to the completion of the airstrip. In the meantime, the demands of flying and maintenance were still escalating and there was more than enough to occupy their attention.

5

Vung Tau:
May 1966–March 1967

From its new location at Vung Tau, 161's operations in support of the establishment of the task force continued around the clock. The operations were not without incident however. On 1 June, Second Lieutenant Don Cockerell's Cessna was hit by ground fire while on a low-level mission. A bullet entered the floor of the cockpit, severed the elevator trim chain, grazed the pilot's left calf and exited through the side of the fuselage. Unsure of the extent of the damage Cockerell carefully landed back at Vung Tau for repairs to the aircraft and his leg.

After the completion of Operation *Enoggera* on 5 July, the Flight supported 5RAR in Operations *Sydney 1* and *2* from 8 to 23 July. These were the first operations fully under task force control. 5RAR's task on *Sydney 1* was to clear Nui Nghe, a jungle-covered hill outside the northern boundary of Line Alpha, as a preliminary to further operations aimed at restoring control of Route 2 in the northern part of the province. Reconnaissance had shown that the hill was crisscrossed with tracks and dotted with bunkers and trenches.[1] There was evidence of regular occupancy.

Sydney 2 was a cordon and search of Duc My, a hamlet in the Binh Ba village complex north of Nui Dat. The complex had a long history of Viet Cong domination. These operations provided valuable experience for the battalion, and the methods used became models for future operations of the same type.[2] They also provided valuable experience for the supporting units, including 161 Recce Flight. It was a particularly demanding time for Second Lieutenant Rob Rich, who carried out a forced landing on 18 July after his Sioux suffered engine failure. Both pilot and aircraft were recovered safely, the aircraft by Chinook helicopter. For Rob it was a case of déjà vu. Two days earlier he had carried out a forced landing after experiencing engine problems while flying in support of Operation *Brisbane* in the Nui Dinhs, a range of hills west of Nui Dat. Rob was no doubt waiting for the third failure but luckily it didn't happen. Given the level of flying effort and the operating conditions, it was inevitable that such problems would occur. However, that was cold comfort for the pilots concerned. July 1966 was the Flight's busiest yet, with 1585 sorties flown for a total of 750 hours.

Radio rebroadcast

Many extra flying hours were expended in meeting the demand for radio rebroadcast operations in support of the ground forces. As the name implies, a rebroadcast mission involves the aircraft acting as an airborne intermediary to permit communication between two or more parties unable to make direct contact. Communications equipment in the VHF and UHF bands, which includes most military airborne and field communications facilities, is limited to line-of-sight range because transmitted signals are not reflected from the ionosphere to give the extended range possible for communications equipment operating at higher power on lower frequencies. An airborne station with the capacity to receive and retransmit messages can therefore serve as a link between two ground stations that are a significant distance apart, or closer together but separated by an obstruction such as a large hill. In its most simple form, rebroadcast can be achieved by the airborne operator relaying signals from one party to another by listening and then repeating the information. This is repetitive, inefficient, time-consuming and prone to error. Automatic rebroadcast is achieved by installing a second communications set in the aircraft. Signals received by one set can then be automatically rebroadcast by the other.

161 Recce Flight's automatic radio rebroadcast capability was achieved by fitting an extra VHF–FM radio to the Cessna aircraft. On 17 October 1966, two Cessnas flew continuous rebroadcast in support of Operation *Queanbeyan* from 2.45 a.m. until 8.35 p.m. This was the first successful, prolonged radio rebroadcast operation mounted by the Flight.

Behind the operations

Behind the operational scene the development of the task force area continued. The 1st Field Squadron, Royal Australian Engineers (RAE) under Major Warren Lennon was engaged in providing many necessities including adequate drainage, latrines, a garbage dump and an airfield. It was the monsoon season and construction tasks were consequently most difficult. At Vung Tau, 161 was also trying to improve its facilities. Along with the primary business of operations, much construction work was carried out at the Back Beach area to improve living conditions.

The Cessna's operational capabilities were also improved. A trial modification was devised to fit two rocket tubes a side to carry 2.75-inch, folding-fin, white phosphorus (WP) rockets for target marking. Initial firing runs were completed successfully on 14 July. Proficiency was a matter of practice and there was no sighting system. Each pilot, depending on his height, put a chinagraph mark on the windscreen to suit his own needs. However, there was always a catch. Like everything else technical and operational, the modification had to be approved by the RAAF. Major Paul Lipscombe and his troops resorted to subterfuge:

> Our draft modification had duly been submitted and the dreaded RAAF engineering officer appeared on the scene with an Armaments bloke from RAAF Butterworth in Malaysia to check it all out. When we found out they were coming, I told the fitters to get rid of it. So they took it all off, switches and circuit-breakers and whatever, but concealed the wiring behind the wing root panels inside. The RAAF people turned up and humphed a lot and gave the go-ahead and, much to their surprise, the modification was completed in about fifteen minutes. Later, a RAAF team turned up to review the installation and of course 9 Squadron was there by then. The group hopped into a Huey and dropped a ration box in the wash

just off Vung Tau beach. Captain Neville Pinkham took off in the modified Cessna with WP loaded and rolled in and hit the box. And you could see the eyes come out of this Huey like they couldn't believe. So that was with the target-marking rockets. But the RAAF didn't know we had been using high explosive [HE] rockets as well. I was down at the airfield one day and a couple of RAAF senior officers came along and of course, there on the outboard pods on each Cessna were HE rockets. The senior of the two just went off his brain because we had no approval to carry armaments. I suggested that he mind his own business and he duly reported back through the system that Major Lipscombe had been disrespectful to a senior officer. I told his wing commander that although he was senior he was from a junior service and thus only my equivalent. And that got things right off again. That's how sensitive they were. In the event, after Neville's display, we didn't hear another peep out of them about rockets.[3]

It wasn't long before the new capability was being exploited. On 24 September 1966, Second Lieutenant Vic Salmon, with US Army observer Major J. Deloach, fired two rockets at what was thought to be an enemy soldier with a water buffalo crossing a creek. This was the first occasion on which rockets were fired by a 161 pilot in an operational role. Bigger and better pods and rockets were to come as 161's pilots sought over the years to improve the offensive capabilities of their aircraft.

Long Tan and its aftermath

For the battalions at Nui Dat, the first major engagement with the enemy was at hand. SAS patrols and intelligence from Vietnamese agents indicated a concentration of enemy forces to the northeast of the now empty village of Long Tan. Meanwhile, during July, 6RAR mounted Operations *Brisbane* and *Hobart* in the eastern and western sectors of the task force TAOR respectively. The aim was to detect and counter enemy activity which threatened the security of the task force base area.

Hobart was an eventful operation. Bravo and Charlie Companies of 6RAR made close contact with elements of D445 battalion on 25 July. Bravo Company's 6 Platoon came under heavy fire and incurred several casualties including two fatalities. The operation continued until 6RAR was recalled to Nui Dat on 29 July to counter the threat of a possible large-scale assault on the task force. The battalion had been blooded but had performed well in its first serious engagement with the enemy. The gauntlet had been thrown down by the Australians, and intelligence indicated that the enemy was reacting by concentrating forces in and around the TAOR to mount a strong attack on the Nui Dat base.[4]

The attack did not eventuate, and task force operations to open up the province beyond Line Alpha continued. Then, on 17 August, the base came under mortar attack and casualties were suffered. The previous weeks had been particularly frustrating for the task force headquarters staff. While specialist unit 547 Signals Troop reported consistent indications from radio direction-finding that an enemy force was closing from the east, infantry patrols had been unable to confirm the threat.[5] However, when 6RAR went out to search for the mortar positions and pursue the attackers, their persistence in following enemy tracks drew them into a major engagement with enemy forces. The historic Battle of Long Tan ensued. Not surprisingly, available records suggest little if any direct involvement by 161 Recce Flight in this intense encounter in heavy monsoon rain during the late afternoon and evening of 18 August. There was little that the Flight could have contributed in the prevailing conditions and with heavy artillery fire concentrated in the contact areas. The story of Long Tan has been told many times and is not repeated here. Suffice to say that it put paid to enemy ambitions of a successful assault on the task force.

While August 1966 was most notable for Long Tan, the month saw sustained operations by the task force and consequently by the Flight, which racked up 1061 sorties for a total of 711 flying hours. Flying in Phuoc Tuy was becoming more dangerous as the enemy was more closely engaged. On 30 August, Second Lieutenant Don Cockerell again took ground fire and sustained damage to the starboard wingtip and port aileron. Cockerell recovered the aircraft to Vung Tau where it was quickly repaired by fitters already adept at patching bullet holes.

Possum Master Two

August 1966 also brought a change of command for 161. It was time for Possum Master One, Paul Lipscombe, to go home. He had brought

161 through its challenging first year. His relief, Major Laurie Doyle, arrived on 31 July and took command on 14 August. Major Doyle was the first of six Gunners to command the Flight. He was a career officer of fourteen years' seniority who had done his pilot training on Austers with 16 AOP Flight at Canberra. He was appointed Chief Flying Instructor on Cessna 180 aircraft prior to the formation of 16 ALA at Amberley on 1 December 1960. He had anticipated command of 161 since the beginning of the Australian commitment.

Major Doyle saw the relocation of 161 to Nui Dat as his first priority. He was keenly aware of the implications of the change in the operational environment from Bien Hoa to Phuoc Tuy. The engagement at Long Tan and the subsequent activities of the task force reinforced his eagerness to move to Nui Dat. He wanted 161 to be a visible, integral and more responsive element of the task force, not a support unit located fifteen minutes' flight time away. He spoke of his feelings on taking command:

> I was daunted more than a little by the fact that this was the first war for Army Aviation, although I was the second Possum Master, and there was a new phase entering as the Australian task force went into Phuoc Tuy province. We were our own masters answering to a general at Long Binh, whereas when Paul was at Bien Hoa he was one step further removed. I felt comfortable, really comfortable, about commanding a unit which was part of what I recognised was an infantry brigade; a bit light, we were short one battalion, but this was what I was used to. But I was daunted by the fact that this was the first time that we had launched a structure like that with an aviation element.[6]

Conflicting viewpoints: Pacification versus the war of attrition

The fierce repulsion of the enemy at Long Tan pushed back the threat to the task force and gave Brigadier Jackson more latitude to structure the activities of his units. The US forces were also putting in place a strategy for the longer term involving both the engagement of enemy main forces and pacification activities. Pacification was the general term applied to the process of restoring government control among the people, often referred to as the 'other' war, and was conducted in parallel with the campaign of attrition waged in higher level engagements.[7] The success of pacification depended on the ability of troops to protect the village people and their produce from the guerilla forces of the Viet Cong; otherwise their cooperation would end in brutal reprisals. During 1966, in parallel with their own rapid escalation of forces, the Americans placed great emphasis on retraining and equipping ARVN forces to deal with guerillas in pursuit of pacification aims while it pursued the 'conventional' war of attrition against enemy main forces.[8]

Keeping the enemy separated from the civilian population was a central plank of the counterinsurgency operations mounted by the Australian task force, a practice founded in successful operations of this type during the Malayan emergency some years earlier. The selection of the Nui Dat area as the task force base reflected that aim, as it was ideally positioned as a barrier between the Viet Cong strongholds in the north of the province and the populous, productive areas in the south. Unlike the US forces, and to the displeasure of the American commander General Westmoreland,[9] the task force commander did not see the Australian role as confronting enemy main forces while leaving the pacification program to the ARVN Division in Phuoc Tuy province. Instead, the task force 'practised the "oil slick" technique of methodically spreading its influence and consolidating gains within the province, while maintaining readiness to confront main force units'.[10] Following the encounter at Long Tan, Brigadier Jackson followed this policy by concentrating on clearing out the remnants of enemy bases and installations from within the TAOR and completing measures for the security of Nui Dat. An extended program was put in place to establish effective perimeter defences to reduce dependence on intensive patrolling and discourage any large-scale attack by enemy forces. Security measures for Nui Dat included constant VR sorties by 161 Recce Flight. Side by side with operations, the task force also followed a program of civic action in the villages.[11] Aid projects such as the installation of water pumps and assistance with health care were important elements of the pacification process.

Operations in the mountain strongholds

Brigadier Jackson's pacification strategy did not rule out offensive operations in areas where enemy strongholds threatened task force objectives. He initiated clearing operations in the Nui Thi Vais and

Nui Dinhs in the southwest of the province, vantage points from which the enemy could monitor the key Route 15 from Vung Tau to Saigon and mount ambushes. As a safe haven for enemy forces, it also posed a continuing threat to the central regions of the province including Nui Dat itself. It was a very rough area, honeycombed with tunnels and caves tailor-made for booby traps and ambushes. Several operations including *Vaucluse* (8–24 September), *Canberra* (6–10 October) and *Queanbeyan* (16–26 October) disrupted the enemy's activities in this stronghold and destroyed several bases and camps.

The Flight's pilots soon found themselves in the thick of things. On 6 October, Second Lieutenant Bob Askew was flying direct support for 6RAR on a recce mission east of Binh Gia when his Sioux developed a severe engine vibration and lost power. The terrain was unsuitable for an emergency landing, but he managed to put the aircraft down on a narrow road. He was highly commended for his presence of mind and skill in saving his aircraft, and was later awarded the Queen's Commendation.

It was during Operation *Canberra* that 161 lost its first aircraft and almost incurred its first fatality. On 10 October, Second Lieutenant Bill Davies crashed on Route 15 after his Sioux was hit by sniper fire while flying DS (Direct Support) for 5RAR. The aircraft was totally destroyed after striking a telephone pole at the side of the road. 'It turned over on its side and crashed straight into the bitumen, turning over and over as the tremendous momentum of its rotating parts expended itself.'[12] Davies was seriously injured and was medevaced to Australia after medical treatment at the US 3rd Field Hospital in Saigon. He recovered from his injuries after further treatment.

Operation Queanbeyan, *17–26 October 1966*

5RAR distinguished itself in its conduct of *Canberra* and *Queanbeyan*. The 161 Commander's diary is laconic in its reference to tasks in support of *Queanbeyan*, merely recording that several pilots had evacuated 5RAR casualties during the period 17–21 October. One such incident was particularly notable. On 17 October, the 5RAR headquarters group was ascending a steep path up Nui Thi Vai to their intended location 1200 feet above. They took cover from rain under a huge rock, 'like a large triangular prism resting on one of its edges, leaning on and supported by some huge trees'.[13] It was some 50 feet long and 30 feet high, with a roughly horizontal top of approximately the same dimensions. As the group moved higher, it sustained two casualties from close contact with the enemy. There was no suitable LZ in the immediate vicinity for a Dustoff[14] Iroquois to take the wounded on board. The nearest clearing was at the foot of the hill, several hundred yards away, over very rough ground which would have entailed a slow and painful effort by a stretcher party. The surface of the large rock encountered on the advance up Nui Thi Vai suggested itself as an alternative which might, just might, accommodate a Sioux helicopter. It was big enough, but trees interfered with the approach and any attempt to recover the wounded would entail a very delicate piece of flying.

Second Lieutenant Bob Askew, the irrepressible DS pilot for 5RAR that day, examined the situation from the air while some trees were removed by the Assault Pioneer Platoon to permit access. The line of approach was barely wide enough for the Sioux's main rotor blades and the limited space meant that he would have to back off the rock until he could rotate the aircraft and make the translation to forward flight down the hillside:

> It was an acid test of his judgment because once he was committed to the landing it was not possible to pull out at the last moment without grave risk of crashing. However, like all of the pilots of 161 Reconnaissance Flight who had flown so much for us since we had been in Vietnam, often up to eleven hours a day, we knew that Askew's judgment was to be relied upon. Captain Bob Supple guided the aircraft in. An additional danger which the pilot had to face was the risk of being shot down by a sniper from the enemy group further up the slope. While on its final approach, the aircraft was virtually a sitting duck and the pilot had no protection apart from a flak jacket. The surface of the rock was saucer shaped with a high lip on the eastern side, the side from which we could climb up onto it. The rotor blades cleared this lip by about two feet so no one could approach the aircraft while its blades were still spinning, and Bob Supple had to bring the aircraft in right alongside him to avoid decapitation.[15]

A few minutes later, Askew took the first casualty, Captain Brian Ledan, aboard and carefully reversed out from the rock. He then transferred his passenger to the waiting Dustoff before learning of the second casualty, Corporal Womal, and returning to the rock. Sadly, this soldier died from his injuries before he could be evacuated. Askew again made a successful withdrawal from his precarious perch and flew the body to Vung Tau before resuming his more usual duties in support of the operation. His skill and courage that day are fittingly recognised in the annals of 5RAR.

Four days later, another 161 pilot distinguished himself while flying DS for 5RAR on Operation *Queanbeyan*. Second Lieutenant Charles 'Chic' Barron's efforts on 21 October resulted in the award of a Mention in Dispatches (MID):

> The battalion's companies were widely separated on the steep slopes of the mountain mass with a resupply problem due to the difficult terrain. It was essential for the continuation of the operation that supplies were delivered to the fighting troops. The ground in which the battalion was operating was extremely difficult and consisted of steep covered slopes and rocky outcrops, which only provided small and dangerous landing points, the approaches to which were covered by enemy fire through which [Second Lieutenant Barron] had to fly before he reached the comparative tree-bound safety of the landing points. He repeatedly flew his helicopter into small gaps in the jungle and effected resupply to extremely hazardous positions by hovering and resting the helicopter's skids on piles of debris, or rocky outcrops. His rotor blades had marginal clearance with the surrounding jungle and he was obliged to reverse his helicopter out in all cases but one.
>
> During that day, he flew forty resupply missions into these critical landing points which were made even more hazardous by the heavy loads he carried and the unfavourable and gusty wind conditions prevailing. When, during the mid afternoon his relief was due, he immediately requested permission to continue as he alone was familiar with the few landing points and the highly fluid tactical situation. By the time of his final task, after last light, he had flown nearly eleven hours and completed forty nine sorties in a fine showing of initiative and flying ability.[16]

Continuing operations in late 1966

As 1966 drew to a close, task force operations continued with the dual aims of pacification and the extension of the TAOR. Notable operations were *Hayman* (6–12 November), to clear Long Son Island in the marshy Rung Sat zone, and *Ingham* (18 November–3 December), to locate and destroy the Viet Cong D445 battalion. The latter objective was not achieved but the operation was successful in locating and destroying the enemy base and recovering large stores of rice. On 23 November, Lieutenant Colin Scott's aircraft was fired upon during operations in support of *Ingham*. He was not injured and the aircraft was undamaged.

By this time 161 pilots were becoming very familiar with the province and the operational techniques they had developed and practised for more than a year in country. On 6 November, 6RAR showed its appreciation for 161's support. At a presentation ceremony, Second Lieutenant 'Chic' Barron received a captured ChiCom machine gun on behalf of the Flight.

Developments in Possum territory

Battalion operations aside, every effort was still being made to enhance 161's effectiveness, with particular emphasis on reconnaissance operations. All pilots received instruction on the use of a night vision aid, the Starlight Scope, to determine its suitability for use on night recce sorties. Fixed wing commander Captain John Wright made a most valuable contribution to the development of 161's reconnaissance tasks, a contribution later recognised by the award of an MID. He flew many night sorties, developing and practising techniques for using the Starlight Scope and establishing the ideal heights for its use under various conditions of visibility. He also worked with his pilots to improve daylight VR techniques, showing that results and safety were optimised if the reconnaissance was carried out at treetop level and just above stalling speed.

Along with improved VR techniques, pilots' needs were also addressed by the replacement of their old Owen guns with M-16 automatic rifles. Their comments were very favourable after their first range practice. However, some felt that it would be nice to be able to hit back with a little more firepower when fired upon in flight, and this possibility was to engage their interest and creativity throughout 161's service in South Vietnam.

The pace of operations continued to increase. The increased flying hours in support of task force operations brought management problems and unique solutions. When the aircraft strength of the Flight was raised to nine in mid-1966, it was authorised to fly 70 hours per month for each aircraft on establishment, a total of 630 hours per month. It was quickly apparent that this allocation was inadequate for the needs of 1ATF, and by 1968, it was almost doubled to 1200 hours per month.

The increased flying hours flowed through to maintenance tasks. The allocation of flying hours was a major factor determining the manning of the workshops and the scaling of spare parts held at the unit. For example, the increase from 630 to 1200 flying hours necessitated an additional five D servicings[17] each month, about 280 man-hours of work. As well, more time was needed for other scheduled servicings and repair tasks arising from the higher flying hours.

For Major Doyle, the rate of aircraft usage meant that major overhauls had to be carried out on his Cessnas before the anticipated move to Nui Dat in early 1967. An E servicing[18] program meant weeks of down time for each of the three aircraft in turn. The Flight did not have adequate servicing facilities, but luckily the RAAF's 9 Squadron found some space in its Iroquois servicing hangar. It probably helped that 161's senior maintenance fitters were RAAF. The OC gave Sergeant Doug Kennett the job of managing the program.

The E servicing program posed another problem for Laurie Doyle. It meant he would have four fixed wing pilots but only two aircraft available at any given time. He hit upon a good solution to this problem, one which would also increase the knowledge and expertise of his Cessna pilots:

> I thought there had to be a constructive solution. Now, I'd met Major George Shallcross, the CO of the 54th Aviation Company which operated the big, single-engined Otters out of Vung Tau. The Otters, call sign 'Big Daddy', were hash and trash carriers.[19] They were able to get into places where other short field aeroplanes couldn't, not even the Caribous. I explained my problem to George and asked if he could take an experienced stiff-wing operator who could be checked out on the Otters to fly right-hand seat and get some extra experience on those kinds of operations. He agreed readily, and of course did more than that. He provided a full conversion to Otters for all of my fixed wing pilots.
>
> Lieutenant Vic Salmon was the first pilot to go to the exchange program with the 54th. And one day, a very harassed American Army warrant officer air traffic controller has a whole stack of traffic and out of the blue came 'Vung Tau Tower, this is Big Daddy 701. I'm 25 miles south; do you read?' And without thinking, all the guy in the tower hears is the

Australian accent and he says 'Roger, Possum 701!' There's a pause and then this plaintive voice says 'Vung Tau Tower, this is BIG DADDY 701!' There were four Possums on the net, including me, and we all heard him. Did he ever get a drubbing! Vung Tau, this is BIG DADDY!!!

So we had our bit of fun and the Americans found out very quickly that we had well-trained, mature young men and they trusted us with their aeroplanes. 'Big Daddy' with an Australian accent became an often-heard cry. Now, I couldn't justify the same thing with the chopper pilots, but after I left it turned out that they managed to do something similar for them. A number of young men got some very good experience flying a wide variety of aircraft: Iroquois, Cobras, the Cayuse and so on.[20]

Just as importantly, the detachment of pilots for a month at a time, to fly with US personnel, forged friendships and understanding in ways that would not otherwise be possible. From the beginning of its deployment until the end, 161 enjoyed close and cooperative relations with US forces and learned a great deal about both the strong and the weak points of the American way. A story told by Laurie Doyle was illustrative of the trust and mutual esteem which came with experience:

I'm sitting in my office on the airfield one day and through the door came a Forward Air Control (FAC) pilot called John T. Buck. John, who was to become a general, was a character. He'd come into my office and say 'J.T. Buck, your friendly FAC, sir!' This day he said, 'Do you have a spare aeroplane?' I knew that John would never stuff me around, so I turned to the soldier running the ops radio and said, 'Captain Wright is just taxiing. Get him back here, and tell him not to switch off. He has a change of mission.' So John Buck got in the aeroplane with John Wright and off they went out to the northeast. It turned out that the FACs had run out of serviceable aeroplanes. And what John Buck explained to John Wright was that he had six Phantoms about to taxi at Bien Hoa, loaded with grape—to use an old expression. So, away they went to run the air strike. Before I returned to Australia I stayed with John Buck. One night after dinner he handed me a big, blue box and said, 'Give this to John Wright. That mission he flew so well for me was one of my best ever. The Phantom drivers had their new CO with them and he was so impressed with the mission that he awarded me an Air Medal. But it belongs to John Wright.'[21]

Operations in early 1967: Revisiting the task force area

In January 1967 the focus of task force operations shifted to 'operations designed to reassert authority over the central region of Phuoc Tuy'.[22]

Operation *Caloundra* was a cordon-and-search of the village of Xa Binh Ba in the Binh Ba rubber complex to the north of Nui Dat. Operation *Bravo* commenced in mid-January to clear the area around Nui Dat past Line Alpha to the now-established 12 000 metre Line Bravo, the limit of the range of 105mm artillery operating from Nui Dat. On 16 January a cordon-and-search operation was mounted at Hoa Long village, the site of a struggle between Australian civic action efforts and Viet Cong attempts to control the villagers through terrorism and murder.[23] A succession of brief operations continued through February and brought another narrow escape for the Possums when Second Lieutenant Mike Meehan took ground fire during Operation *Tamborine*.

Engagement with the enemy: Operations Bribie and Renmark

On 17 February, Operation *Bribie* was mounted in retaliation to a Viet Cong attack on the coastal village of Lang Phuoc Hai, south of Dat Do. This became a major engagement as 6RAR confronted determined resistance from a substantial enemy force. In the ensuing firefight the Australians suffered their heaviest casualties since Long Tan. The 161 DS chopper played a useful part in guiding APCs to assist in the withdrawal of a beleaguered Bravo Company.[24]

Operation *Bribie* was followed immediately by *Renmark*, a search-and-destroy operation into the Long Hai hills in the south of the province. On 21 February, Bravo Company of 5RAR was moving in a line of APCs when one of the carriers was destroyed by a huge explosion when it triggered a booby trap. Three soldiers were killed and nine injured. Minutes later, two more were killed and nineteen wounded when an anti-personnel mine was detonated. Captain Tony White, the battalion medical officer, was taken at once to the horrific scene by the DS pilot, Captain Jim Campbell. More than 30 soldiers, most of them wounded, were trapped in the middle of a minefield. Despite the risk of triggering mines with his helicopter's skids and rotor downdraft, Captain Campbell landed repeatedly in the minefield, first bringing in Captain White and then removing casualties one at a time to a safe evacuation point.[25] He was awarded the Distinguished Flying Cross (DFC) for his part in *Renmark*, the first of fourteen such awards to 161 pilots during the Vietnam campaign. This quietly courageous officer remains one of the legends of Army Aviation.

As February gave way to March and 1ATF mourned its losses during *Bribie* and *Renmark*, the date for the relocation of 161 to Nui Dat approached and efforts to maintain operations in support of the battalions while preparing for the move fully extended the Flight's capabilities. A new and long chapter in the Flight's history was about to begin as it finally found a permanent home with the task force.

6

Relocation to Nui Dat

Task force commander Brigadier Owen Jackson officially opened Luscombe Field at Nui Dat on 5 December 1966. Major Laurie Doyle, with Captain John Wright as co-pilot, had made the first landing on the strip on 31 October. Laurie didn't want to get beaten to it by the Americans or the unscrupulous RAAF pilots from Vung Tau.

The airfield was named after Captain Bryan Luscombe, the first Air Observation Post pilot trained in the Australian Army. He was killed in action while serving with the British Commonwealth Division in Korea in 1952. At the opening ceremony, Laurie Doyle presented a brass plaque to Brigadier Jackson which he attached to the airfield sign. The plaque told Captain Luscombe's story and was later incorporated in a permanent stone marker maintained by 161 as a memorial to him.[1]

The Luscombe runway ran roughly east-west. In air traffic control parlance, it was Runway 10 to the east and 28 to the west. On take-off to the west, the dominant feature facing the pilot was a chain of high hills, the Nui Thai Vais and the Nui Dinhs, which overlooked the vital Route 15 from Vung Tau to Saigon and afforded the enemy a grandstand view of the centre of the province including Nui Dat. Beyond the hills the mangrove labyrinth of the Rung Sat provided a thousand waterways for the enemy to infiltrate the coast with men and supplies. Turning south over the village of Hoa Long, the provincial capital, Baria, would be under the nose of the aircraft. Beyond lay the Vung Tau peninsula jutting into the South China Sea. In the background to the left would be the populous and productive agricultural area of the central south of the province, with the villages of Dat Do, Long Dien and An Ngai providing familiar landmarks. Further south, the pilot would see the range of hills called the Long Hais, another enemy stronghold, extending out to the sea.

Continuing his circuit left, the pilot would be facing the comparatively isolated Xuyen Moc area in the eastern sector of the province. The bulk of the May Tao massif would catch his eye next, near the border of Long Khanh province to the northeast. It was to the central highlands of South Vietnam rising beyond the hills of Long Khanh that the Ho Chi Minh trail disgorged a constant stream of men and equipment to support the insurgency in the south. As he continued his circuit to the north, still climbing, the pilot would note the Thua Tich area and the forest extending to the west; across to the Hat Dich area where the provinces of Phuoc Tuy, Long Khanh and Bien Hoa met. This area, with its supply routes from the coast via Hat Dich, was the operational home of the enemy's 274 and 275 Main Force Regiments. In the left foreground now was the Binh Ba rubber plantation and, in the distance to the north, the large Courtenay rubber complex. The ribbon of Route 2 could be seen running north from Baria to access these plantations. Saigon and the huge Long Binh-Bien Hoa military complex lay over the horizon to the northwest. Completing his circuit left, the pilot could line up on the threshold of runway 28 as he headed west again. During his tour with 161 he would come to know all of these areas very well, from both a safe altitude and down amongst the trees where the enemy established his base camps and dug his tunnels and bunkers.

Home is a rubber plantation

The opening of Luscombe Field enabled 161 to move from Vung Tau to its new home at Nui Dat, on the northern side of the runway near its eastern threshold. Detachments from the Flight to Nui Dat had

RELOCATION TO NUI DAT   69

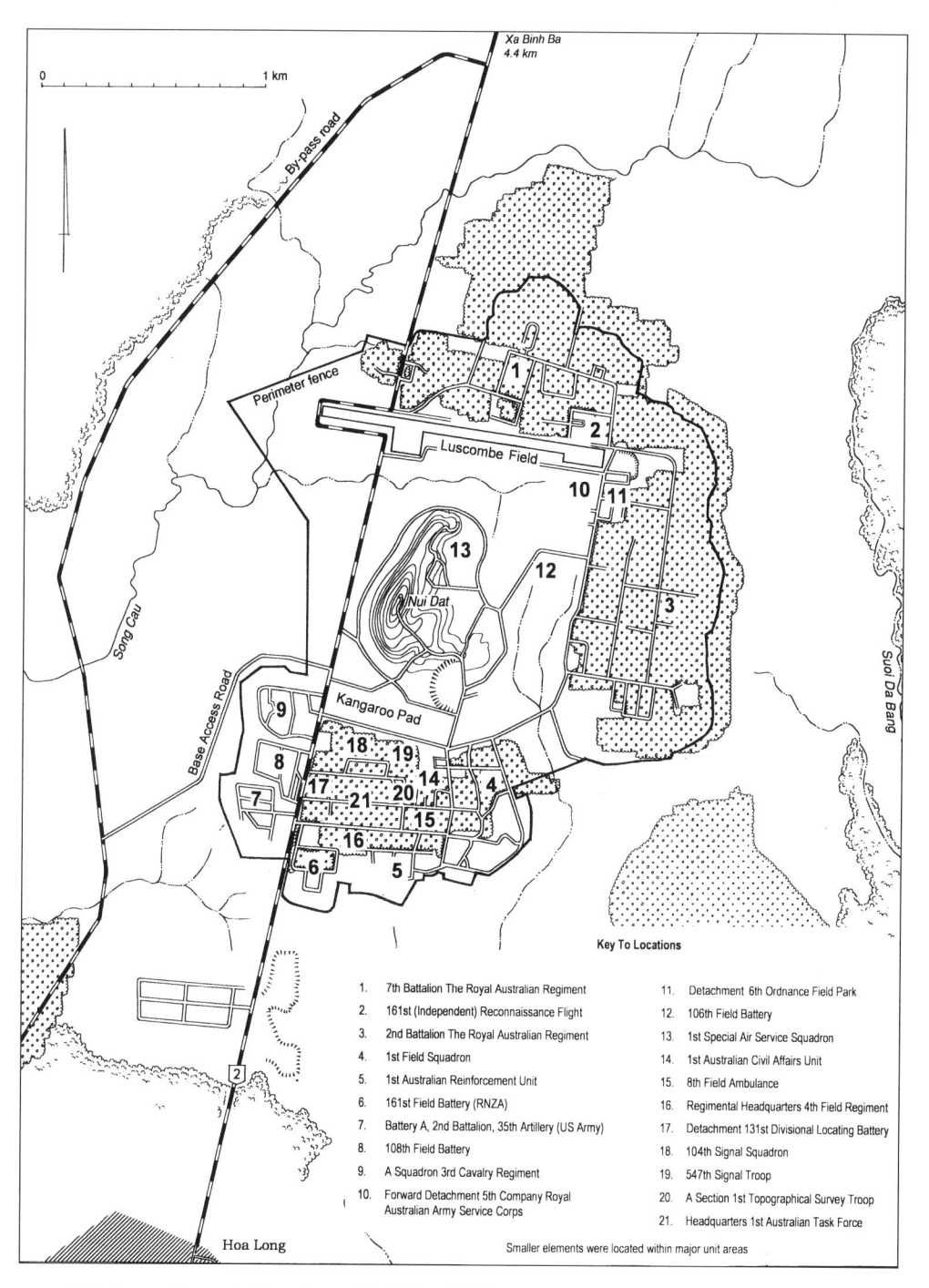

Key To Locations

1. 7th Battalion The Royal Australian Regiment
2. 161st (Independent) Reconnaissance Flight
3. 2nd Battalion The Royal Australian Regiment
4. 1st Field Squadron
5. 1st Australian Reinforcement Unit
6. 161st Field Battery (RNZA)
7. Battery A, 2nd Battalion, 35th Artillery (US Army)
8. 108th Field Battery
9. A Squadron 3rd Cavalry Regiment
10. Forward Detachment 5th Company Royal Australian Army Service Corps
11. Detachment 6th Ordnance Field Park
12. 106th Field Battery
13. 1st Special Air Service Squadron
14. 1st Australian Civil Affairs Unit
15. 8th Field Ambulance
16. Regimental Headquarters 4th Field Regiment
17. Detachment 131st Divisional Locating Battery
18. 104th Signal Squadron
19. 547th Signal Troop
20. A Section 1st Topographical Survey Troop
21. Headquarters 1st Australian Task Force

Smaller elements were located within major unit areas

6.1 Australian task force base, Nui Dat, 1967.

begun six months earlier in June 1966, with an officer and two ORs to act in the capacity of task force aviation officer and to provide an artillery advisory service. On 28 November, Captain Mike Webster and Privates D. Keating, W. Muller, J. Rankin and J. Ruttley arrived at Nui Dat to begin preparations for the Flight's relocation; the first of many detachments until the move was completed on 24 March 1967. 1 Field Squadron, Royal Australian Engineers (RAE), had built the basics: the shells of the maintenance hangar, administration building, operations and ordnance huts. A kitchen area and toilet pits were thoughtfully provided for refuel and evacuation purposes. In regard to the latter, it seemed that 161's new home was connected to the 1/83 Company US Artillery area on the southern side of the runway by a geological fault line. When the latrines were fitted out with appropriate seating—drums with seats poised over the drop zone—the morning relief parade was a memorable affair. Each seat would be occupied by a soldier, usually reading the US 'Stars and Stripes' propaganda magazine. The 1/83rd's big 8-inch and 175mm self-propelled guns would fire, the shock wave travelling underground to emerge as a blast of foul-smelling gas through the apertures covered by manly Australian bottoms. As one, the troops would rise on the columns of gas, involuntarily nodding and bowing to each other as if in courtly preparation for the next dance. As the blast passed they would settle gracefully again and await the next. Old hands didn't even lose their places in the Stars and Stripes. However, their olfactory mechanisms were impaired forever.

Setting up maintenance operations

Captain Peter Robinson, RAEME, was the first engineering officer to command the 161 Workshop. He was a formidable man with a bristling ginger moustache that gave him his sobriquet 'Bush Moosh'. Possum Master Laurie Doyle commented on his management style: 'It wasn't mine, but Jesus, the people in that workshop knew who was boss and they knew very quickly how that boss wanted things done. And, because of that, we were able to produce serviceable aeroplanes whenever they were required.'[2]

While his tongue could be rough when the occasion demanded, Peter Robinson came to the Flight at the right time. The increasing demands for aviation support aside, the workshop was still not properly equipped to carry out its task. Its ground support equipment (GSE) was suited to exercise conditions, not active service. An innovative mind was needed at the top to improvise and plan. Peter Robinson set about his job with vigour. Fortunately, he had completed aircraft maintenance training with the US Army. His certification as an Aircraft Maintenance Officer (AMO) enabled him to authorise and supervise repairs to US aircraft. Friends he had made on his training courses were AMOs serving in Vietnam, providing a network of colleagues in the aircraft maintenance business. Brownie points were gained by 161 for repairing US aircraft operating in the area. In return, the network enabled 161 to access tools and parts to supplement its own stores system in the maintenance of its American-built Cessna and Sioux aircraft.

RAEME engine fitter Geoff 'Stork' Deacon arrived on the first of the two tours with 161 on 10 May 1967, shortly after the unit moved to Nui Dat. He noted that the maintenance facilities and stores systems were rudimentary but found the challenges enjoyable:

> What struck me first was that it was like going on exercise where you only had the basics. We had the old tin shed we called a hangar. For heavy lifting, we only had an A-frame that fitted on the front of a Landrover. Bush Moosh had designed it. We had to lift out engines with it, which was a pretty precarious exercise. Jimmy Jones [Corporal Jones, engine fitter and larrikin] broke it lifting an engine plus its container. Bush Moosh was enraged and banished him from the hangar for a couple of weeks.
>
> The store was just beside the hangar and most of us learned how to use it because you'd be on duty crews, you'd do shift work, night work, whatever. You needed to be able to find whatever bits and pieces you needed. We were more self-reliant then than later, I think. There was plenty of work, seven days a week, so you didn't sit around wondering what it was like at home. We always did the work properly without compromising safety, but improvisation was a big thing. You had to work around problems; you bartered and you did whatever was necessary to keep things going. Many of us were ex-apprentices. We could go to another unit that had a RAEME element and we were bound to run into an ex-apprentice. You'd find one and get things there.
>
> We wrecked a lot of aircraft in 1967 and we put a lot of work into resurrecting others. And we fixed up a few bullet holes. One occasion I remember well was the first time we did a major servicing on a Sioux overnight. We took the head off, mast out, engine and transmission out, and

built another one up. We put that back in, replaced the mast, head and blades. The cooks made us a feed at midnight. And anyone standing around—it didn't matter whether he was on guard, or from the orderly room or wherever—we'd get him doing something, simple things, like greasing hanger bearings, to take the heat off us while we got the rest of it done. I liked the close-knit set-up, and it didn't matter what part of the Flight you were from. We had our separate messes but we'd still get in together at the OR's Mess for a piss-up and we'd have everyone there regardless of rank.[3]

Unit facilities were built and fitted out on an opportunity basis using the Flight's own manpower and supplies either allocated by the task force or scrounged from the Americans. Timber framing and plywood were much in demand. Craftsman Felix Mitchell recalled the Great Plywood Scam:

A lot of our building materials came through the Harold Holt requisition system. Anywhere you saw sheets of ply that were nailed to walls for lining—the Messes, the OR's boozer and the workshop sections in the hangar—the Harold Holt system supplied that. Geoff Pike had a lot to do with it. He made friends in the Chinook outfit when he was the guard out on the airfield at Vung Tau. There was a whole bunch of plywood there, and one day he and some mates went down and asked if they could have some. The Yank in charge said 'No problem, guys. You sign here and you can take delivery of your allocation.' So they signed for two bloody great piles of ply. And Pikey is wondering how to shift it when he remembers he has friends who own Chinooks. Shortly after, a Chinook arrived at Nui Dat and dropped off several tons of ply. Being resourceful Australians, we took to it like Argentinian ants and it disappeared very quickly. The Yanks did eventually turn up and wanted to know if we'd been on the receiving end of a large quantity of plywood. Fortunately, we'd never seen it. By then it was part of the buildings.[4]

The provision of electrical power to meet the Flight's needs was another ongoing drama. It was the expertise of RAEME engine fitter Craftsman Felix Mitchell and electrical fitter Sergeant Jack Ellis that kept the lights on, if a little dimly at times. Felix became known as 'The Generator Man':

It was powered by an old Ford V8 engine, the one they had in the 'B' Model Ford from 1932 on. Mate, it was ancient. We put it near that corner between the boozer and the kitchen. The bloody thing kept breaking down. You'd hear it running on six cylinders instead of eight. The lights would be blinking and it was just a pain in the bum. Bush Moosh found out I'd had a B Model Ford and told me to look after the generator. It was kind of him, but he was like that. Anyway, I kept it going. At 0800 every morning I'd warn everybody and just shut it down. I'd clean the plugs and fill it with oil again and I even put a different exhaust on it to try to get a bit more guts out of it. We needed a new generator badly.[5]

Felix, a religious man, was often heard speaking to God about the recalcitrant generator and his prayers were eventually answered. It happened that a convoy delivering new equipment to the task force had a breakdown while passing 161. The errant vehicle was carrying a 35 KVA generating set. The drivers were offered hospitality while repairs were made by the Flight's very helpful mechanics. The following day there was a disturbance on the other side of the base when a large, empty box was unloaded. Life became a little difficult when the generator, identified by its serial number, was discovered at 161. However, the generator remained in its new location after some fairly heavy bartering behind the scenes.[6]

Catering section gets the drum

Another innovative feature which testified to the expertise of the Flight's fitters was the oven. Among the kitchen staff was one Gary Channells, a pastrycook by trade who lamented the lack of proper catering facilities. It was important that the cooks be happy people, so the troops built him an oven. The business section was a 44-gallon drum with a hinged door and angle iron brackets inside to support the baking tray. The drum was packed around with mud for insulation and another 44-gallon drum sat over the top with a chimney going out of the back. For fuel there was an ingenious drip-feed system using aviation turbine (AVTUR) fuel. Gary could produce almost anything, including pies, in this unconventional kiln. His major problem was getting the ingredients.

The oven aside, the cooks did a great job with what they had. It wasn't always flash, but it was edible. And for those who were a little overweight, it was no bad thing to bypass breakfast now and again when the smell of preserved eggs cooking was too much to bear on top of the morning session with the latrine and the guns.

It was in this way, through hard work, innovation and nefarious means, that 161's basic living and working areas were established for the third time to form the basis for ongoing improvements. Meanwhile, the pace of operations was escalating and the demands on the Flight were ever-increasing. There would be little time for the niceties during the next eighteen months.

New faces, new demands

Unlike the battalions, 161 Recce Flight was manned using the 'trickle' system of personnel replacement. March and April 1967 saw new blood in the Flight while old hands marched out. Flight Sergeant Mick Swain arrived on 3 March to take up the post of NCO in charge of maintenance. Mick had distinguished himself earlier in his service with Army Aviation when he was the passenger in a helicopter crash. He dragged the injured pilot clear of the blazing aircraft, sustaining severe burns himself. He was awarded the George Medal for his bravery. Meanwhile, RAAF airframe fitter Sergeant Doug Kennett left for Australia with an MID for his role in managing the Cessna major servicing program at Vung Tau. Captain Dick Knight, who as 2IC was responsible for so much of the unit's success at Vung Tau and then carried much of the burden of preparatory work for the move to Nui Dat, went home at the end of April. With him was Bob Askew, who was presented with the Queen's Commendation for Brave Conduct on 29 April by task force commander Brigadier Stuart Graham. Knight and Askew flew two Sioux aircraft onto the *Sydney*. The new 2IC, Captain Phil Roberts, arrived with Second Lieutenant Ross Hutchinson and two replacement helicopters. Cessna drivers Second Lieutenant David McFerran and Lieutenant Kevin Peacock arrived to complete the fixed wing section. New faces were always welcome because they brought news, idiosyncratic behaviour, fresh jokes and new ideas.

Managing operations: The crowded sky

Two vital elements of the Flight's operations at Nui Dat were its command post (CP) and air traffic control (ATC) facilities. Pilots had to be properly briefed to meet task force headquarters requirements. There were liaison tasks and radio nets to be monitored. There was much helicopter traffic into and out of Nui Dat and a mélange of visiting transport aircraft. FAC aircraft and ground attack jets operated in the area, and many other aircraft overflew Nui Dat. An air traffic advisory service was essential if conflicting traffic was to be safely avoided. As the resident aviation unit, 161 was responsible for providing this service for Luscombe Field in addition to its already established artillery warning and control centre (AWCC), Kangaroo Control.

The CP was manned from 20 minutes prior to the first scheduled aircraft departure each day until 20 minutes after the last sortie was completed. It stayed open as required for night operations. Like everything else in 161, it began as a rudimentary facility. Second Lieutenant Don Trick (now Don Dennis) arrived in August 1967 as Operations/ATC officer. He described the CP as 'a dim little room cluttered with radios and telephones, nothing like the nerve centres I'd admired in movies such as *The Dam Busters* or *Twelve O'Clock High*'.[7] Don set about its reconstruction, stealing materials from the Engineers' stores depot and space from the Flight's administrative office which occupied the other half of the building. He was pleased with the result:

> Our command post now looked the part. Its walls were covered with maps, a flight schedule board and Playboy centrefolds. A long bench crammed with radios and field telephones filled one end of the room. Three rows of folding canvas chairs faced a large map of the province. But there were still none of those WAAFs with long sticks, pushing little airplane models around a plot table. One touch I'd added was a bulky Second World War microphone rescued from a junk pile at a US base. I'd scrubbed the chrome plate to its original art-deco glory and put it in a place of honour on the bench among the radios. Beneath it was a sign: SPEAK TO THE PILOTS—ONLY 100 PIASTRES.[8] By picking it up and screaming obscenities, it served as a means of letting off steam. It was used regularly.[9]

Don played a leading role in the development and implementation of an information management system for briefing purposes. There were no desktop computers in 1967, so much painstaking manual effort was required to compile the Intelligence Register, an indexed system of map sections and data sheets which recorded information from pilots' mission reports and briefings. A pilot preparing for a mission could review the grid references, dates and details of every sighting in the assigned area. Intelligence information was also provided by the task force, but the 161 pilots came to rely a great deal on their own local knowledge and records.

The CP facilities also included boards showing the daily task list, readiness states of aircraft, a log of messages and clearances received, current artillery and air strike warning areas and a host of other information. Communications links included the 161 Recce Flight command net, task force air/administrative net, Kangaroo Control monitor, telephone facilities via the unit switchboard, a direct line to Seagull Air[10] at task force headquarters and an intercom system linking key unit appointments. There was an alarm system to signal stand-to and emergency conditions. The unit switchboard was adjacent to the CP and was manned by a small detachment from 104 Signals Squadron which also operated a sub-station on the task force command net.

Ever a man with a sense of the ridiculous and a flair for description, Don Dennis described the atmosphere at night:

> During night ops, the CP's dimmed lighting and black hessian curtains gave it a conspiratorial atmosphere, full of whispering shadows like the secret lairs haunted by Nazis in old B-grade movies. However, instead of a portrait of Adolph gazing sternly down from the wall, our Führer was a pouting Miss September with her knees draped over her ears and a belly full of staples.[11]

The ATC section also grew from humble beginnings. Originally there were two operations staff on the unit establishment, one warrant officer and one sergeant, who manned the CP at Vung Tau and who also set up Kangaroo Control at Nui Dat. When the Flight joined the task force the Ops/ATC staff became responsible for manning the Luscombe Airfield control tower when it became operational. Until then, Sergeant Jack Jewell did his best to fill the gap by using a radio-equipped vehicle to guide troop-carrying Iroquois helicopters (slicks) in and out of the airfield when the battalions were being deployed on operations:

> I used to sit on the bonnet of the Land Rover and put the slicks in a holding pattern and get them sorted out. It was a pity that the tower didn't work but they just didn't have the gear. They did get it working later on. There's been some funny stories come out of that tower. They worked a lot

of aircraft through there in the later years. Of course, they had the equipment then. Not like that Second World War shit they saddled us with.[12]

After the move to Nui Dat, another radio operator was posted in. The new arrival, Corporal Peter Blissett, recorded some 'reccelections' of his tour:

> About half of my posting was at the task force headquarters working at Kangaroo Control. The control centre's job was to separate aircraft and artillery rounds. It was an interesting job, with each area in South Vietnam having an AWCC. Ours was the only one manned by NCOs; others were manned by officers. We provided the aircraft with the location the artillery was firing from, the maximum height and the target location. If an aircraft did not have a map of the area, like most US aircraft, we would provide a safe track under the artillery. We also provided a flight watch,[13] and a relay service when necessary. It wasn't long before someone decided we were doing such a good job with the guns that we should go on operations with them. The last time was to fire support base (FSB) Anderson two weeks before I was due to return to Australia. I was not impressed.
>
> The other half of my tour was with the Flight in Operations. I think it was August 1967 when Captain Phil Roberts and I opened the first Luscombe Tower. We had acquired an old observation tower from the perimeter and had it put on SAS Hill. The radio was a PRC-25 set and I had never spoken to an aircraft in my life. There is no way I can relate the stories of the events that occurred in the first few weeks of operation of the tower. Phil Roberts, a Signalman named Brian Sullivan, myself and Don Dennis ran 'Luscombe Advisory' until qualified air traffic controllers like Sergeant Dave Brown arrived.[14]

From this ad hoc beginning, the ATC section became much better equipped and was staffed by three properly qualified controllers. Later, a new tower was built, with improved facilities and a better location near the runway. 161 even finished up with a Fire Section. But in the second half of 1967, it was all new. The learning curve was steep but somehow the job was done.

New tasks, new techniques

When 161 Recce Flight moved from Bien Hoa to Vung Tau in 1966, its operational capabilities were limited by its strength of only four aircraft and the equipment that could be fitted to them. However, its expansion to become 161 (Independent) Recce Flight, with nine aircraft and a corresponding increase in manpower, allowed it to become more versatile and effective in terms of the scope and number of tasks undertaken. The period at Vung Tau saw the Cessnas acquire the capability to launch target-marking and HE rockets, and radio rebroadcast became much more widely and effectively used. But there was much more to come during the years at Nui Dat as the build-up of the task force and its operations continued.

First, the number and variety of administrative support and liaison tasks increased. Some were daily commitments, for example the special delivery service for signals traffic which was carried by an RA Signals soldier in a helicopter from Nui Dat to and from staff at Vung Tau, Long Binh and Saigon. Others were ad hoc requirements. There were more sorties for area familiarisation for new or visiting senior officers. There was pilot training for the new commander of Australian Forces in Vietnam, Major General Don Vincent. During a period of chronic delays in mail services, 161 established a mail service to Tan Son Nhut with Lieutenant Tom Guivarra flying the original run. The popular service was inevitably known as 'Possum Mail'.

The Cessnas were seldom allocated for direct support work because the aircraft needed an airfield rather than the rough landing zones that sufficed for Sioux operations. They had their own special functions and operations. Major Laurie Doyle recalled that the fixed wing element worked almost exclusively for the intelligence staff at the task force headquarters. 'We got our reconnaissance tasking every day, and it was pretty standardised. We did some new things, too, like providing a platform for airborne electronic intelligence missions.'[15]

Signals intelligence operations

Planning for the Australian task force recognised the need for a specialist unit to provide signals intelligence (Sigint) in the same way that the Radio Research Unit at Bien Hoa fed intelligence to the 173rd Airborne Brigade. 547 Signals Troop arrived at Nui Dat on 15 June 1966. Its operations were highly classified and the source of the intelligence it provided was strictly 'need-to-know'. It took some time for 547 Troop to establish its bona fides. When it warned of the approach of a main force enemy headquarters in the days before Long Tan, its information was questioned because of the lack of corroborating intelligence from other sources. After that historic engagement, 547's contribution gained respect and became a vital factor in the planning of battalion operations.

Airborne radio direction finding operations quickly became a major commitment for 161's fixed wing aircraft, with daily tasks requiring two sorties of two hours each. The aircraft carried specialist equipment and an operator from the Signals Troop. The flying itself was quite demanding, with accurate results depending largely on the pilot's ability to position his aircraft accurately and to fly a constant heading and airspeed while the operator was recording data. The degree of difficulty increased as the enemy became aware of the purpose of these sorties and began to implement countermeasures. For example, an enemy operator observing the aircraft could tell when it was starting a recording run and cease transmitting. Or an enemy commander might send his operator off to a site remote from the main force location to carry out transmissions and thus mislead the task force intelligence staff as to the location of the enemy headquarters. It became very much a cat and mouse affair.

As noted, 547's operations were very hush. However, while the need for security was recognised, it was not possible to conceal from 161's technical personnel the purpose of the intelligence-gathering sorties. The Cessnas had to be fitted with the direction finding equipment, including the externally visible, wheel-shaped housing of the antenna. Newcomers to 161 would raise their eyebrows, but would be warned that the topic was off limits by a finger raised to the lips, rolling eyeballs and a hissed warning. The 547 sorties thus became commonly known as 'shush' missions. Like all of 161's tasks, shush trips were not without incident. In September 1968 Lieutenant Steve Tizzard and his 547 operator, Corporal Dick Schafer, experienced propellor pitch control problems and force-landed in a wet paddy near the Courtenay rubber plantation 20 kilometres north of Nui Dat. The aircraft was badly damaged but was recovered to Nui Dat by Chinook. Unfortunately, load stability problems led to it being dropped from about 30 metres and it wasn't much good for anything after that.

Security requirements meant that 547 operators were largely unrecognised for their role. They deserved high commendation for their work and the risks they shared with the Possums who flew them. So too did the many observers from 161 and other units who flew on specific missions requiring an operator, or just went along as an extra pair of eyes and a weapon to make whatever contribution they could.

Visual reconnaissance operations and techniques

Apart from patrols and ambushes intended to keep the enemy off balance along their supply routes and near local villages, continuous patrols were necessary to ensure the security of the task force base. Ground patrols supplemented by aerial reconnaissance kept the perimeter under constant surveillance. VR sorties commenced at dawn, with a Sioux covering the four-kilometre inner zone to Line Alpha while a Cessna checked the outer zone to Line Bravo at twelve kilometres. The daily program also covered other areas within the TAOR as required by the intelligence staff for operational planning. Last-light sorties supplemented the dawn patrols, while night sorties were undertaken when weather and visibility permitted. It was a demanding and unending routine for the pilots.

A VR sortie typically covered an area of nine map grid squares in meticulous detail. A pilot or observer needed considerable mentoring and practice before he could readily detect signs of enemy activity. Over forested areas this entailed an ability to ignore the canopy and look for shapes or movement on the ground below. Over cleared areas it meant being able to detect footprints or other signs such as bent grass to mark the passage of traffic, instinctively noting details such as direction and likely numbers. When a trail or route was in regular use, a trained VR pilot could notice differences in usage from day to day and provide a close estimate of times and numbers. Likely launch positions within mortar range were visited regularly. Areas showing signs of activity were subjected to harassment and interdiction (H & I) artillery fire. Creek crossings and likely supply routes were noted and monitored. Gradually, each pilot built up a picture of the province. Back at the CP data were collated and filed to update the Intelligence Register. OC Laurie Doyle was impressed by the expertise and depth of knowledge gained by his pilots:

As well as the Sigint sorties for 547 Signals Troop and courier tasks, the fixed wing pilots concentrated on visual reconnaissance, especially in the areas further out. They were tasked through the G2 (Air) on the task force headquarters staff, at that time Major Ian Power. He would present the request in the form: 'I want you to look in these grid squares and what we are looking for is a base camp or whatever.' Tom Guivarra was an extraordinary example of the skills needed for this job. He had the usual skills to be not put off by what looked like just green canopy. Like others, he could look through it to see what was underneath it. But he also seemed to have very acute vision and a real feel for what might be out of place in an ordinary scene. I often wondered how those fixed wing pilots put up with it—John Wright the section commander and his pilots Salmon, Guivarra and Colin Scott, and later David McFerran. They flew over the same canopy seven days a week, 52 weeks of the year. They established all sorts of landmarks. For example, they would talk about the 'grey tree'. One day I asked one of them about it and we jumped in an aeroplane and he took me out and here's this tree with a grey branch. In that sea of green it had become a significant landmark and it was used by them as a reference point, like 200 metres or two klicks to the north of the grey tree. They fed information to each other, day in and day out, and they were pretty successful.[16]

Lieutenant Tom Guivarra was indeed a very good VR pilot and a notable personality who, like a number of other Possums, went on to a distinguished career in Army Aviation. His family came from North Queensland, the blood of the Torres Strait Islanders and the men and women of a half-dozen other nations their heritage from the old pearling days in the Torres Strait. Tom's skill and daring were recognised in his citation for an MID:

> As a fixed wing pilot, he displayed a remarkable skill on visual reconnaissance missions. He was responsible for many new sightings of enemy locations and constantly showed great determination in following up small indications of the presence of the enemy . . . His ability to note minute detail invariably led to more significant findings . . . During a tour of duty in which he flew over 800 hours, his personal skill and cool daring enabled him to secure the information he sought.[17]

Intelligence: A challenge in information management

While 161 was a significant contributor to the task force's intelligence, its reports were too often overlooked. The management of intelligence was undoubtedly a challenge. The intelligence function as described in the official history sheds some light on the problem while acknowledging 161's role:

> The four major sources of intelligence were battlefield intelligence ... information from agents, informers and enemy personnel who were either captured or defected; information from flanking or superior formations; and signals intelligence ... Specialist intelligence-gathering units in the task force included the Army Aviation reconnaissance flight.[18]

The overall flow of intelligence from these various sources was huge. Difficulties inherent in information overload are also mentioned:

> A mass of raw reports also flowed into the task force from the reporting agencies within the province. This flow of information, according to one senior Australian intelligence officer, 'was voluminous and embraced the whole range from useful information to the rubbish of pedlars (sic) and fabricators. Sorting the wheat from the chaff was an endless task'.[19]

Whether these difficulties were widely known and appreciated is difficult to say. However, the consequence appears to have been that some intelligence officers were regarded as incompetent. For 161, there was often frustration among the pilots at the apparent lack of regard for their eyewitness information. Fixed wing section commander Captain Bernie Forrest was very blunt in his view:

> I'll tell you, intelligence was the greatest failure up there. Our people had no idea what to do with the stuff they were given. For example, there was that SAS attack up on what we called the 'diamond clearing'. On the map there was a diamond-shaped clearing where the road went up through the rubber and came out on Route 2 near Courtenay. We'd been reporting tractor activity on that clearing for months. It was the wet season and the tracks were obvious and we'd been reporting it every day after the first light recce. One day the OC was going over to the briefing and I said, 'Why don't you ask them why we're reporting this stuff day after day and nobody does anything about it?' So he got up at the meeting and said all this and the Commander gave the Int people a rocket and they got on to SAS. They made up a plan and on their first night in there the SAS got the whole bloody lot of them. The tracks were like a road through the clearing by then so the SAS guys dug their hole, planted their bomb and that was it. They got the tractor, the trailer and sixteen bodies scattered all over this clearing. They took enough supplies for ten days but they were lifted out the following morning.

> That's the sort of nonsense that was going on. We'd just report stuff day after day after day. The SAS blokes, we'd take them on a reconnaissance. A section corporal would come out and he'd say, 'Okay, I want these nine grid squares.' They might be due north of Binh Ba or out from Binh Gia or somewhere like that. So we'd take him out and all the tracks would be heavily used and he'd say, 'On our Int briefing we've been told that there's no activity in this area.' And here they're putting five troops out into the bush with that rubbish as intelligence.[20]

Civic action

The task force was joined in mid-1967 by the 1st Australian Civil Affairs Unit (1ACAU). This unit's function was to carry out civic action projects in support of task force operations in a general expansion of 'helping' activities already undertaken. Popularly known as the 'winning hearts and minds' program, civic action was considered to be a very important aspect of counterinsurgency operations. The Flight became involved as well. Possum Master Laurie Doyle explained:

> There were other programs going on, for example there was a village nearby called Xuyen Moc. We adopted that village as 161's target for civic action because it had an airfield for fixed wing aircraft. It had a US Army refuelling point. If someone wanted something delivered quickly to Xuyen Moc, like 200 pounds of skim milk for the hospital, we'd throw it into whichever type of aeroplane was most suited and go out and back. So there were a lot of spontaneous sorties under the general heading of Xuyen Moc.[21]

Staff Sergeant Bob Young, 161's medic for a year from September 1967, received an MID for his fine contribution to the Xuyen Moc program. His citation reads in part: 'Staff Sergeant Young also volunteered his services to his unit Civil Affairs program and in his capacity as a medical assistant treated over 3000 Vietnamese patients in the village of Xuyen Moc and accordingly earned their gratitude and admiration.'[22]

As 1967 progressed and Nui Dat became home, the war continued to escalate. Operational commitments meant that there was little time for anything else. Forgotten were the travails of life on the back beach at Vung Tau, and those who had endured the rigours of Bien

Hoa had long since gone home. Unlike the previous two locations, there were no nearby facilities where the troops might seek cultural exchange in a dark bar. At Nui Dat, no one crept back past the sentries or along the beach in the early hours. Other distractions had to be sought, and in time they were. But for now, it was down to business.

7

Nui Dat:
March–December 1967

During 1967, the war intensified as the build-up of Allied forces continued with the aim of taking the offensive. The enemy matched the increasing commitment, with the flow of troops and supplies along the Ho Chi Minh trail continuing uninterrupted despite all efforts at interdiction. The United States was concerned at the prospect of an extended campaign but stopped short of all-out war. The growing number of Allied casualties, together with the lack of decisive and permanent gains, encouraged public opposition to the war in the United States and in Australia. In Phuoc Tuy province, the task force had secured its base, made its mark on the local enemy forces and was ready within the limits of its operational capabilities to mount both offensive and pacification operations. In this respect, it was hampered by the lack of a third infantry battalion to give it full brigade strength.

The task force had a new commander in Brigadier Stuart Graham, MC. In his most recent post, he had been responsible for training infantry battalions for service in Vietnam.[1] Graham had firm ideas about his approach to the task ahead. Like his predecessor, Brigadier Owen Jackson, he felt that his mission 'was to help ensure the security of the main areas of population and resources of Phuoc Tuy and so enable the government to restore law and order and get on with the job of developing the social, economic and political life of the province'.² As already noted, this view ran counter to the US strategy of destroying the enemy's main forces while leaving the security of the towns and villages to ARVN forces.

A factor which assisted Graham to focus on extending operations in the east and southeast of the province was the allocation of US forces to the north of Nui Dat in early 1967. The 11th Armoured Cavalry was based at Black Horse and the US 9th Infantry Division at Bearcat, 30 and 42 kilometres distant respectively. These forces threatened the enemy main force 274 Regiment in its northern stronghold, leaving Graham to concentrate on the principal support area for the enemy D445 battalion in the east and southeast of Phuoc Tuy.³

Protecting the rice harvest: The Horseshoe and the fence

In March 1967 the task force launched a major effort to deny the Viet Cong access to the rice-growing area of the central south via approaches from the east. The first phase of the operation was to establish a permanent forward base at a feature called the Horseshoe—the elevated remnants of a small volcano in the Dat Do district south of Nui Dat. The occupying force would be a rifle company and a troop of artillery. 5RAR would establish the force and then build a barrier fence and minefield from the Horseshoe south to the sea. The occupation was completed and work began on the barrier fence in mid-March. The barrier comprised two barbed-wire fences 100 yards apart with a minefield in between.

Phase two of the plan was Operation *Portsea*, 'a massive thrust to be made out to Xuyen Moc to clear the country from the coast to over fifteen miles inland of Viet Cong and their bases, caches and other installations'.⁴ *Portsea* was conducted by 6RAR with supporting US and ARVN forces. The operation commenced on 21 March and proceeded to secure the eastern approaches to the rice-growing areas while repairing Route 23 to open access to Xuyen Moc. *Portsea* coincided with 161's move from Vung Tau to Nui Dat. Nevertheless, 161's pilots flew 171 hours in support of the operation from 21 March to 16 April. Captain Jim Campbell and his rotary wing pilots recorded their activities in a series of reports such as the following compiled by Second Lieutenant Chic Barron after a day as DS pilot on 22 March:

> Tasks consisted of six liaison, five recce, two resupply and one AOP sortie. All liaison trips consisted of transporting passengers to or from EAGLE FARM helipad at Nui Dat to the forward area or the Horseshoe. Recce sorties were as follows:
> (a) Troop leader of APCs recced route to be taken by APC Sqn—a second recce arose from this when I overflew the move—on this occasion I reported two huts, one of which was searched by APCs and destroyed.
> (b) Recce by CO over all of the area of operation.
> (c) Recce requested over area where enemy contact was made. On this recce I received four rounds of small arms fire and reported the grid from which it came. Just after this, a 6RAR company reported mortar primaries from this direction and an airstrike was put in about 30 minutes later. Before the airstrike Lieutenant Guivarra flew low over the area and reported two huts which he marked. I flew low and confirmed these huts plus signs of a prepared position. I was in contact with the FAC calling the strike and asked him to save half his ordnance for this target which I marked for him with smoke.
>
> I returned to this area for a bomb damage assessment after the strike—huts were undamaged—returned on several occasions and as light conditions became more favourable, observed a rice cache in one of the huts—estimated it as up to 400 bags. The AOP sortie just on last light was designed to record this area as an H & I target for the night to prevent possible removal by the enemy.
> (d) The two resupply sorties flown were from Kangaroo for the APC squadron at the forward location.[5]

Barron's report concluded with the comments that communications had been good and that he felt the aircraft had been well used. He flew almost eight hours for the day, a fairly typical one for a DS pilot.

Later during the operation, on 8 April, Second Lieutenant Ross Goldspink took a round through the cockpit bubble of his Sioux. Luckily he and his passenger were uninjured. It was all in a day's work for the redheaded 'fling wing' pilot and his fellow operators.

Optimising the aviation role

As 1967 progressed, 161 Recce Flight met the growing demands of the task force by increasing its flying rate and developing better maintenance facilities. Possum Master Laurie Doyle saw his role as ensuring that the Flight continued to mature in light of its experience with concomitant improvements in its versatility, responsiveness and effectiveness. At the same time, the task force headquarters staff and the battalion commanders were learning how to maximise the benefits of 161's services without requesting the impossible. Laurie explained his philosophy of operations:

> It started with Paul Lipscombe at Bien Hoa, continued through me, and right to the end to Tub Matheson who brought the last detachment home. We set out to do it the way we thought it should be done. The task force learned pretty quickly that we could be trusted. We were reliable. If we stuffed up there was blood on the carpet and what have you, but we were there as soldiers, flying aeroplanes, to serve soldiers. It was as simple as that.[6]

There were limitations imposed by the aircraft type and carrying capacity and there was a limit to how hard the OC could push his pilots. But very rarely did 161 say 'no'. Laurie felt that he was lucky in terms of pilot experience:

> I had two pretty experienced soldiers leading them in Jim Campbell and John Wright. When you've got that sort of talent, and an old sweat like Dick Knight as second in command, it helps a lot. With the flexibility that the light helicopter offered, most of the company commanders and the COs of battalions were very quick to know what they could and couldn't do. A very healthy two-way communication developed about that. The COs learned quickly too that there were places where you couldn't put an Iroquois, but perhaps a little Sioux could get in; like Chic Barron did that notable day when he flew eleven-and-a-half hours on operations. Half of the time he was putting one skid on a rock while they loaded or unloaded the aircraft. In a couple of cases that was with casevacs; soldiers who were wounded and could have died if he wasn't able to pluck them out.[7]

New battalions: 7RAR and 2RAR join the fray

Both 5RAR and 6RAR had rendered signal service in establishing and securing the task force area as well as in the conduct of subsequent operations. They were replaced by 7RAR and 2RAR respectively over the period from April to June. The first New Zealand infantry contribution was Victor Company, which joined 2RAR. The combined force, later augmented by a second New Zealand rifle company, became the first ANZAC battalion.

Operations continued unabated, and 161 flew a record 916 hours during May despite the loss of a helicopter for several weeks as a result of engine failure. On 2 June, Lieutenant Ross Hutchinson lost power and crashed his Sioux en route from the Horseshoe to Nui Dat with an Engineer officer as passenger:

> I flared into a paddy field and should have made it but for a bund [earth wall] hidden in the long grass. The tail hit the bund and bounced me into the dirt. I got seven compressed vertebrae and a fucking big headache. My passenger suffered similar injuries but was knocked unconscious in the crash. I recall thinking I was dead, so why was I worried about the sound and smell of spilt fuel hitting a hot exhaust? Luckily I was able to extricate myself and my passenger, and a RAAF Dustoff about to depart Nui Dat had us both in the Vung Tau hospital in less than 30 minutes.[8]

The Sioux was almost a write-off after cartwheeling into the paddy. Airframe fitter Sergeant John 'Skeeta' Ryan had been in country only a few weeks when he was called upon to help recover the aircraft and to rebuild it if possible:

> Recovering the aircraft was interesting. A couple of times angry bees went past us and the battalion had protection out for us. It put a bit of excitement into life. Rebuilding the aircraft was probably the most challenging and satisfying job in the time I was there. Basically, the only undamaged bit was the data plate. And we were able to straighten out the main pan frame of the seat and the side walls, but we needed a bubble and a new centre frame and a whole lot more. We estimated six weeks' repair time, but took less than five weeks from pull down to rebuild.[9]

Meanwhile, Ross Hutchinson was recovering in hospital at Vung Tau. Usually an irrepressible larrikin, he was feeling a bit down as he contemplated the probable end of his flying career:

> Enter some American friends of mine, who smuggled me out of the hospital one night on a stretcher on the back of a US jeep. Where did we go? Well you may ask. We went straight to the Grand Hotel where the beer flowed freely and the women were cheap and vice versa. I of course got pissed. Drinking while lying prostrate has that effect on one. There I was strapped on this stretcher and telling all the strap-hangers [non-combatants] to get a real job. Not a wise thing to do. The ensuing fight meant we had

to leave the premises and do our drinking elsewhere. Sometime next morning my 'friends' took me back to the hospital whereupon I was severely chastised. Somehow I don't think that I was representing the Australian Army in a good light.[10]

In an interesting footnote to this adventure, Hutch's M-16 rifle was damaged in the crash and he was later fined $17.50 for repair to a weapon damaged 'Not Fair Wear and Tear'. He wrote that 'the moral of this story is you can write off a capital item worth oodles of dollars but don't bend your Banger!'[11]

Operation Paddington (6–16 July)

Operations in the first months of 1967 had confined most enemy units to the more remote regions of the province. Unfortunately, the task force lacked the mobility to pursue them.[12] The extension of pacification continued through the proven effectiveness of search-and-destroy operations such as Operation *Paddington*, in which US forces were to participate in a sweep through the May Tao high country in the northeast of the province. The aim was to find and destroy the base and support elements of 5 VC Division, whose 274 and 275 Regiments were the enemy main forces operating in Phuoc Tuy. However, intelligence indicated that the 5 Division Headquarters and 274 Regiment were weathering the monsoon about eleven kilometres to the northeast of Xuyen Moc.[13] The focus of *Paddington* was switched to that area, with an eventual combined American, South Vietnamese and Australian force supported by APCs, engineers and 161 Recce Flight. American air and naval support was also available. The complete task force headquarters was deployed forward in the field for the first time.[14] However, the enemy slipped the net following delays in key force deployments.

During *Paddington*, 161 Recce Flight's DS choppers flew 85 hours in support of 2RAR and 7RAR. The fixed wing section was also involved. Cessna pilot Lieutenant Colin Scott was later awarded the DFC for his sustained efforts during *Paddington*:

> On 13 July he sighted a large enemy party but could not inform friendly troops as his radio had failed. He returned to base and, in a new aircraft,

returned to the scene. By this time the enemy had disappeared so he flew at treetop height in the area that he expected the enemy would be, well knowing that the Viet Cong in the face of such persistent reconnaissance would attempt to shoot him down. Balancing these odds against the requirement to locate the enemy, Lieutenant Scott showed courage and determination of the highest order and through his persistence found the enemy, estimated at two companies, in position. As he repeatedly flew low over the enemy position to gauge its extent, his aircraft was subjected to heavy fire from small arms and automatic weapons. Lieutenant Scott, after confirming the Viet Cong locations, called for strike aircraft. He was directly responsible for three successful airstrikes against the enemy.[15]

Late on 14 July Scott located another large camp estimated to contain two enemy battalions. He was fired on repeatedly as he flew low to confirm his sightings, and he then successfully directed artillery and led airstrikes on to the enemy position. He called for a relief aircraft when his fuel ran low and in blinding monsoonal rain and failing light marked the target for his relief before diverting to the nearest airfield to refuel. He returned to base in the dark after a mission lasting nearly five hours. His debriefing led to two more successful reconnaissance missions on the morning of 15 July when he personally led strike aircraft to two more occupied positions.

Possum Master Three

Major George Constable, Royal Australian Artillery, took over command of 161 from Laurie Doyle on 22 July 1967. The new OC was a popular, charismatic figure who led from the front. His flying skills were highly regarded. A Duntroon graduate, he completed Air OP training and later served with 16 ALA from December 1960 until October 1961. He was recalled to the Artillery fold until he returned to flying in 1966 as Officer Commanding 16 Squadron after the formation of 1 Aviation Regiment. He served there until he took over command of 161 at Nui Dat. Don Dennis, who served as his operations officer, described him thus:

> He had a way with people, a way of making those who served with him want to perform well—not from fear of retribution, but to be able to hear from him the brief compliment of 'Well done'. That in my opinion is the sign of a true leader.[16]

Major Constable arrived at an interesting and demanding time. The war was still 'hotting up'. After Operation *Paddington*, the task force returned to interdiction operations against Viet Cong supply lines and bases with Operations *Cairns* and *Atherton*. Then, early in August, Operation *Ballarat* in the Hat Dich area brought a significant engagement now known as the Battle of Suoi Chau Pha. On 6 August, Alpha Company of 7RAR made contact near a creek, the Suoi Chau Pha. The contact turned into a savage, close-quarters encounter between Alpha Company and an aggressive force of equivalent size from the enemy main force 274 Regiment. Artillery support finally turned the conflict in 7RAR's favour, but not before significant losses were sustained. Once again the enemy had shown that he would resist fiercely attempts to break his supply lines in the north of the province.

The task force commander was equally determined to cut the enemy off from the villages which were sources of recruits, food and other necessities. From 31 August to 21 September, Operation *Ainslie* was mounted to resettle villagers from an area known as Slope 30, fifteen kilometres to the north of Nui Dat, to the purpose-built village of Ap Suoi Nghe only three kilometres to the north of the base. Slope 30 was known to be the main area for the procurement of supplies for 5 Viet Cong Division.[17] A feature of Operation *Ainslie* was that the task force Civil Affairs Unit played its first major coordinating role. The operation required the commitment of the full resources of the task force. It was achieved and took from the enemy what had been a vital supply area. For the villagers, it was less successful as Ap Suoi Nghe did not prosper.[18]

Psychological warfare operations (Psyops)

At Nui Dat, 161 acquired voice broadcasting equipment comprising a tape recorder which could play messages through a solid-state, one kilowatt amplifier feeding a bank of large, heavy duty speakers. The amplifier and speakers were fitted externally on a Sioux, while the recorder was operated in the cockpit. The equipment was also fitted to a Cessna, with special brackets used to mount the amplifier and bank of speakers in the passenger doorway. However, it was generally easier and quicker to mount it on a Sioux despite the added limitations it imposed on that aircraft's weight-carrying capabilities.

One of the author's favourite memories is of George Constable's test flight of the Cessna fitted for psyops. George wanted to see how 'this pile of crap hanging out of the door' would affect the low-speed handling and stall characteristics of the little aeroplane. We took off and circled around the area before trying a couple of stalls. George was a professional but also a joker. 'Never did get a handle on stalling these things,' he grumbled as we mushed along to the music of the stall warning horn. 'Fuck it,' he finally said. 'It seems alright.' And it was.

Many psyops missions were flown during the latter half of 1967. There was the 'Chieu Hoi' program, which entailed flying over known enemy locations and playing tapes which exhorted enemy soldiers to leave the dark side and enjoy the rewards of working with the Allies. These operations often drew an unfriendly response, and were flown at 1500 feet above ground level to make the aircraft a difficult target. Other psyops sorties involved assisting the battalions with cordon-and-search operations against the enemy's infiltration of local villages. The troops would position themselves around the target village in the early hours to cut off escape routes while avoiding detection. A voice aircraft would arrive to inform the villagers of the search operation and to give them instructions to assemble for identification and interviews.

There were other, non-operational uses for loudspeaker-fitted aircraft. A notable example was 161's farewell to New Zealand's Victor Company when it left after its tour with the ANZAC Battalion. It is still remembered fondly by NZ veterans:

> Victor Company had an excellent relationship with 161 (Indep) Recce Flight. On the day we left, 13 November 1967, they put up a loudspeaker aircraft and circled the Nui Dat base and played 'The Green, Green Grass of Home' over and over again. We were seen out in style. Once again the Australian brass were not impressed, but we were. The memory of that day lingers on, and the song is forever etched in the memories of Victor Company. Sadly, it's now the song played at funeral services for our fallen comrades-in-arms.[19]

Chemical warfare, Possum style

Sometimes frustrated pilots took matters into their own hands. Second Lieutenant Mike Meehan once decided that he, like everyone else, was tired of reporting that the Viet Cong were netting fish every night in coastal lagoons east of Nui Dat when the task force intelligence people did nothing about it. Inspired by a number of beverages and with the able assistance of operations officer Don Dennis, Mike built a device consisting of explosive and soap powder which he launched into one of the lagoons the following morning.

On his return, the story leaked to task force headquarters staff, who wanted to know who had launched an unauthorised act of chemical warfare against the Viet Cong. Possum Master George Constable was carpeted, not for the first time. (According to Don Dennis, George used to routinely walk into the brigadier's office backwards to facilitate the kick in the arse so he could get down to business.) He somehow calmed down the brass, and returned to 161 where he administered a promised 'kick in the backside' to the offenders. The offenders bent over at the bar while George executed the punishment and then bought a round of beers for all.[20]

It is said that, when Mike Meehan went back to check on his handiwork, the Viet Cong had their washing hung out in the trees around the lagoon. 'You've got to hand it to the bastards,' he mused. 'They use everything.'

Pushing back the enemy

As 1967 approached its close, the task force continued to work towards extending its TAOR to encompass virtually all of Phuoc Tuy.[21] From September through December, Operations *Kenmore*, *Santa Fe* and *Forrest* disrupted the enemy in his formerly secure areas away from the population centres and denied access to the rice harvest. The Possums flew psyops sorties in support of cordon-and-search operations and more than four million leaflets were dropped by air.[22] By year's end, good progress had been made in pushing the enemy back towards the fringes of the province and consolidating the gains made.

The latter half of 1967 also saw Australia come under sustained pressure from the United States to increase its commitment to the conflict in Vietnam. In July, Britain had announced its decision to withdraw its forces 'east of Suez' and the Australian Government was struggling with the implications of that decision for its own commitment to regional defence in other areas of Southeast Asia. Its senior staff in Vietnam had pointed to the need for a third battalion, tanks and increased air support to enhance the task force's limited capabilities as a 'two battalion' brigade. After much consideration, the Australian Government decided on 6 September to augment the task force with 'a third infantry battalion group with helicopter support, a squadron of Centurion tanks, a joint RAAF/RAN helicopter squadron, as well as additional engineering construction personnel and headquarters staff'.[23]

In October, Brigadier Graham was replaced as task force commander by Brigadier Ron Hughes, an experienced veteran of the Second World War and Korea. The pattern set by Graham was continued by Hughes, who nevertheless brought his own approach to command of the task force and within months had come to favour a more aggressive stance.[24] The upgraded task force gave him the capability to deploy and support his forces more widely.[25] That in turn meant more flying hours for 161.

The maintenance challenge

Keeping up with the demand for aircraft in the face of losses and operational damage called for a maximum effort by 161's maintenance personnel. Sergeant 'Skeeta' Ryan remembered well the challenges faced by the fitters:

> There wasn't much off-duty time. In hindsight I realise how fortunate we were that we didn't have failures because of fatigue and the 'can do' attitude of the maintenance blokes. I remember seeing Chuck Fellenberg, exhausted to the point where he's got a connecting pin in his teeth and two cables of the elevator control pushed together, and he's trying to put the pin in. But there was no way in the world his head would go through the frame to get there. He was determined to do it, but just too bloody tired to realise that physically it was impossible. I said to Chuck: 'Out of here. Get to bed.' And he slept; slept dead for ages. That's how tired the blokes were at times as a result of the pace that they worked at.
>
> And how many times did we patch bullet holes and say, 'There's the hole, how did it miss the fuel tank?' And the night the Sioux came home with a hole in the fuel tank and the fuel level had dropped to where it was

just dripping, but it was dripping down onto the turbocharger and flashing as the aircraft was landing. You can't put the fire extinguisher on it because the turbocharger would just explode and there'd have been hot lumps of molten metal flying everywhere. And you can't just leave the fuel falling on it with the flames flashing up towards the rest of the fuel in the tank. We were lucky. It didn't go bang and it didn't burn.[26]

At times there was just a run of bad luck. Evidence of how tight the DS chopper sorties could be was provided by Lieutenant Ross Goldspink in a series of incidents involving tail rotors. Captain Peter Robinson, as befitted a good maintenance engineer, was not impressed:

> Helicopter pilot Ross Goldspink distinguished himself in one seven-day period during 1967. His first effort was to back his Sioux into a tree. Fortunately, the tail encountered only the softer foliage and small branches. The strike tabs were bent so the tail rotor was replaced. Two days later, departing from a small helipad, the said Goldspink managed to put the tail rotor into a mound of dirt, this time deflecting the tabs rather a lot and damaging the tips sufficiently to suggest impact damage. We fitted a new tail rotor and gearbox. There were also a few words said by the engineering officer and the OC. Not content with the double, pilot Goldspink completed the hat trick at Xuyen Moc when he flared for landing and 'a large rock struck the tail rotor'. His record stands.
>
> Operations around Xuyen Moc cost 161 quite a few tail rotors. Lieutenant Ross Hutchinson engaged a barbed wire entanglement with one. He and the tail rotor lost. Then, on 26 May, Second Lieutenant Blair Weaver was en route from Xuyen Moc to Nui Dat when he heard a loud noise behind him and experienced a sudden yaw. On looking behind him he could not see a tail rotor. In fact, there was no tail rotor, guard, gearbox or extension tube. He called in a Mayday, entered a steep descent and with great skill executed a copybook running landing in a small clearing. It was unfortunate that, just at the end of the landing run, the left skid struck a tree stump in the grass and the aircraft rolled sufficiently for the main rotor to strike the ground. When the whole mess came to rest Blair was able to step out. He took his survival kit and the radios and concealed himself in the tree line until he was picked up fifteen minutes later. We were unable to extract the remains before last light so the aircraft was destroyed by rocket fire. The following morning I was inserted with a couple of the maintenance fitters courtesy of 9 Squadron, together with a section of grunts and a couple of gunships to give us cover. We recovered the remains of the tail and other critical items. By chance the Operations Officer on the *Corpus Christi Bay*, the helicopter Depot Repair Ship anchored in Vung Tau

Roads, had been my neighbour in the US. Tests in the metallurgical laboratory showed traces of bullet casing at the root of the extension tube.[27]

Of Possums and Bird Dogs

Maintenance issues aside, the increasing tempo of operations entailed corresponding increases in the Flight's other intelligence-gathering and administrative support roles. With only three Cessnas, the fixed wing section had reached the limit of its capabilities. A partial solution, and a novel one, was to borrow an aeroplane. Possum Master George Constable arranged for the loan of a Cessna O-1 'Bird Dog' light observation aircraft from the US Army's 54th Aviation Company at Phu Loi. The loan arrangement was facilitated by Captain Peter Robinson's status as a US-trained Aircraft Maintenance Officer, which enabled him to authorise servicing and repairs. For major servicings, the aircraft would be flown back to Phu Loi and a replacement aircraft provided. It was as simple as that.

On 28 August 1967, a Cessna lifted off from Nui Dat bound for Phu Loi to the north. Aboard were George Constable, Peter Robinson and fixed wing section commander Captain John Wright. On arrival at Phu Loi, George completed a dual check and flew the Bird Dog back to Nui Dat with Peter Robinson occupying the rear observer's seat. John Wright followed, a little enviously perhaps, in the Cessna. For the next week, George flew the aircraft regularly on operations. On 7 September, Captain O'Malley of the 54th at Phu Loi checked out newly arrived Captain Bernie Forrest and Lieutenants David McFerran and Tom Guivarra on the aircraft. Bernie takes up the story:

> After my checkout with Captain O'Malley on the Bird Dog, I did a flight in it on the 8th and later that day Tom Guivarra ran it into the ditch at Black Horse. I don't know what it was that put him into the ditch but we'd only just been checked out. I did my solo from Luscombe to Black Horse and return. We were just using Black Horse to do a practice landing somewhere else. And that's what Tom was doing. You've got to remember too that most of the strips up there were very narrow. We used to operate from Bearcat, and the strip there was really just a road with quite big storm water drains either side.[28]

The Black Horse incident was not simply a landing gone wrong. Second Lieutenant Glen Duus recalled being told that a Chinook helicopter was hovering alongside the strip and the downdraft literally blew the Bird Dog off the other side.[29] Nevertheless, the incident was a blow to Tom Guivarra's professional pride. He was disappointed that it happened at the end of his tour and he had no opportunity to demonstrate further his mastery of the Bird Dog. The aircraft was recovered and repaired, resuming operations on 14 October.

From August 1967 to May 1968 the Bird Dogs flown by 161 clocked up more than 900 hours. This invaluable contribution was even more important in the context of aircraft losses during 1967. Blair Weaver's crash in May and Ross Hutchinson's involuntary landing in a paddy field in June would have been enough. Two more helicopters were lost in late November in quick succession. On 20 November Lieutenant Paddy O'Brien, newly arrived from Australia, was conducting a VR in the vicinity of the task force perimeter with Warrant Officer Brian Quee aboard as observer. They detected movement in the forest below and had turned back to investigate when the Sioux lost power and crashed through the trees. Despite suffering injuries, the pair escaped from the wreckage and were rescued by a RAAF Iroquois. Two days later, another Sioux piloted by Second Lieutenant Roger Colclough, with Officers' Mess steward Private Moore as passenger, fell victim to a booby trap when he investigated a Viet Cong flag apparently caught in a treetop. The flag had been sighted by a Cessna returning from a sortie and advice was passed to Colclough who was nearby. He checked out the scene and found not one, but two flags fluttering in the treetops. A FAC pilot, Jade Zero Six, had also heard the call and had designs on the flags. However, Roger had the whip hand in his Sioux and, despite his misgivings that it might be a trap, his passenger leaned out and retrieved one of the flags. He was eager to try for the second but, even as Roger made the decision to leave well enough alone, their luck ran out. Operations officer Don Dennis takes up the story as related to him:

> At that instant everything turned red. The chopper felt as if it had been struck from beneath by a giant sledge-hammer. We were thrown forward and up. There were clanging sounds like gravel on a tin roof. The tree had been mined! Fortunately, the engine behind us took the force of the blast;

otherwise I'm sure we would have been shredded as fragments ripped through the aircraft.

My immediate reaction was to get the hell out of the place. Surprisingly, the engine still responded. I nudged the rudder pedals and turned away, but as I did so I heard Jade Zero Six call over the radio: 'Better put it down, son. You're on fire.' Because he said it so calmly, yet with such fatherly authority, I didn't ask questions. I autorotated, pulled pitch and flared a few feet above the ground. As we lost speed I knew Zero Six wasn't bullshitting; flames that had been forced back by the slipstream now blew forward and wrapped around the cockpit. We skidded to a halt, scrambled out and ran for our lives.[30]

The FAC called in covering fire from gunships and F-100s while Colclough and Moore were extracted by a Dustoff chopper. The remains of the Sioux were recovered to Nui Dat by Chinook. Another lesson had been learned, and 161 had lost its second aircraft in quick succession. It is said that Roger no longer goes near flags and refuses to salute them, even on Anzac Day.

Arming the Cessnas: Bigger and better rocket pods

It was sometime during the closing months of 1967 that Captain Bernie Forrest, who took over command of the fixed wing section from John Wright in September, seized upon an opportunity to give the Cessnas a little more firepower than was afforded by the four 2.75-inch rockets they could carry at the time:

> I was at Long Binh waiting for fuel. This old Spec 5 was there (like one of our Flight Sergeants) and I was talking to him. I said, 'Gee, I'd love a set of those 7-pods on one of our Cessnas, but we don't have any sequencing switches.' He said, 'You don't need sequencing switches. It's all built into the pod.' So we unloaded the 2-pods, took them off and put them in the back of the Cessna. He picked out a couple of good 7-pods for me and put them on, wired them up and checked them. He said, 'Yeah, they're both good. I suppose you want some rockets?' So he sent his troop up to get some rockets. We'd been using the little 11-pound WP and HE warheads. The kid came back with HE 17-pounders and so I did a sum and it came up to about 250 pounds in each rack which we were entitled to carry. So we loaded these rockets and I headed back to Nui Dat. I landed there and went and saw George Constable. I said, 'George, I've got something to show you.' We walked down to the aeroplane and he saw it

and said, 'Forrest, you'll get me shot!' I said, 'No, I don't think so because we're under approved weight.'

Anyway, I convinced George and he said, 'Let's go out and try them.' Now, we had an area just south of the Horseshoe, not far off the Long Hais, which we never hit with artillery fire because there were no targets big enough. George said, 'We'll go out and we'll blast that.' So we went up and rolled into the area from about 2500 feet and lined it up and let go with the rockets. We punched in fourteen rockets, better than two rounds out of a battery because our rockets had bigger warheads. We weren't even back on the ground when George said, 'We'll keep 'em.' Being a Gunner he could really appreciate what you could do with them.[31]

The comforts of home

Successful flying and maintenance operations left no room for complacency. A Digger likes his home comforts and it was apparent to the soldiers that the Flight was there alongside the strip, nestled into the rubber, for the long haul. So, despite the heavy workload, efforts continued on an opportunity basis to maximise creature comforts. The gentrification phase was to come later; in 1967 the accent was on the basics. Craftsman Paul Lidster recalled asking Captain Peter Robinson's permission to take a vehicle on an 'acquisition mission' to the construction site at the task force Ordnance Depot. A lot of timber had been seen heading in there, and 161 needed timber for several projects including the completion of the ORs' Sundowner Club. Bush Moosh, always with an eye to the main chance, agreed to the use of the vehicle on the condition that floorboards to complete his tent were part of the deal. He also asked where the timber would be found but was told that it was on a need-to-know basis and he was not one of those in need.

It was decided that a bold mission stood the best chance of success. At the front gate to the Ordnance Depot site, Corporal Bob Little, the leader of the raiding party, asked a young soldier the whereabouts of the sergeant in charge of the timber area. Paul Lidster continues the story:

> The kid doesn't know much, but says, 'All of the timber is down the back there. He's probably there.' We get there and Bob jumps out of the truck and yells a few orders at the top of his voice like a good corporal should.

But there's no one there. Bob had a list of the timber we needed so we loaded it on the vehicle. As we drove out Bob had the hide to tell the bloke on the gate, 'Thanks, mate. We found him and you were right. All of the timber's down the back.' And away we went. We'd taken the precaution of taking the TAC [unit identification] signs off the vehicle before we left. So the poor bastard never even knew who it was. Bush Moosh got his floorboards and we got the timber for our boozer extension.[32]

Not a white Christmas

No account of 161's operations during 1967 would be complete without a Christmas story. Craftsman Felix Mitchell's day is stamped forever in his mind:

I'll always remember Christmas '67. George Constable was the OC then. He came across to me as an outstanding figure, a person respected because of his appearance and bearing. There were grubs you wouldn't bother with, but George was one guy who really made an impression and commanded your respect. He'd ordered a few bottles of champagne but a few cases turned up instead. At the Sundowner on Christmas Eve we got a bit lashed on George's champagne and our own booze and it was midnight and we're still down there and singing.

Next morning, there were some very seedy people around including me. George came back. I remember that somebody had put a bloody great pile of empty beer cans outside my tent and I sat on it cross-legged to try to hide it. Then I thought, 'Shit. It's Christmas Day. I should put my hat on and salute him and wish him a Merry Christmas.' So I did that and apologised for not getting up and made some feeble excuse and he looked round and said, 'Felix, I'll give you fucking Merry Christmas.' That's all he said, and he walked off. And I thought, 'Oh God, I'm in the shit; very deep shit.' About an hour later the call came. 'Mitchell, Matthews and Smythe. The OC wants to see you.' So we go up to the Orderly Room and there's George. And he was a bit annoyed that so many of us got absolutely pissed and were like mongrel dogs at six in the morning. I can understand now that this was not a good thing. He had to have people ready for ops. So we were chosen to show others the lesson that had to be learned. On Christmas Day, Mitchell, Matthews and Smythe had to rebuild the sandbagged enclosure where the rockets were stored. We pulled this thing apart and we didn't have any new sand so we had to fill new bags from the old, rotting ones. Smythe is chucking these rockets around—WP rockets that had oozed and were stored in this drum of oil awaiting disposal because they were dangerous. Meanwhile, Matthews is lying over the wall we'd just rebuilt spewing his ring up. Mate, he was crook. This went on until about 12.30. Next thing, the duty officer came down and said, 'Mitchell, the OC wants to see you.' So I went up there and I threw him the snappiest salute you ever saw and said, 'Yes, sir?' He said, 'I've been watching you and you've done a wonderful job down there. I think you should go and have Christmas lunch now. Merry Christmas.' And he was grinning from ear to ear. Mate, I was so crook that I just managed to make it away before I was sick. But there was no way I was going to do it where he could see me.[33]

A new phase beginning

By the end of 1967, Nui Dat had indeed become home. As Christmas came and went, a shadow loomed on the horizon. A new word, 'Tet', was about to become familiar to all. The traditional Vietnamese New Year festival at the time of the full moon, Tet marked the beginning of a period of savage fighting for the Allied forces. For much of early 1968 Australian infantry soldiers and support elements would be deployed outside Phuoc Tuy province. It was to be a testing time for all.

Part 3

The Tet Offensive

8

The Tet and Second General Offensives:
January–July 1968

By January 1968, the United States had committed almost 500 000 troops to the war in Vietnam. The build-up of enemy forces had been equally large. It was a war of attrition, with neither side being able to turn the tide in its favour. The enemy sought to break this deadlock by launching the Tet Offensive, with the dual aims of striking a debilitating blow against the US-led forces and inspiring a popular uprising by the South Vietnamese people against their government and its foreign supporters.[1]

As the lunar new year festival of Tet at the end of January approached, intelligence sources indicated that a major offensive was likely, but it was difficult to predict where the enemy might strike in strength. In Phuoc Tuy, signals intelligence reported an uncharacteristic radio silence. As Saigon and the nearby military installations at Bien Hoa and Long Binh were clearly prime targets, the Australian commander, Major General Vincent, committed the task force to operations outside Phuoc Tuy province in support of American forces defending the northern and eastern approaches to the capital. Operation *Coburg* saw the deployment of 2RAR/NZ and 7RAR to an area of operations some 55 kilometres to the northwest of Saigon. The battalions were supported by A Squadron 3 Cavalry Regiment, 1 Field Squadron, 161 Recce Flight, the RAAF's 9 Squadron and US artillery and aviation resources.² Rotary wing pilot Second Lieutenant Glen Duus recalled the lead-up to *Coburg*:

> I took Brigadier Hughes up to Long Binh a couple of days before we deployed forward on 24 January. I didn't know his purpose. About three kilometres south of the perimeter of Long Binh he said, 'Go down. I want to look at the trees.' I wasn't very happy about it. He's the only brigadier we've got. We did a run parallel with the southern border of Long Binh, about one or two kilometres out. He asked how high the trees were and I told him they were 60 to 80 feet. He said, 'Okay, off we go.' We went up to 'Head Shed' [Headquarters II Field Force Vietnam]. The Australian liaison officer met the Brig and off they went and eventually I picked him up again and took him back to Nui Dat.
>
> I was duty officer at 161 a day or so later when the OC was summoned to task force headquarters. It was about 7.00 p.m. and quite unusual. I got him over there and alerted the 2IC, Phil Roberts, together with Paddy O'Brien and Bernie Forrest who headed up rotary wing and fixed wing. Usually, something like this was an indication of undiscovered crime and the Brig was about to have someone's head. We couldn't think of anything we might have done. George Constable came back and called a conference in the ops room. We got Mike Boland, the workshops officer, in as well. George wanted to know if we could support 'x' aircraft away from base for a longish time. Bernie and Paddy were okay with it. Mike wanted to know what 'x' was and George couldn't tell him. I'm not sure he knew. So eventually Mike said, 'Fine, whatever.' George disappeared back to task force and it was all a big mystery.³

Operation Coburg (24 January–1 March 1968)

It wasn't a mystery for long. The distance to the *Coburg* operational area from Nui Dat required task force elements, including a detachment from 1 ALSG, to be positioned at the huge US logistics base at Long Binh to the northeast of Saigon. Long Binh was a logical target for any major offensive aimed at the fall of Saigon and the discouragement of American forces. It combined with Bien Hoa air base to form a huge complex, vulnerable to attack by enemy forces now equipped with 140mm and 122mm rockets with ranges in excess of ten kilometres. The role of the task force was to deny the enemy access to suitable sites from which to launch these weapons against the complex.⁴

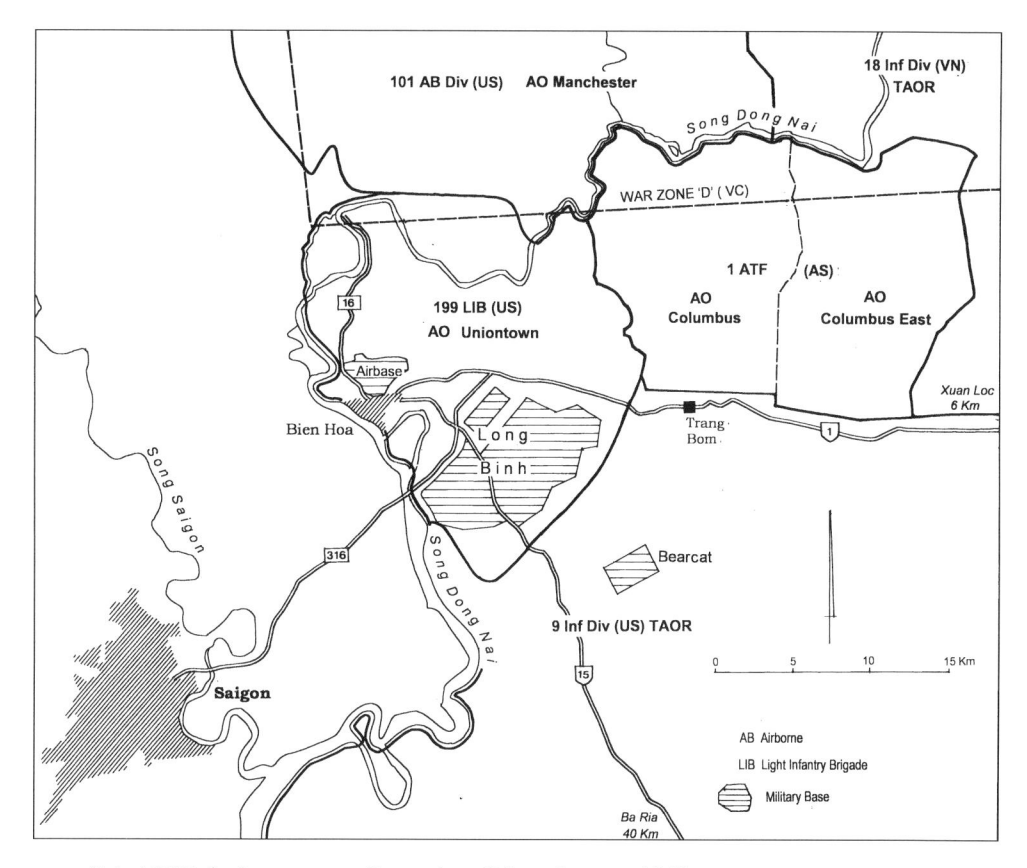

8.1 1ATF deployment on Operation *Coburg*, January 1968.

The Australians operated from fire support bases (FSBs) Andersen and Harrison in Columbus, a large area of operations to the northeast of the Long Binh–Bien Hoa complex. The forward tactical headquarters was located with 2RAR at Andersen, while 7RAR operated from Harrison. Glen Duus was among the 161 pilots deployed:

> *Coburg* came and off we went up to Bearcat. Accommodation had been arranged for us. We were close to the aircraft and everybody was prepared to refuel us. The task force headquarters was shifted up to FSB Andersen, north of Route 1, which we took over from 199 Light Infantry Division. We set up another FSB called Harrison. The battalions started working, with 2RAR first into Andersen. We were very much involved, of course, in our routine DS work with the battalions and recon and other tasks. The Cessnas did a fair bit of recon. We were rotated back and forth from Nui Dat.

Recce work in the FSB Andersen area was extremely dangerous because it was on the approach into Bien Hoa. Pete Spoor took off one day and looked up and he could see the rivets on a pair of F-100s doing a GCA.[5] He was frightened fartless. Another day, I was sitting at 2500 feet and it's real early and there was fog. There was a bloody 707 at about 1000 feet, trying to get through the fog into Bien Hoa. That was scary, too.[6]

On 31 January, the enemy launched 'heavy ground, rocket and mortar attacks against most of the provincial capitals and autonomous cities, including Saigon and the former imperial capital of Hue, as well as many district capitals and smaller towns'.[7] After fierce fighting, the enemy attacks were repulsed in most areas and the hoped-for general uprising of the civilian population did not eventuate.

One of 161 Recce Flight's boldest, Lieutenant Ross Hutchinson, took an active part in the defence of Bien Hoa on 31 January. He had been detached to 334 Helicopter Assault Company, US Army, at Bien Hoa and was on hand when the attack began. His MID citation describes a busy engagement:

> He was detailed to fly as an observer for a heavy fire team operation over the Australian TAOR during Operation *Coburg*. At 0200 hours, when the heavy fire team was refuelling at Bien Hoa, the base came under heavy rocket and ground attack. An attempt was made to get all available aircraft into the air but there were insufficient pilots due to many of them living off the base. Consequently Captain Hutchinson [who was a lieutenant at the time] flew co-pilot in a gunship for Captain Rubin, United States Army, and proceeded to the eastern end of the air base which was under heavy ground attack. Captain Rubin's aircraft with Captain Hutchinson flying co-pilot engaged the enemy for the next hour during which time both the crew chief and the gunner were wounded by enemy ground fire.
>
> At 0300 hours, the aircraft returned to re-arm and refuel and because there was still a shortage of pilots Captain Hutchinson then took command of an aircraft as the only pilot aboard and proceeded to engage opportunity targets in the Bien Hoa area. Captain Hutchinson's aircraft landed again to re-arm at 0400 hours and by this time some experienced pilots had arrived on the airbase, so Captain Hutchinson returned to flying co-pilot and continued to engage opportunity targets until the Viet Cong attack was broken at dawn.[8]

Fixed wing commander Captain Bernie Forrest also remembered operations on *Coburg* clearly:

> Fixed Wing was operating mostly out of Bearcat. They allocated us an area east and northeast of Bien Hoa and Long Binh. We did VR in that area

because, as you know, Charlie got into Bien Hoa. They were up on the water tower for three or four days before they got them off. It could have been quite nasty if it hadn't been for a lucky sighting. The story goes that there were American door gunners hanging out on their straps, feet hooked in the doorframe and getting some cool air as they did sometimes, and one of them looked down and the fields were just crawling with people. He pulled himself back inside and told the skipper to do a U-turn and have a look. As they turned round, the pilots looked down and there was just a swarm of people coming across and heading for Bien Hoa and Long Binh. They say they just got the gunships, the artillery and whatever else they could lay on the area and got into them. After Tet, you wouldn't fly under about 3500 feet around there because of the stink of rotting bodies. There were thousands of them. You can imagine what would have happened if they hadn't picked them up there; if they'd actually gotten into Long Binh and Bien Hoa. A big force into those places and they'd have been history.[9]

These accounts show that the deployment of allied forces in defence of Long Binh and the Bien Hoa airbase did not succeed completely in preventing attacks on these facilities. Repeated incursions by 5VC Division caused considerable damage. As a result, the task force's mission was 'quickly changed from reconnaissance-in-force to a blocking operation designed to intercept enemy forces as they moved back from their attacks',[10] and considerable casualties were inflicted on the enemy as they withdrew. Reconnaissance-in-force operations over an extended area of operations resumed until 1 March, when the task force withdrew to Nui Dat. It was commended for its contribution to the defence of Long Binh–Bien Hoa by the Commander of II FFV, Lieutenant General Weyand. The Royal Australian Regiment and 3rd Cavalry Regiment were later awarded one of the five battle honours approved for the Vietnam War.[11]

The success of the task force in conducting *Coburg* 'helped to establish the case for ongoing extended operations outside Phuoc Tuy'.[12] Further operations of this type were mounted during the enemy's second major offensive in May 1968.

Tet and Phuoc Tuy

In Phuoc Tuy, the local Viet Cong D445 battalion positioned its troops for an assault on the provincial capital, Baria. The attack commenced on 1 February, with the Viet Cong quickly occupying key positions. Simultaneous attacks were made on some of the larger villages including Hoa Long, Long Dien and Dat Do.[13] Elements of 3RAR, with support from APCs and aircraft of 161 Recce Flight, were deployed from Nui Dat in support of South Vietnamese forces against the Viet Cong offensive. Casualties were sustained during operations in Baria. An attempt to extract the wounded by Dustoff chopper failed because access was blocked by power lines. Captain John Coggan ignored the risks and flew three successful casevac sorties in his Sioux. He was awarded the DFC for his skill and courage during this action. Operations continued over the next week at Baria and other points of attack, in particular at Long Dien, until the enemy temporarily ceased its offensive. The task force promptly sought to maintain a positive regard by the local people by resuming its civic action programs to assist the worst-affected civilians.

The fallout from Tet

The Viet Cong forces in some areas of South Vietnam were so weakened by their losses during Tet that they had to rely increasingly on the support of North Vietnamese reinforcements to continue the insurgency in the South. Tet, although presented by some Western media as a victory for the insurgents, did not achieve its aims. No major centres were taken and there was no popular uprising. The offensive did however cast doubt on the possibility of a decisive victory by either side and led to a call for peace talks by the United States. Opposition to the war in Vietnam increased in both the United States and Australia, with public sentiment again fuelled by media reports of allied casualties.

Operations February–April 1968

When the task force returned to Phuoc Tuy from Operation *Coburg*, there was much to be done. The resumption of operations and civic aid programs promised a busy post-Tet period. Intelligence pointed to a regrouping of communist forces in Phuoc Tuy. Cordon-and-search operations *Oakleigh*, *Dandenong* and *Clayton* quickly followed. During Operation *Clayton*, a 161 Sioux voice aircraft was used to broadcast intentions and procedures to the inhabitants of Long Dien. The operation involved the interrogation of thousands of villagers in the largest operation of its type yet mounted by the task force.[13]

The next thrust of the task force was to the area south of Nui Dat, towards the Long Hais, in an attempt to locate and destroy Viet Cong bases which continued to pose a threat to the south of the province. Commencing in late February, Operation *Pinnaroo*, and its subsidiary operations *Ashgrove Tram* and *Cooktown Orchid*, aimed to clear and take control of the Long Hais. It was a milestone operation, using Australian tanks for the first time and calling in B-52 strikes prior to reconnaissance-in-force operations by the infantry. The memories of the casualties suffered by 5RAR in Operation *Renmark* a year earlier were still fresh, with booby-traps and enemy mines constituting a major threat. A sustained campaign of airstrikes and artillery fire was followed by clearance operations by infantry, armoured and combat engineer elements. Extensive enemy facilities were found and demolished. A disturbing feature was that the only enemy mines recovered were of the M-16 type used by the Australians in their barrier minefield south from the Horseshoe.[14] The enemy was able to use the minefield as a source of supply because insufficient Australian and ARVN resources were available to patrol its boundaries effectively. In hindsight, the decision to establish such an extensive minefield was questionable. It remains a controversial issue. This factor aside, the difficult and complex operation was counted as a successful foray into a very inaccessible and formerly secure enemy stronghold. A great deal of damage had been done to long-established infrastructure.

High jinks at 161

At this time, 7RAR was preparing for its departure from Vietnam on 9 April. Its CO, Lieutenant Colonel Eric Smith, was particularly impressed by the support which had been provided by the Possums and US Army aviators over the preceding year. He admired their competence, bravery and 'can do' attitude under all conditions.[15]

Before he left, the Colonel was called upon to act as a character witness for 161's resident chief larrikin, Lieutenant Ross Hutchinson. Hutch had been involved in an escapade related to the SAS attack [described in Chapter 6] on an enemy group that was using a tractor to move arms by night. Following the successful operation, he picked up a recoilless rifle (RCL) from the scene and flew it back to the task force where it was taken by headquarters staff 'for intelligence purposes' and placed in the task force museum. This caused some angst among both the SAS troops who had blown up the tractor and the 161 members whose intelligence had sparked the operation and who had recovered the weapon. They felt that the RCL should be theirs instead of being locked away in the museum. Some drinks were taken to minimise the pain of their loss and, as the alcohol inspired creativity, a plan evolved by which justice might be done. They would steal the RCL, have it split down the middle by machinists on the US repair ship *Corpus Christi Bay*, then present the halves to each other as a token of mutual esteem. One of the party, Second Lieutenant Glen Duus, recalled the subsequent debacle:

> I was the driver when we stole it from the task force museum. Hutch had the bolt cutters. Don Dennis was there too. And there was another vehicle with the SAS contingent. Now, what fouled us up was that they'd put a sentry on the museum, which we hadn't expected. He was told to piss off or get garotted. Unfortunately, he told his boss. Anyhow, we took the RCL back to the Sergeants' Mess and discovered that, if you filled it up with beer cans, you could shoot them out of the thing. The next morning, Paddy O'Brien flew it down to the *Corpus Christi Bay* to be cut in half. As Paddy was coming back, he got a message from George Constable: 'If the miller has cut it, put your head under the miller.' So Paddy went back to the ship and retrieved the RCL.
>
> An investigation was conducted by Colonel Reggie Gardner from the Field Regiment. He was responsible for the task force museum. His offsider was one Stuart Mitchell, Captain, who came across to take depositions. To give him his due, he was suitably embarrassed. And since we didn't know what to say, we all went to see George. And George said, 'Admit taking it and nothing else.' So Stuart ended up with all these pages saying 'Yes, we took it.' The poor bugger. Anyhow, the RCL was never seen again up there and it's now in the Infantry Museum. George obviously got a kick in the arse. We knew we had dropped him in the shit, but he didn't can us or do anything. We were very quiet for the next few months.[16]

Operation Toan Thang 1: The battle at FSB Coral, April–May 1968

The First Battalion, commanded by Lieutenant Colonel Philip Bennett, replaced 7RAR on 9 April. Now on its second tour, 1RAR just had time to complete its work-up phase on Operation *Blaxland* in the Nui Dinhs before Australian forces once more left Phuoc Tuy province to help counter an expected second offensive against Saigon and the Long Binh–Bien Hoa complex.[17] Operation *Toan Thang* (Complete Victory) was launched in the III Corps area by US and South Vietnamese forces on 8 April to mop up remaining enemy formations involved in the Tet Offensive. The operation soon became a defence of Saigon and the Long Binh–Bien Hoa base area when, on 5 May, the enemy launched full-scale attacks on Saigon and its surrounding government and defence installations in a re-run of Tet called the Second General Offensive.[18]

The task force's involvement in *Toan Thang* began in late April when 3RAR was deployed north into Bien Hoa province to block enemy routes into the Long Binh–Bien Hoa area. The deployment became a multi-battalion operation, with the battalions rotating through the area of operations (AO) to ensure sufficient forces were available at all times to maintain the security of Nui Dat. On 12 May, the task force moved from its operational area east of Saigon to AO Surfers, 45 kilometres north of the capital, to cover enemy withdrawal routes. The Australians first occupied FSB Coral, located roughly in the centre of Surfers to provide artillery support to 1RAR's designated sector. Coral also became home to the task force forward headquarters and support elements.

The occupation of Coral on 12 May almost ended in disaster. The insertion of the Australian forces was delayed and it was not possible to establish a coordinated defensive area before nightfall. Further, the strength of the enemy forces was underestimated. It was to be the first time that Australian troops met North Vietnamese Army forces in regimental strength.[19] That night, Coral was attacked by a battalion-strength force. This first encounter was a close-run affair in which the enemy overran 1RAR's mortar platoon and two gun positions of 102 Field Battery before its forces were beaten off by supporting fire. Over the next two days the defences of Coral were built up and reconnaissance patrols were commenced. The enemy struck again with a

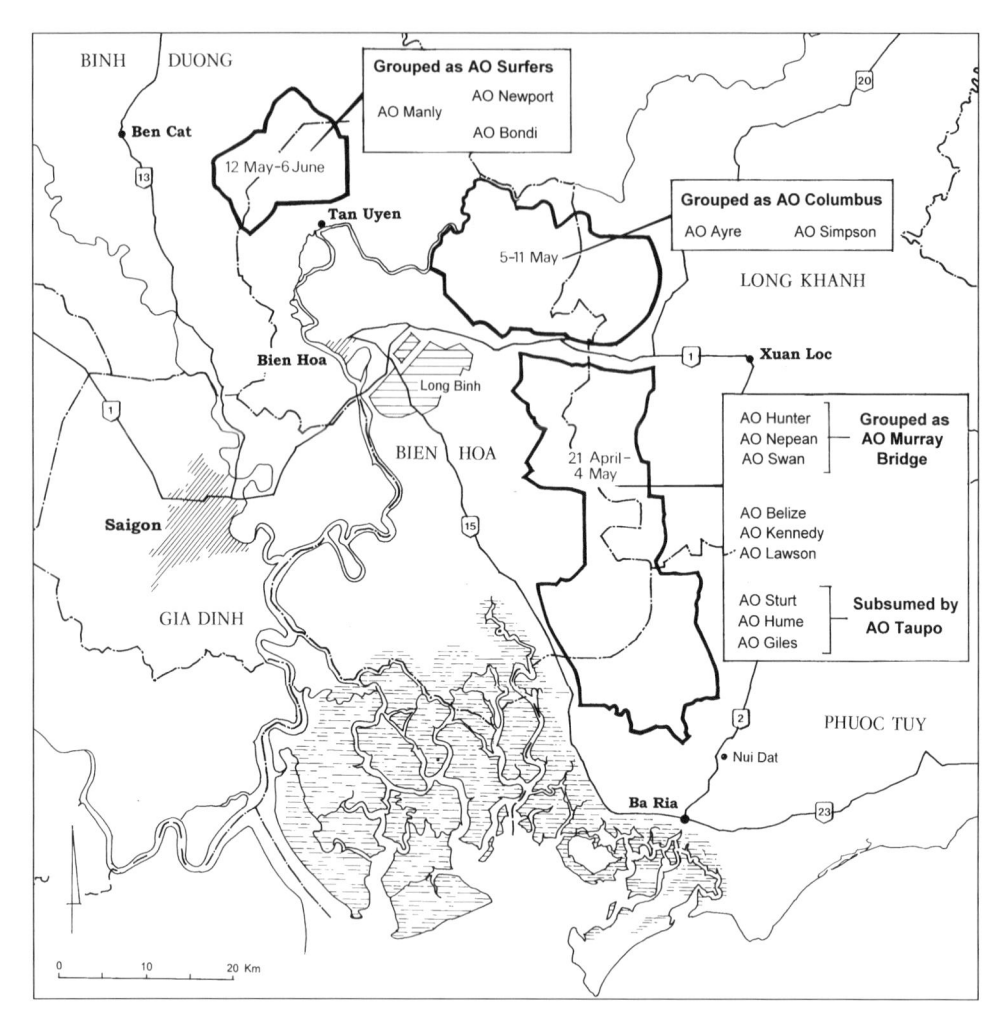

8.2 1ATF deployment on Operation *Toan Thang 1*, April–June 1968.

regimental strength force on the night of 15–16 May. Once again, the weight of supporting artillery fire and airstrikes available to the Australians turned the tide and, as day broke, the enemy forces withdrew. However, the North Vietnamese soldiers had won the respect of the task force for their evident courage and battlecraft.[20]

It was during this period that Second Lieutenant Glen Duus, heading north but looking east, almost collided with a tree during DS operations from Coral:

We got up to Coral and it was a big shitheap because of stuff-ups with the deployment of forces into there. Lots of things happened after the big contact that first night. On about Day Two, I took Lurch [Major John Kemp, the Engineer major] for a recce to find water. Otherwise it would have to be freighted in. We went off to the north a bit and there was a stream there. We crossed to the other side and the place was full of Charlies. They were in an entrenched camp. They just looked up at us and it didn't seem like they gave a shit. Anyway, we went back to Coral and I told Major Tony Hammett about this. Next thing, Hammett's company is heading north looking for these Charlies. And Tony said, 'Come and show me where this camp is.' So we went up and I'm flying along with my head out, eager to show him that I could find it, when he looks ahead and sees this bloody great dead tree sticking out. He just said, 'Tree. Tree. Tree. TREE!' On about the fourth call I woke up and looked up and said, 'Yes, tree.' And I went around it. But had he not seen it I would have hit it. He was a helicopter pilot himself, of course, and he'd once had a tree strike.[21]

Possum Master down: The loss of Major George Constable

On 22 May, Centurion tanks were moved forward from Nui Dat to provide close support for the infantry battalions deployed on Operation *Toan Thang 1*. 161's fixed wing pilots flew convoy cover. The convoy had almost reached Coral on 23 May when Major George Constable departed to provide air cover for a logistics convoy returning to Vung Tau. He was engaged in this task when he crashed and was killed.

It appears from various accounts that George flew along the convoy to its head at low level before climbing sharply, perhaps to turn back along the other side. The aircraft crashed and burned a few moments later between the road and a nearby village. Reports of gunfire and the apparent loss of control of the aircraft suggested that George was severely wounded or killed by ground fire. The exact manner of his death is of less importance than the fact that he was lost. The cause of the accident was eventually listed by the RAAF Directorate of Air Force Safety as 'Operational hazard—ground fire'.[22]

The news quickly found its way back to Nui Dat as is the way when an aircraft goes down, and many felt stunned disbelief even when official confirmation was received. Fixed wing commander Captain Bernie Forrest talked about his memories of that day:

> I was coming back from a trip when I heard on the net that there was a Cessna down, and by the time I landed I knew it had been George shot down in the Bird Dog. Everybody felt it. But you've got your own things to do and yes, it was a shock, but there was no service. The padre didn't come over and say 'On Sunday we'll have a little memorial service.' There was nothing. Absolutely nothing happened in the unit. I think it's just the way it was. I suppose it's the same for the troops on the ground. If somebody gets killed beside you, you just can't throw it in. You just have to keep on doing what you were doing, particularly if you're actively engaged in a firefight or something like that. You'd do what you could to help, but in the end you'd have to get back to what you were doing. And I think that it was like that for the pilots. Everybody was affected by it in their own way, but there was never any collective reaction.
>
> As FW section commander I really thought that somebody would have asked me to write a report on the aeroplane or the operations leading up to the crash or whatever. But there was nothing. To my knowledge, no accident report or crash critique was ever written.[23] We had the aeroplane on strength from the US Army and I don't know of any paperwork that ever went between our unit and their unit about writing off that aircraft. I've just never read or seen anything written at all about the actual crash and the loss of George.[24]

There is no doubt that the ORs were devastated. George was a much-loved and respected person. More than that, many were proud of him in a way enjoyed by only a select few leaders. For those who knew him less well, it was still a sobering time. Second Lieutenant Don Moffatt, a short service commission pilot who had trained at Scheyville with National Service officer candidates before earning his wings, had arrived in country on 29 April 1968. Don was an assertive, mature individual for his years and was later appointed RW section commander as a Second Lieutenant when Captain Paddy O'Brien returned to Australia. He recalled his feelings about George's loss:

> I'd not been in country long when George went down. It certainly brought me back to earth because, when you go to a place like that, you don't really think much about being killed. It shocked the whole Flight. I think we all thought we'd go over there and do a year's flying and come home. It put a bit of a jolt through the blokes. Suddenly you think, 'Jesus Christ. You can cop it.'
>
> I think it took the blokes who'd spent a long time there with him longer to get over it than those of us who were new. George checked me out when I got there. I didn't know him; I'd never met him until I got to

Vietnam. And I didn't get the chance to know him very well. But it shocked me, I know that. It left a little bit of a hole in the old gut, probably because you're thinking, 'Well, it could have been me.'[25]

The absence of any group manifestation of grief at George's loss may be indicative of the shock that this first death in 161 caused. Or perhaps it was just that grief tended to be a more private emotion in those days and indeed it was not considered manly to shed even a private tear. The George Constable the author knew would not have had it any other way. 'Just get on with it and don't stuff up,' he would have said. And because of the person he was, his death is mourned to this day by those who knew and flew and worked with him.

Fire Support Base Balmoral (May–June 1968)

When George Constable was killed the Flight's 2IC, Captain John Coggan, assumed temporary command. There was no relief from operations. On 24 May, 3RAR established FSB Balmoral in the northern sector of Surfers, less than five kilometres north of Coral. The following day Bravo Company of 1RAR became engaged in a vicious firefight midway between the two FSBs while escorting four Centurion tanks to Balmoral. The protection and firepower of the tanks was used to good advantage, once again showing their worth as armoured, mobile support for infantry operations.[26] Their arrival at Balmoral was timely as the enemy attacked on 26 May. Balmoral's defences held with the assistance of close air support. An infantry/tank action was launched against the scene of the previous day's contact and the three-hour engagement that followed again demonstrated the effectiveness of armoured support.[27]

The Possums continued their DS and reconnaissance roles throughout. On 27 May, a Sioux sustained damage from ground fire while carrying out a tactical recce in support of operations from Balmoral.[28] An airstrike was called in and, with supporting artillery fire, severely damaged what appeared to be an enemy headquarters. Balmoral was again attacked by enemy regimental forces after midnight on the 28th. Once again the enemy was beaten off with heavy casualties by a combination of defensive infantry and tanks, close air support and artillery fire.

For the Australians, the sustained conventional warfare engagements at Coral and Balmoral were unlike any previous battles including Long Tan. Operation *Toan Thang 1* concluded shortly after. A significant feature of the operation for 161 Recce Flight and other support units was the establishment of a forward maintenance area, at Bearcat from 25 April to 13 May and then at Coral until 6 June. Forward logistics support was also a key factor in the operation. The operation demonstrated that the task force could deploy quickly and effectively.

Possum Master Four: Major Harry Benson

It was little more than two weeks after the loss of George Constable when Major Harry Benson took over as Possum Master Four. Like his predecessors, the new OC had an impressive professional background. A Gunner, he trained as a fixed wing aviator before undertaking a rotary wing conversion some years later. Along the way, he completed the fixed wing instructor course at the RAF Central Flying School. He was posted to flying duties with the British Army in England, Germany, Hong Kong and Malaya. During this period he gained experience in both fixed and rotary wing operations similar to those undertaken by 161 Recce Flight in South Vietnam. He then attended Staff College in 1964 before serving for two years on the military staff at the Australian Embassy in Washington, D.C. His attendance at staff college and duties in Washington had taken him away from Australian Army Aviation for some time, but he had already been warned for duty as the next Possum Master before George Constable was killed. He knew personally very few of the people he would command in Vietnam, and had much to think about during his hurried departure to take over the Flight:

> I had a long time to think about what I was going to do while I was on the flight to Saigon. The people who were there, the pilots and so on, were pretty young and many had limited experience about the expectations of the Army. Many had clear personal objectives to pursue after their service in Vietnam. Now, I knew that, and there was no way I could change that even in the year that I was going to spend there. I simply wanted to do what I thought was best for them.

> I can tell you that it was an incredibly difficult thing for a human being to take over from a ghost, but that's what it was like. He was an excellent person, and I knew him reasonably well. He was with me for some time. Despite that, I just loved every minute I was in the job.[29]

The new Possum Master had gained valuable insight and experience while on the Army staff in Washington D.C. He was accredited to the US Army Aviation Centre in the Pentagon, where he made lasting friendships and had access to the latest developments in US Army Aviation doctrine and flying training programs. At the Fort Rucker Aviation Centre, he gained multi-engine qualifications and experience on both fixed and rotary wing aircraft including the Iroquois and Chinook. He had thus learned a great deal that was directly relevant to his command of 161.

Major Benson's experience led him to a conservative and thoughtful approach to his command; an approach that was not always understood or appreciated by his younger, less experienced pilots. Sioux pilot Second Lieutenant Peter Rogers was undergoing Battle Efficiency training with Harry when the news of George's death precipitated Harry's sudden departure for Nui Dat. He followed soon after and his memories of that time provide insight into the pilots' reactions to the new Possum Master's approach:

> With a couple of notable exceptions, I think our line pilots were young Turks. We were given the freedom and heavy responsibility of operating largely on our own with an enormous amount of firepower available to us at the press of a transmit button. We angrily resented the delays in getting clearances and approval for offensive action, and were not tolerant of those commanders we saw as having the big picture but not the nitty gritty experience of seeing the baddies *right there*. We didn't make life easy for Harry with our attitudes, but I have the greatest respect for him now. Although I didn't know George Constable at all, I understand that he was fairly gung-ho and gave his pilots a lot of latitude. Harry was more cautious, and we resented him for it. It wasn't until years after that I appreciated his concerns.[30]

Harry had much more to think about than his pilots' attitudes. He was also concerned that some of the senior officers who flew with the DS pilots might not understand fully the implications of the directions they gave to their drivers:

> Some pilots got remarked upon by the commanding officers of the battalions who, for some reason, imagined that when they got in the helicopter it was somehow secure. A CO might have been to a particular place where there'd been a contact. He'd say, 'I want to go and have a look there.' And the pilot might not be happy about that because he knows it's a big risk for little gain. I mean, what is it about getting into an aircraft that makes people feel secure? So the pilot might say, 'Look, if you can just get someone to go and throw smoke where you want us to look at, then okay.' Because that meant that somebody had to go and report what was there. Some of the COs really didn't understand. They'd just be thinking about the disposition of their companies and they'd imagine what it would be like and get into the helicopter and ask to be taken up there as if it was a secure area. Now, the pilots had to look at the task and decide how they were going to treat it, because they owned the helicopter and the safety of the passenger was their responsibility.[31]

There was another matter to be addressed. The Squadron Sergeant Major (SSM) position at 161 became vacant and task force headquarters decided to fill the post with a Company Sergeant Major (CSM) from one of the battalions. Major Benson was taken aback:

> You can only imagine what happened in the hangar. This guy was an older soldier and he was a CSM through and through. And I think that it happened because the task force commander felt that 161 was a bit of a loose cannon. There wasn't much I could do about it immediately, but I had some good friends in Saigon. I got in touch with one on the General's staff and explained that this situation was just going to murder us. The place was just falling apart. And they did a wonderful thing. There was a new CSM arrived who hadn't been in country before and it was arranged that he should take over. He was an excellent person, just what we needed.[32]

There were other matters that engaged the new Possum Master's attention, but he elected to wield the 'new broom' with care in a measured approach to reform. In the meantime, there was much to keep him busy.

Relief from routine

Life at Nui Dat was not always so serious. For young men engaged in dangerous activities comic relief was always welcome. Second Lieutenant Don Moffatt recalled fun and games in the Officers' Mess:

We had some hilarious times. Don Dennis had one of the greatest senses of humour you'd ever see; a funny, funny man. One night, we were just sitting in the Mess and, for no apparent reason, he does this skit. He didn't actually talk, just made some noises, and to cut a long story short he was taking off Douglas Bader [a Second World War fighter pilot who flew with artificial legs]. He gets the siren going and there's an air raid. He must have been relaxing because he puts his legs on and they're a bit tight and squeaky so he has to oil the things. This is all done without any talk. Anyway, he gets in his Spitfire and takes off and he crashes. His legs get mangled up in the pedals and he can't get out. So he gets his lunchbox and gets out the can opener and cuts his legs off to get out of this thing. And he survives. Well, mate, he put the scarf on and he put the leather helmet on with the goggles and all. Now, you couldn't do that, could you? If I tried to pull that with you it'd just be bullshit. But he had everybody just about rolling on the floor. He did other skits, but that's the one that really sticks in my mind; how clever and how funny it was.

It was great up there when a new bloke arrived, because you've run out of all the stories and everyone knows everyone's jokes. It could get pretty bloody boring at those times when you didn't have new blood coming in. So you needed people like Don within the old bunch who could be funny. To pull a stunt like this Douglas Bader thing was just marvellous.

I remember another funny night. There was this bloke, a black American called Major Whitehead of all things. He came down from somewhere up north for a month or six weeks with us. He got dropped off by a Bird Dog, and he got out and had his gear and he walked up to the Mess. We had drinks and drinks and more drinks and he got fairly pissed on his first night. He hadn't said what he flew, so someone said to him after about twelve Fosters, 'Oh Major, do you fly fixed wing or rotary wing?' The major was affronted. It was clear that he felt there could be no doubt about what a real man flew. He drew himself up and said, 'My boy. Ah'd rather have a sister in a whorehouse than a brother what was a starched wing pilot.'[33]

Back to the grind: Operations in Phuoc Tuy

There was little respite for the Possums after Tet and the subsequent deployment to Bien Hoa province during April–June which included the operations at Coral and Balmoral. During July 1968 the task force swung back into full operations in its own TAOR, revisiting the Long Hais and the Long Green and Light Green areas in the southeast of the province (so called because of the colours used on maps to designate them). The aim was to knock out the local Viet

Cong C25 company known to operate there when it came out of the Long Hais.

Operation *Elwood* was a cordon and search of the hamlets of La Van and Vinh Thanh, in Ngai Giao village. It was supported by a Sioux equipped for voice operations. The plan was for the Possum aircraft to circle the village just before dawn on 23 July, broadcasting its message to the people below. The broadcast directed them to collect their identification documents and go to the village square, reassured them regarding their safety and advised that they should cooperate for the best and quickest result. Unfortunately, the voice chopper, piloted by Second Lieutenant Glen Duus, was sent out a day early. To the horror of the 1RAR company commander who was engaged in a preparatory recce of the area with another Possum, he duly broadcast his message. The villagers did as directed but of course there was no one to do the business. When these things happen, heads must roll:

> The air operations officer at task force headquarters bore the brunt of retribution for this blunder, but in the considered opinion of other officers present at Nui Dat he was the scapegoat for another and more senior officer. The junior officer was sent to be training officer at the reinforcement unit. The whole event quickly became known and was recounted with varying degrees of amusement throughout the task force and back in Australia.'[34]

The show must and did go on. Operation *Platypus* saw the battalions return to the Hat Dich area to harass the enemy. On 2 August, a large mine was triggered by an APC proceeding along a fire trail. The driver was killed instantly and other casualties were sustained. The 1RAR medical officer, Captain Dick Crane, was flown in by Sioux. 'With more bravado than he actually felt Dick told the pilot, Don Moffatt, that he would appreciate it if they did not land on another mine.'[35] Luckily, Don managed not to. He and Dick Crane became friends and remain so to this day.

Army Aviation becomes a Corps

July 1968 was a significant month for the Flight for reasons other than operational highlights. On 1 July the Australian Army Aviation Corps was formed. While this had no effect on 161's operations, it was a major milestone in the history of Army Aviation. It meant that aviation was recognised as a permanent and professional element of the Army's overall structure. Another notable happening was the arrival of the first Royal New Zealand Army pilot to fly with 161 in Vietnam. The Flight had gone ANZAC. On 25 July, Captain Ted Brooker arrived at Nui Dat, still rather bemused by his posting:

> I was serving in 3 Squadron. I'd done about 200 hours on Sioux, for a total of about 1000 hours all up, when I was invited to do a tour in Vietnam with 161 Recce. I was actually invited, but it was made pretty bloody clear that if I didn't take up the offer then my career would be severely limited. So I got on this Hercules and flew to Singapore and stayed over in a Brit Army Mess. I was by myself. Nobody seemed to know that I was coming or anything about me. I was never told how it was arranged.[36] I had no briefing, none at all. I flew on a Bristol Freighter into Tan Son Nhut and then to the Dat. I got out there, went over to the 161 Officers' Mess and met Paddy O'Brien. We'd just sat down to have a beer and this bloody gun battery across the road fired. Fuck, I was under the table that fast it wasn't true. It gave me the fright of my life. Of course everyone in the place thought it was a howler of a joke.
>
> We had a mentor system, and Glen Duus was my mentor. He used to say, 'Look through the bloody trees, not at them!' I remember flying around when I was new there, and he'd say, 'Look down there.' I couldn't see a bloody thing. Anyway, Glen taught me the ropes and he's always had a special place in my memories. He was really, absolutely first class. And Pete Rogers, when he came I was his mentor. It worked well.[37]

The Scheyvillians: A new breed

During 1968, graduates of the National Service Officer Training Unit at Scheyville who had subsequently completed pilot training began to arrive at Nui Dat. Because of the time involved in their officer and pilot training, there was little left of their two-year National Service obligation to put their training into practice. All but two who served at Nui Dat took short service commissions to enable them to serve a full tour in South Vietnam. So technically, they were not 'Nashos'.

Scheyville was an essential new source of aircrew to meet the growing demands at Amberley and in the Vietnam conflict. Indeed, it was the initial training ground for most Army pilots for a decade from the mid-1960s. Of the 94 Australian and New Zealand pilots who served with 161 Recce Flight from 1965 to 1972, 47 were Scheyvillians.[38] They won their share of decorations, with six being awarded the DFC and two more Mentioned in Dispatches.

Like other graduates of Scheyville, pilots gained the skills of an infantry platoon commander as well as being familiarised with the use of Armour and Artillery. Thus, when they flew on operations in Vietnam, they were not only competent airframe drivers but also possessed insight into the tactical situations experienced by the infantry forces they supported. They were able to offer relevant and informed observations to the commanders they flew around Phuoc Tuy. Small wonder that they were highly regarded, and that a number went on to very senior positions in Army Aviation.

Also they fitted in well in the fairly relaxed flight line atmosphere. Many Army pilots tended to have less formal relationships with the men who maintained their aircraft than with other soldiers. Captain Tub Matheson, himself a Scheyvillian who flew with 161 during 1971–72, explained:

> 161 was a funny sort of a unit. The RAEME troops, everybody, I think we'd all grown up together. I remember as a young officer, the rule was that you wouldn't call a Digger by his Christian name and he would never call you by yours. That was bullshit. The Army Aviation experience was that you went away, maybe for a month or more, with your 'all trades' fitter. 'Take that aircraft to Western Australia and we'll see you in six weeks.' You live together, you sleep together. I don't know how many times I've played mobile crane—a strap around my neck, lifting engines in and out of Army aircraft. You went to Christian names. And like I said, you grew up together. We went up in the flying business while they went up in their RAEME stream. Like with Len Avery. He finished up as WO1 Artificer at the same time as I finished up as CO of School.[39]

Looking back; looking forward

Almost three years had passed since 161 Recce Flight was raised at Amberley for deployment to Bien Hoa. Much had changed in the war and in the Flight. Now in its third location, it was much larger and had amassed a great deal of experience. It had suffered only one fatality, an almost miraculous record given the operational hazards its pilots faced every day. It had lost several aircraft and there had been injuries, some severe. Its new OC, Major Harry Benson, was taking stock of all aspects of his command and formulating his ideas for change and improvement. He was keen to ensure that the Flight was ready for whatever came next.

9

The aftermath:
August 1968–February 1969

The Tet and Second General Offensives were over and a new trend in operations was to follow. General Westmoreland was relieved as the US commander in South Vietnam by General Creighton Abrams, who instigated a gradual shift in US strategy that saw Westmoreland's favoured large-scale search-and-destroy missions move towards smaller unit operations. The latter were more compatible with established Australian tactical doctrine and preferred method of operations in counterinsurgency.[1] There would be more emphasis on pacification in the years to come.

Following Tet, task force commander Brigadier Hughes resumed his strategy in Phuoc Tuy comprising 'operations in depth against the enemy's remote base and logistics areas while continuing to drive the enemy back from the populated areas in the south'.[2] The progress made in pacification during 1966–67 had suffered badly during Tet and there was much to be done. However, while Tet was nominally over, its aftermath would see task force elements continuing to deploy outside the province until March–April 1969. The task ahead was daunting.

A challenging period

At 161, Possum Master Harry Benson was learning the ropes like any other new pilot. While he was well qualified and had enjoyed opportunities to fly the latest and best US military helicopters, he had to gain experience in the operational zone and the techniques employed. It was a busy time, and he might not have been mentored to the extent that he would insist on for other pilots. However, he met the challenge and the 'Harry era' was established. Like all of the Possum Masters, he brought his own unique qualities to the post.

In September 1968, there was a substantial changeover of pilots. Captains Coggan and Forrest left, together with stalwarts Glen Duus, Roger Colclough and Peter Spoor. Fixed wing driver Peter Garton and operations officer Don Dennis had also gone home in August. New names like Barry Donald, Stan McClymont and Steve Tizzard began to appear in the Commander's Diary. Second Lieutenant Don Moffatt recalled the period well:

> I had been there with those blokes who were a year or two ahead of me in the structure. And I thought the world of them. Now, they went home almost en masse, and that's when I got promoted to rotary wing section commander. All the new blokes, bar one, were junior to me. It became a whole new era. It just changed almost overnight.[3]

Another notable change was in the way VR missions were conducted. Major Benson began to authorise sorties with a fixed wing aircraft flying at around 1500 feet above ground level as 'top cover' for a VR chopper down among the treetops. Captain Ted Brooker was a strong proponent of this method as he had been taught the technique in New Zealand by an American instructor. Harry Benson recalled introducing the system:

> I brought it in so that the fixed and rotary wing people could work together. The high person would be the fixed wing pilot. The guy down below could concentrate on looking and finding. So that worked all right. It didn't always happen. Some people would go out and prefer to do it on their own. On some sorties it would be done because of risk factors, particularly in the valleys where the VR aircraft was more vulnerable. On other VRs you didn't need it at all.[4]

The high-low VR technique became a routine procedure when the Jades, the FAC pilots based at Vung Tau, took over the top cover role. This saved 161 from having to allocate its own scarce fixed wing hours and strengthened the already close bond between the FACs and the Possums. It was during 1968 too that regular detachments of 161 rotary wing pilots to American Army helicopter units commenced. On these detachments, the pilots flew Iroquois, Cayuse, Cobra and, later, Kiowa aircraft. Second Lieutenant Bill Heron even gained experience on the larger Chinooks. As well, the link with the 54th Aviation Company at Vung Tau established by Major Laurie Doyle continued, with the fixed wing pilots getting the opportunity to fly the big, single-engined Otter aircraft. Others flew FAC aircraft, including the Cessna O-2 'push-pull' model that began to replace the O-1 Bird Dogs in the late 1960s. These were great learning experiences and at times hair-raising, particularly during operations when Possums like Second Lieutenant Peter Rogers found that some US pilots had less regard for survival than might have reasonably been expected.

Continuing operations

The battalions and their supporting units were kept busy during the latter half of 1968. Pacification continued, with the concomitant goal of boosting the morale and effectiveness of ARVN units. A change of tack came with Operation *Road Runner* in early September, an operation mounted to protect US ammunition convoys of up to 140 vehicles transiting the Australian TAOR on Route 15 from Vung Tau to Saigon. In September, Operation *Hawkesbury* saw 1RAR in the Hat Dich area with 4RAR in a 'hammer and anvil'[5] operation in operational area Tuggerah, which 'covered the axis of a known, traditional and well-used supply and infiltration route from the North and from the Mao Tao mountains'.[6] SAS patrols and VRs by 161 indicated that the enemy was sticking to the northern sector of Tuggerah, an area that was 'extremely thick and difficult and lacking in suitable landing zones for helicopter operations'.[7] Despite these difficulties, Operation *Hawkesbury* resulted in fourteen enemy killed.

The Possum pilots were commensurately busy on their never-ending round of reconnaissance and direct support operations. In an interesting reflection of Major Benson's concerns about the interaction between his young Possums and their senior passengers, RW section commander Don Moffatt told an interesting story of a cockpit power struggle:

> I did a lot of direct support for the battalions. 1RAR was commanded by Lieutenant Colonel Philip Bennett, who later became Sir Philip Bennett. There was nobody in 161 who wanted to fly with him. They hated it, just really hated it. So when there was DS for 1RAR I used to program myself because I got along okay with him. In the beginning I had to stand my ground with him a bit. He was one of those blokes who thought he could get on top of the pilots and this was the problem. He'd tell them to do things that, you know, they just couldn't do or shouldn't do. So he needed to be told in the correct manner that the pilot is the captain of the bloody ship and it doesn't matter what rank you are when you're sitting next to him. And I told him that. I put it, I think, in a fairly reasonable manner because he didn't go off his brain. He argued a bit. I said to him that the pilot was responsible for getting both his passenger and himself back safely. That was a big part of his mission. I said, 'If he goes out trying to kill you both, you've got the wrong bloke flying.' He said, 'I'll be the judge of that.' And I said, 'No you won't, because you're not qualified to make that judgment. I'm not being rude here but the pilot has done the correct training; he's got the signature in the logbook that says he's done the correct training, and a big part of his training is making those sorts of decisions.' So anyway, he sort of wore that and I think I did err his way a bit if he wanted to do something I thought was a bit 'Oh, shit.' But not every time. I ended up having great rapport with Bennett and Harry Benson did as well.[8]

The 'people sniffer'

During 1968, yet another new task was introduced for the Siouxs with a sensor device called the Automatic Personnel Detector (APD), more commonly known as the 'people sniffer'. The sniffer used a probe mounted on the front of the chopper to detect ammonia traces from human bodies in thick jungle where normal VR methods were less effective. Operations in late 1968 in the north of the province called for sniffer sorties to locate enemy groups in heavy cover. Intelligence from this source was intended to be an important aid for the platoons engaged on search-and-destroy operations in the area. However, it was not always effective as the sensor could detect emanations and residue from non-human beings. The mission technique was to fly the sensor and its operator at low level over the target area so that any significant emission levels detected could be recorded, and the grid reference of the source noted. A second aircraft operated as top cover to assist the low-level chopper to navigate accurately and to relay messages back to the task force.

The Sioux pilots had reservations about both the technique and the results achieved. The technique involved flying in straight lines at low level and low speed, a practice normally avoided because the enemy could start to predict the line the aircraft might next take. Second Lieutenant Peter Rogers was also sceptical about how the results were used. He gave two examples:

> First, as one of our pilots was flying over an area he saw three or four enemy on the ground with weapons. So he got the top cover aircraft to call up and request using artillery on them. And the duty officer at task force headquarters refused on the grounds that it would compromise the mission and none of us could understand what that was about. I mean, I thought we were there to find them!
>
> On the other occasion I was flying along with the sniffer gear and there was an open paddock with just bare grass, nothing, no sign of digging, and I knew the area pretty well. Right in the middle of it was a dead tree. In the dead tree would've been probably 30 or 40 birds' nests and we flew directly over it and the operator said, 'Mark 10', which was the maximum. I immediately radioed and said, 'No, cancel that, we've just flown over a tree full of birds' nests.' Too late! It went into the books. The next day they put a B-52 strike on the tree. They blew up a pile of bird shit.[9]

The people sniffer missions were taken over by the RAAF's 9 Squadron, and this took some of the pressure off 161's operations as the helicopters were fully extended on other tasks in support of the battalions.

Maintaining the links

Operation *Capitol* in November provided an example of the variety of services provided by 161's DS pilots. An account of this operation by 1RAR highlighted the requirement for routine personnel administration to continue even while the troops were absent from the task force area. The DS choppers were used for this purpose, flying in support personnel, ranging from pay clerks to padres, to address ongoing needs and issues. There were many and varied sorties of this type: a soldier might be due to leave on R and R, or a malaria case might need evacuation; a company commander might have to be relieved temporarily while he got over a case of gut cramps; it was important for morale that mail be delivered to wherever the action was at the time; during a lull in the operation, a CO might wish to be taken to Vung Tau to visit his wounded in the field hospital there. The services provided by the DS chopper, for whatever administrative or operational purpose, were deeply appreciated by the battalions. However, they were seldom mentioned in accounts of operations as the DS Possum was always there and its availability and versatility were taken for granted. Kiwi pilot Captain Ted Brooker spoke of one unusual task:

> I think it was Charlie Company, I forget which battalion. They were surrounded and they couldn't be resupplied because they were in thick, primary jungle. So they wanted a chainsaw and fuel to cut a pad. And they were short of ammo. And bloody 9 Squadron wouldn't do it, or they weren't available or whatever it was. So anyway, I got the job of taking this chainsaw and this engineer sergeant with a whole pile of rope. We got over the top and hovered above the trees—there was a lot of gunfire—and this sergeant lowered this chainsaw hand over hand down through the trees. Then he lowered the fuel down. All this time we're in the hover and how the hell we were never hit I don't know. We were in a hole and Jesus, I was pleased to get out of it. Then of course they wanted some ammunition, machine gun ammo, so we filled the Sioux up with as much as we could get away with and we went back over there again. This time he kicked one container of ammo out. We got the response, 'Yes, great!' So we kicked another three or four boxes out and then went back and loaded up again. By this stage they had the chainsaw going and they didn't want us to drop any more in case we hit somebody. They made the pad and an Iroquois got in to do the resupply and took the casualties out.[10]

The daily grind continued over Christmas 1968, with a nominal 24-hour ceasefire on Christmas Day. Lunch was flown out to the rifle companies in the field. There were even Christmas drinks as wily sergeants pulled bottles of spirits, carefully stored away for the occasion, from their heavy packs to ensure that their Diggers didn't go without. There was even a Father Christmas in a red suit with false whiskers and a small present for every man. The officers served the modest meal and a can of beer before eating their own lunch. It was very important that these simple, traditional things happened to keep up the morale of the troops. A few hours later the ceasefire was over and the action resumed.

Operations *Tiger Balm* and *Goodwood II* in January 1969 heralded 1RAR's swansong as the end of its second and last tour approached. An interesting incident on 17 January involved 161's DS chopper. Major Bronx Honner, commanding Charlie Company, had sent out an ambush patrol from 8 Platoon after the company had occupied its night defensive position:

> About 30 minutes later, the patrol commander reported that he had a very sick soldier whose illness made it impossible for the patrol to continue. Major Honner radioed for the Dustoff but the American helicopter had already departed from the forward headquarters of the task force for its own night base. The 161 helicopter was the only aircraft available and it also was about to depart for Nui Dat. However, unless Major Honner could guarantee the security of the landing point, Lieutenant Colonel Bennett would not agree to the Possum being used.
>
> The patrol was in open ground—paddy fields with visibility for some hundreds of metres—and the half-platoon size patrol could not possibly secure such an area. However, dark was falling quickly, so Major Honner told the patrol commander to take three men with a machine gun to the far side of the fields in an attempt to cover as much of the ground as possible. He then informed Lieutenant Colonel Bennett that the landing zone was secure.
>
> The Possum duly arrived, entered the Charlie Company radio net and was talked down by the patrol. As its skids touched the ground, before the sick man was aboard, there was a burst of automatic fire from an undetected group of enemy. Major Honner thought that he had caused a helicopter to be shot down. The Digger scrambled aboard, the pilot pulled pitch and the Possum soared up and away with no damage.[11]

Despite his good intentions, Major Honner was not popular with his CO. He apologised and the pilot shrugged it off as 'one of those things'.

Possums, FACs and F-100s

One of the more graphic stories told by Second Lieutenant Peter Rogers was about the morning he cadged a ride in a Cessna O-2 FAC aircraft to get a bird's eye view of an air strike:

The Aftermath: August 1968–February 1969   133

The FAC was actually a Kiwi, who shall remain nameless. He was putting two F-100s onto a target marked with white phosphorus grenades by Phil Stevens in a Sioux. The fighters each had four 500-pound Hi-Drag bombs, with fins that popped out after release and slowed the bombs down so they could be delivered accurately from a low pass. The cloud base was only a couple of thousand feet, so the fighters were turning very tightly to stay in the area. The FAC organised them to run in from east to west, and after each run Phil would zip in, check the area and drop another marker. The trouble started because there were in fact three F-100s and the FAC kept confusing the call signs. He cleared a fighter in 'hot' while Phil was still over the target. Realising his error, he panicked and instead of telling the fighter to break it off, he yelled at Phil to get out of there. Worse, he got disoriented and said to break to the west.

Phil, a fairly unflappable type, dutifully rolled out of the turn and set off to the west at something more than 60 knots as he realised that things had taken a rather decided turn for the bad. He wasn't much of a match for the F-100 coming in behind him at 400 knots. I watched with sick horror as the 500 pounder came off the fighter's wing, knowing that Phil was well within blast range. Amazingly, the Hi-Drag didn't Hi-Drag. The fins didn't pop and it continued at 400 knots into the trees past the target, ricocheted into the air and caught up with the Sioux (now in a 45-degree nose-down acceleration) and was momentarily in perfect formation on the right before dropping back into the jungle.

Apparently, if the fins didn't pop the bomb didn't arm itself—but we weren't to know that. I could almost see the look on Phil's face as he curved away to the south and back to Nui Dat without another word. We finished the strike and the FAC dropped me back at the Dat. I walked up to the mess to find Phil there on his own—at ten in the morning—having a stiff drink and muttering to himself about FACs in general and Kiwis in particular.[12]

Pete Rogers' reminiscences include other experiences with F-100s, one of which featured a long-odds shot that came off:

I was marking a target in the Long Hais. I was in a sort of open bowl surrounded by higher ground and feeling uncomfortably vulnerable. In the middle of the bowl was a colossal rock about the size of a two-storey house, under which was a tunnel with a full-size door as an entrance complete with jambs and lintel. Inside, I could see a set of steps going down to another door at 90 degrees, and on the first pass a little man disappearing into it.

I had two F-100s, again with 500-pound Hi-Drags. They made seven passes, dropping one bomb each time. All they did was knock chips off the rock, which I guess is why Charlie put his entrance there. I reluctantly told the FAC and the fighters to give it away, as nothing short of a direct hit would do any good. That was like a red rag to the lead, who had one bomb left. He came in very low and slow and released the bomb just before he scraped over the rock. The bomb disappeared straight into the doorway. It could only have had a few inches' clearance either side. There was stillness for a second, and then a great whoosh of dust out of the door. The rock cracked gracefully into about a thousand pieces and collapsed into a pile of rubble over the tunnel. I couldn't stop hollering, it was so spectacular. I gave the bomb damage assessment as one killed by air as I figured the Charlie I'd seen couldn't have survived. Mind you, he could have been a kilometre away underground by that time. The fighter jocks were a bit put out; I guess the damage assessments they got were usually more imaginative.[13]

Fixed wing operations

The chopper pilots did not have all of the fun by any means. Captain Bernie Forrest described a Cessna sortie with a difference:

I remember this occasion when the Americans laid a trail of CS gas[14] across the Rung Sat where there was a rice area, south of the line which marked the extent of the water. Charlie was coming into the rice belt to steal the rice from the villagers, so the Americans put a CS gas trail down to stop them infiltrating across that line. Now CS gas is not really a gas; it's a superfine powder. When it's dropped, it settles on the trees and when you walk through you knock a tree and all this stuff falls and gets up your nose and you wish you weren't there. So when Charlie bumped into these trees there was a lot of snorting and wheezing going on.

Anyway, I went and did a mark for these drops. They gave us a briefing and marked a line on the map and we went out and the Yanks had a Chinook. It was just like a ship laying depth charges. They had the tailgate down and they rolled these containers out one a time. The containers had this timing device on the side which was set to explode at a predetermined height, I think it might have been 350 feet. That was the optimum height for these drums to explode to lay the CS trail. So there was a massive cloud of this CS stuff about but only a light wind. They wouldn't do drops in a strong wind for obvious reasons.

They did a test run and by that time the far end marker had gone out so I came back and lined up again and put two more markers down. They went around and lined up the two markers from about 2000 feet and just started rolling these drums out at about 30-second intervals. There'd be a great 'Whoomph!' as each one exploded.[15]

Bernie also found time to do some pilot instruction while he was at Nui Dat. Major General Don Vincent, then Commander Australian Forces Vietnam, had begun flying lessons in Australia during Exercise *Barra Winga* in late 1966. The general had a keen interest in Army Aviation and decided to gain some experience. Bernie was Vincent's instructor on *Barra Winga* and resumed his instructional duties in Vietnam:

> I remember going over to Long Binh on Sunday mornings to pick up General Vincent from Saigon. We'd fly back down through Bearcat and he'd have a few circuits there. If he was up to it he'd go solo and do a couple more on his own. He'd pick me up and we'd fly down to Nui Dat. We'd do the same on the way back if he wasn't running late. He used to fly us back all the time. So that was my role on Sunday mornings, first thing.[16]

Possum down—Captain Ted Brooker

Captain Ted Brooker and his observer, Signaller Bob Vallance, were shot down while carrying out a VR on 19 February 1969. Ted's memories were vivid:

> At the time we were trying to stop the Viet Cong from shipping out the rice harvest. I found this obviously well-used trail south of the Binh Ba rubber. I followed it to the edge of the plantation and searched in circles for further signs but couldn't see a thing. I had Signaller Bob Vallance with me. He was quite a good observer. I saw a slot between the rubber and a cashew nut plantation, about 80 to 100 metres long, which looked wide enough for a fast run under the trees to have a look. I was pretty sure I had the location right. Well, bugger me. I lined it up and it was tighter than I thought and I slowed down a bit more than planned and got down below the trees. There it was; a bloody great stack of rice. Vallance was sitting forward, looking out through my legs to see it when the first burst goes right through the cabin. It went over his back. He'd have been dead if he'd been sitting up. Then I got a round through my hand; made a hell of a mess. I tried instinctively to get out of there. I had a lot of power on and tried it forward and the bloody thing rolled to the right and just wouldn't correct. I suddenly realised that the top of the pole had been shot off and I was holding it while the pole was to the right. By then we had rolled over 90 degrees and I saw that we were too close to the ground for corrective action. If I grabbed the stick we'd just go in sideways and that'd probably kill us. It was just so quick, but I thought it was better to let it roll because it would probably land completely upside down which would give us a better chance of survival. That's exactly what happened. The main rotor hit

> the dirt in front of us and this fucking great clod of dirt went flying off into the trees. The blades went and as we hit the ground the engine was screaming, with no load on it and me winding the crap out of it, and then it stopped. And there we were hanging in our straps. My top cover man, the Jade up top, said 'Possum 20, I cain't see you!' I tried to respond but nothing was working and I couldn't tell him anything.[17]

Brooker and Vallance managed to extricate themselves from the wreckage and look for cover on the side away from the enemy position:

> SOP's say that if you go down, you take the radios with you. I remember thinking, 'Fuck the radios.' I was off. I hit the ground with Vallance and I got out my field dressing kit and patched my hand up a bit and turned on my search-and-rescue beacon. And then the bloody world exploded. The Jade had seen us upside down and then saw us run. He assumed rightly that the baddies were behind us, so he lined up and he put every bloody rocket he had on ripple and put this wall of flame and smoke between us and them while we got up and ran. It was amazing shooting. You've got no idea what it was like, the noise. God, I'd hate to be underneath that. He was flying one of the push-pull O-2s. They carried a shitload of rockets. Anyway, we buggered off and fired flares up through the canopy to tell people where we were and used the beacon. Somebody gave us directions where to go and we were about to head off again when this bloody 9 Squadron guy flew an Iroquois in through the trees. That's why I'm not too rude about 9 Squadron. There was this green haze as the main rotor chopped a pad for them. It was just such an incredible sight. We jumped into the Huey and the gunners were firing as we took off.[18]

The Sioux was recovered to Nui Dat, where it was written off. For Ted, the war was over. He was casevaced to Vung Tau for treatment to his wounded right hand before being flown home to New Zealand.

Déjà vu: Fears of a new Tet Offensive

As 1969 dawned, the anniversary of the Tet Offensive approached, and once again activities in Phuoc Tuy were disrupted. In early 1969, the task force returned to Bien Hoa province on operations *Federal* and *Overlander* as fears of a repeat of Tet were fuelled by regular rocket attacks on Long Binh. However, no large-scale attack eventuated.[19] The task force resumed pacification operations in Phuoc Tuy province and a more settled period began.

Official opening, Luscombe Field, Nui Dat, 5 December 1966. Maj Warren Lennon, OC 1st Field Squadron, RAE and Maj Laurie Doyle, OC 161 Recce Flight.
Photograph courtesy 161 Association.

Cessna 180 with radio direction finding equipment fitted, Nui Dat, 1967.
Photograph courtesy 161 Association.

Flight line, Luscombe Field, Nui Dat, 1967. RAAF Caribou in background. Note Sioux fitted with loudspeakers for 'voice' ops.
Photograph courtesy 161 Association.

Pastry chef Gary Channells with purpose-built oven courtesy of RAEME ingenuity, Nui Dat, 1967.
Photograph: Gary Channells.

Jimmy 'Combat' Jones armed for bear, Nui Dat, 1967.
Photograph: Jimmy Jones.

Fitters Bob Zitzelsberger and Geoff Deacon using sheerlegs rigged on Land Rover for Sioux engine change outside hangar, Nui Dat, 1967.
Photograph courtesy 161 Association.

Early days of Kangaroo Control and Air Traffic services; Sgt Jack Jewell with communications vehicle, Nui Dat, 1967.
Photograph: Jack Jewell.

RAEME fitter Chris Hills and RAAF FSgt Mick Swain on the flight line, Nui Dat, 1967.
Photograph courtesy 161 Association.

Sergeants' Mess opening, Nui Dat, 1967. L-R back row: Sgt John Harmer
(103 Sig Sqn), Sgt Peter Bootes, Sgt Jack Ellis, Sgt Ken Elson, F/Sgt Mick Swain,
Sgt Jim Allman, Sgt John Solomon, Sgt Jack Jewell. Front row: Sgt Stu Wools-Cobb,
WO2 Terry Phillips, Sgt Ron New, WO2 Howard Nichol, Sgt Allan 'Bomber' Harris, DFC.
Photograph: Jack Jewell.

Bird Dog on loan to 161. Major George Constable was KIA in this aircraft on
23 May 1968.
Photograph: Bernie Forrest.

105mm howitzer allocated to 161 for local defence in 1967. L-R Maj Laurie Doyle with 2IC Capt Dick Knight behind, 2Lt Bob Askew, USAF FAC pilots. In front Capt Peter Robinson, 2Lt Ross Hutchinson and Capt Mike Webster. *Photograph: Laurie Doyle.*

Capt Bernie 'Father' Forrest at home in the rubber, Nui Dat, 1967–68. *Photograph: Bernie Forrest.*

Maj George Constable and Capt Bernie Forrest departing for test firing of rockets from twin 7-pod rocket launchers fitted to Cessna 180, Nui Dat, 1967.
Photograph: Bernie Forrest.

161 Officers, Nui Dat, 1967. L–R back row: Capt Phil Roberts (RW), 2Lt Adam Fritsch (RW), Ops Officer 2Lt Don Trick, OC Maj George Constable, 2Lt Mike Meehan (RW), 2Lt Kevin Peacock (FW), 2Lt Blair Weaver (RW), OC Workshops Captain Peter Robinson. Front row: 2Lt Ross Goldspink (RW), 2Lt Tom Guivarra (FW), 2Lt David McFerran (FW), Capt Bernie Forrest (FW), Capt John Coggan (RW). Reclining reprobates 2Lt Ross Hutchinson (RW) and 2Lt Peter Garton (FW).
Photograph courtesy 161 Association.

RAAF goes Army. Sergeants David Menzies, John Green and Peter Nolan wearing blue berets presented by OC Maj George Constable, Nui Dat, 1967.
Photograph: Dave Menzies.

Maj Harry Benson, Phuoc Tuy, 1968.
Photograph: Harry Benson.

Sioux armed with M-60, Nui Dat, 1967.
Photograph courtesy 161 Association.

161 Sign and 'Possum Rock', Luscombe Field, Nui Dat, late 1970.
Photograph courtesy 161 Association.

2Lt Steve Tizzard and 547 Sig Troop operator Cpl Dick Schafer after forced landing near Courtenay, September 1968.
Photograph courtesy 161 Association.

Part 4

Pacification:
March 1969 – September 1971

10

Pacification:
March–December 1969

The aftermath of the Tet Offensive gave way by April 1969 to a less reactive basis for task force operations. From mid-1969, the task force settled back into a program of pacification of Phuoc Tuy province. The aim, as always, was to deny the enemy both the comfort of his strongholds and access to the towns and villages. In the task force, 5RAR had replaced 1RAR for its second tour and was experienced in the field. May had seen 6RAR begin its second tour, while 9RAR would complete its tour in December. Morale in the battalions was buoyed by the ongoing success of infantry operations supported by armour. The support units were well established and their capabilities continued to grow. The task force commander presided over a real 'going concern' and structured his operations accordingly.

The period from March to June 1969 was eventful for the Possums. Second Lieutenant Phil Stevens chalked up notable results on VRs with several engagements to his credit. His persistence and skill in pinpointing enemy targets for helicopter fire teams and air strikes was acknowledged by the award of an MID. Later, on 15 May, Possum Master Harry Benson also crossed swords with the enemy in a determined action which contributed to the award of the DFC for his service in Vietnam. His citation relates that:

> An enemy force was reported to be in the town of Dat Do but its precise location was not known. Major Harry Benson flew over the town in an attempt to fix their position. He was unable to see them so he commenced making low passes over the area in an attempt to draw enemy fire. He was successful and the enemy positions were disclosed. Although his aircraft was hit he continued on and made a safe landing in a friendly compound.[1]

As always, the operating environment remained ready to strike down the unwary or those who flew on the edge. Harry recalled an incident in which one of his fixed wing pilots didn't quite make it:

> It was Errol Driver. He'd only just arrived. One of the other guys had taken him out to Black Horse airfield in tandem to pick up some people and take them somewhere else. Anyway, Errol overloaded. He started off down the runway and I can see him now. He would have said, 'Uh oh! No. Yes. No. Yes. Yes. Noooo!' as he went off the end. We got this radio call that he'd gone in at the end of Black Horse. They were not injured, so we went out and brought them back. Well, writing that incident up was one of the hardest things that I ever did. I managed to get hold of the old civilian handbook for the Cessna 180 and I read it very carefully. And it sounded okay, what he had done, the load limit, the ambient temperature and all that stuff, and how I finished up was that it was a 'could have been' thing in terms of temperature and the length of the strip and by and large we couldn't make a big deal of it.[2]

Operation Hammer

Operation *Hammer* (May–June 1969) featured a landmark action in response to an aggressive move by the enemy. On the morning of 6 June, a tank and an armoured recovery vehicle came under fire while moving through Binh Ba en route to the 6RAR fire support base further north. The 1ATF Ready Reaction Force[3] was deployed. Its infantry element, Delta Company of 5RAR, came under heavy fire from rocket-propelled grenades as it entered the village. It was evident that a substantial enemy force was present. Captured documents later showed it to be the 1st Battalion, 33 North Vietnamese Army Regiment, guided by the Binh Ba Guerilla Unit.[4]

The engagement escalated into what became known as the Battle of Binh Ba. Delta Company fought its way into the centre of the village, with its supporting APCs and tanks also drawing heavy fire.

Fierce house-to-house fighting continued during the afternoon as reinforcements arrived. The action was complicated by the presence of civilians who had been unable to escape the area when fighting broke out. Second Lieutenant Peter Rogers was airborne with 5RAR's intelligence officer, Captain Mike Battle, when he reported a significant number of enemy escaping to the south-west. This indicated that Delta Company's counterattack was achieving its aim. Next day, 7 June, Rogers was directed to the village of Hoa Long where Viet Cong were reported in company strength. He found a group of the enemy (possibly those forced out of Binh Ba) occupying a bunker system and directed armed helicopters and ground troops onto the position. Two of the enemy were captured. He continued to direct air and ground forces onto targets until nightfall despite being engaged by ground fire on several occasions. For this and subsequent actions on 15 July and 2 August, Peter Rogers was awarded the DFC.

Binh Ba was a fierce battle in which a large enemy force was defeated by rapid reaction, skill, courage and fire power.[5] The engagement ranks as one of the major military victories of the Australian Force in Vietnam.

Improvements in Possum territory

On 1 April Airframe Fitter Paul Lidster, now a Sergeant, arrived at Nui Dat for his second tour. He immediately noticed significant changes which had occurred since he had completed his first tour ten months earlier. The runway had been extended and it had markings. At its western end, a RAAF Air Movements Section had been established with a large parking and reception area. The Wallaby Airlines Caribous and other transports now picked up and offloaded their passengers and freight there.

Paul also noticed innovations in the workshop. Despite the sustained build-up of operations and flying hours in the two years since 161's relocation to Nui Dat in March 1967, Captain Peter Robinson and his successors as OC Workshops, Captains Mike Boland and Stuart Curnow, had overseen improvements to maintenance facilities and had streamlined servicing and repair tasks. In October 1968, Warrant Officer Keith Scott had arrived at Nui Dat as the first RAEME Artificer Sergeant Major (ASM) of the 161 Workshop. He took over from Flight Sergeant Keith 'Bones' Einam. The period of RAAF supervision of maintenance at Nui Dat was over.

Notwithstanding these efforts, the workshops had still not reached the standards that followed the introduction of Pilatus Porter aircraft later in 1969. Airframe Fitter Craftsman Barry Skinner, who went on to become an engineering officer in 1 Aviation Regiment, described the workshops' situation on his arrival on 24 March and further improvements during his tour:

> There wasn't a lot there. We had the little two-ton pump-up crane to take rotor heads off, and the Hyab truck for engine changes and any other heavy jobs. But any other ground support equipment, no. If you needed something you developed it yourself. The earlier guys certainly made a good start for us, but that big old tin shed that we had as a hangar had its limitations. In late '69 when we got the Porters, we built the larger hangar next to it and that made a huge difference. It was a proper place to work rather than having a Cessna sticking out of the eastern end of the old hangar towards the dust bowl and having to take the wings off to roll the bloody thing in to get your work done. Better electrical, instruments and radio-servicing facilities, with air conditioning, were possible. At last the workshop area began to look like a permanent facility instead of something thrown up to support an exercise. The main jobs, like engine changes, would take about ten hours. When the aircraft finished flying for the day at 7 or 8 o'clock, the D servicing crew would come in and we'd work all night until the thing was finished and ground run and ready for test flight next morning. And then we generally had the movies set up in the hangar and we'd have our booze supply and a feed and we'd sit there and watch the movie before we hit the sack early in the morning.
>
> And they'd put in that pit out back where we used to do the wash jobs and could get in to work under the aircraft. I did a few jobs under there, doing the lateral shaft from the collective control and lockwiring and so forth. I remember Keith Scott and Scatters Curnow coming down one night and saying, 'How are you going under there?' I was nearly finished and they said, 'Good. Here's a beer.' It was one of those things that had to be done; a late job. I can still remember being stuck in the bloody bear pit.[6]

Barry also recalled the effort that went into improving the tent lines and creating recreational facilities to ensure that there were diversions from the daily grind:

> It was the same with our tents. When I arrived there it was all just sandbagged. By the time I left, most of us had corrugated iron around our

sandbags and put little verandas on the front of our tents. A lot of self-help stuff and diversionary activities went on. Through 1969–70 we really got into go-karts. Denis Scott and Ed Bevans—the guys on the engines side—built their frames up and got their little engines together. I suppose they were lawnmower engines, I'm not too sure. But they acquired them from somewhere. They built three or four go-karts and we used to race them on the airstrip against a Sioux. If a Sioux was taking off, you'd tee it up with the pilot and he could tell you what sort of speed you'd get up to. I guess what was done under the belt didn't matter then, and these kinds of diversions helped a lot. You needed them. It saved the guys from going bananas. If there was nothing much going on with one of the crews they had something to tinker with.[7]

Air Traffic Control: The second tower

It was during 1969 that an improved air traffic control facility was built. Sergeant Ron 'Snow' Baxter played a supervisory role in its design and equipment fitout. The original tower near SAS Hill had been a makeshift affair at best. The new tower was positioned alongside the runway, about half-way along on the northern side. It was 60 feet high, with a 360-degree view above the rubber. There was only a vertical ladder for access. Sergeant Mike Croker, a controller on his second tour in 1971, noted that it was a scary climb and descent but it did have the advantage of keeping official visitors and inspecting officers away.[8] Aloft in his cabin, the duty controller was king of his world and safe from the distractions of petty officialdom below. It was even air conditioned, not for the comfort of the controllers but to prevent the communications equipment from overheating. That was their story, anyway.

The Nui Dat airspace for which the controllers were responsible was from ground level to 2000 feet out to a five nautical mile radius. In addition to arrivals and departures using the Luscombe runway, they oversaw movements in and out of Kangaroo Pad and the multitude of smaller pads scattered around the task force area. Control was by UHF-AM and VHF-FM transceivers and the only navigation aid was a non-directional beacon (NDB) which permitted aircraft fitted with radio compasses to home in on the airfield.

Kangaroo Control was still responsible for advising all aircraft in Phuoc Tuy province about artillery shoots, demolition explosions and bomb runs. Luscombe Tower monitored their frequency so that it could advise Luscombe traffic if artillery was operating out of Nui Dat and what bearing it was on. The tower was also connected to the 161 command post and other key locations. The Flight was later provided with a fire section staffed by soldiers who had undergone appropriate training. One of these, Bill 'Baldy' Richards, described the imposing edifice from which he worked:

> The fire shack was a wooden hut built from packing cases, with a tin roof and fly wire covering what could be called windows. The windows were fitted with hoochie drop weather coverings. The shack was painted in red and white squares and stood at the base of the tower on the northern side of the runway. There were six of us firies in the unit, working in two crews. One manned the Early Rescue Tender (a Land Rover) and the other manned the Heavy Fire Tender (a Mk 5; the old red Mk3 had become unsafe and lacked enough water carrying capacity so we built one from scratch).[9]

With such modern and well-equipped facilities, the Possum pilots and all those who visited Luscombe Field could rest assured that they were in safe hands. Well, perhaps not entirely, but the aim was to save people rather than aeroplanes. The tower and rescue facilities were a marked improvement on the days when Sergeant Jack Jewell sat on the side of the strip with a radio and the crash vehicle was a Land Rover fitted with a red bucket marked 'FIRE'. The bucket was apparently to collect ashes from crashed aircraft in case they were needed by the Courts of Inquiry.

Life in the tower was not dull. Air trafficker Sergeant John Custance, who served with 161 during 1968–69, recalled a fiery incident:

> Snow Baxter had just relieved me in the old ATC tower on SAS Hill. Suddenly, one of Charlie's homemade rockets scored a direct hit on the task force ammunition dump at the base of the hill. The next fifteen minutes produced the best fireworks display I've ever seen. There was explosion after explosion and rounds going everywhere. Snow decided that discretion was the better part of valour and abandoned ship just as a load of HE rounds went off. The explosion dumped him on his arse. It took several hours before the fire was under control and the airfield reopened. During this time, Snow carried out his duties as if nothing was going on from the refuge of a nearby bunker.[10]

Sergeant Bill Hudnott, an air trafficker during the Flight's last year in Vietnam, described the ATC procedures:

> The key difference between controlling in Australia and controlling in a combat operational environment is that, in the civilian environment, every aircraft has to be separated from every other aircraft by a certain amount of time, space or height. It's fundamental. However, in the military, you could put any number of aircraft together and you'd treat them as a single aeroplane. The stats from Vietnam—the number of aircraft movements—were huge. But many of those aircraft movements would just be multiples; say a section of fifteen aircraft and that would be put down as fifteen movements. However, it was only one transmission, and the pilots were responsible for their own separation. Our responsibility was simply to advise others that they existed except for when they entered Luscombe's airspace. Then they did as we instructed.
>
> So that was the operating environment. The work was extremely rewarding because there was an instant response to your good work. If it worked and they all got travelling and everything was accomplished safely, then you knew you were doing a good job.[11]

The traffic sign scandal

In 1969 an access roadway to the battalion area behind 161 was cut through the Flight's area between the officers' lines and the rest of the camp. The traffic at all hours created something of a noise problem, with the pilots complaining of being kept awake by trucks. Squadron Sergeant Major Alf Smith, an enterprising and popular infantry veteran who had a good handle on the troops, requested the workshop to make up two replicas of real road traffic warning signs. He had them painted in appropriate colours and carefully printed with the message 'Nuns Cross Here At Night'. He placed one at each end of the road where it crossed the 161 boundaries. Sergeant Paul Lidster recalled the subsequent displeasure of the task force chief padre, who happened to be a Roman Catholic:

> One of the guys is in the laundry, alongside the road near one of the signs, doing his washing. He hears this Land Rover pull up and there's banging and crashing going on and he thought someone had run off the road. He goes out and the first thing he sees is this major trying to pull this sign out. So he says, 'What's up, Sir?' Then the major turns around and he could see the padre's

crosses on his uniform. He has a bit of a rant and rave about the sign being blasphemous so the troop tells him that the SSM is in charge of blasphemy.

Anyway, the unit got into trouble and had to take the signs down. About a fortnight later, a padre from the battalion who used to drink in our Sergeants' Mess decided to have a padres' convention, Americans and all, and wanted to use our Mess for an evening. There were fifteen or 20 of them coming, so we all vacated the Mess after tea on the night of the convention and went to the movies. Afterwards we went back to the Mess and they'd finished their discussions and the padre who organised it is acting as the barman. And he's arguing with this major at the bar. He's saying, 'It's your shout. I don't care what you've been drinking; the shout's only three or four dollars.' It turns out that it's the Catholic padre who attacked the signs who doesn't want to pay. Apparently he was drinking soft drink and it was only ten cents, while beer was fifteen cents. The others were drinking beer, of course, and this guy reckoned he was being dudded. Anyway, he grudgingly pays up and the party goes on and I looked around and saw a RAAF guy there. He was a priest from my home town of Orange. He used to play football and was hard to tackle because he had no neck. I hadn't seen him for at least ten years. So we talk and the night goes on and next thing this Catholic padre is at it again. We hear the SSM saying, 'I don't care who you are. This is my Mess and you'll abide by my rules or get out.' The major is having another go at him about the signs. So the SSM says, 'If you have a complaint, come and see me in my office during working hours. Not in my Mess!' Anyway, the guy behind the bar hears this and I can't remember whether he called this major 'Sir' or not, but he said, 'Why don't you go home? You're giving us all the shits.' And he left.[12]

Possums on patrol

It was in 1969 that the Flight became involved in patrols outside the wire. Possum Master Harry Benson was not excited by the thought of sending inexperienced troops into the field. However, there were issues that had led to a higher level requirement for non-combatant personnel to undertake local patrols. It came to a head and Harry gathered his people together to hear their reactions to the scheme. He explained what was entailed, feeling that it was very wrong:

> Some people volunteered. There were a few who were quite gung-ho at the idea of getting out there with all of their stuff on and some had never had it on in their lives. So they went, and of course about half way through we got a message and we had to get them back. They weren't far enough away to send helicopters to pick them up, so we sent vehicles.[13]

Craftsman Barry Skinner recalled the patrols with amusement:

> The battalions would go out to the Horseshoe or their other fire support bases and so we'd do these patrols. I remember myself, Fred Hardidge and a few other guys went. We'd go out through 5RAR because we were on the wire with them. They'd always have a rear echelon so they'd provide the leaders and away we'd go. It didn't matter what rank you were, you just went out as a rifleman. So we went out and did our thing and we saw there'd been a bit of movement so we put in an ambush. We paired up—I paired up with Freddy Hardidge—and we went into ambush and we were supposed to be two hours on, two hours off. We did well until I went to sleep on watch. The next thing, I thought the whole bloody Viet Cong army had come down on top of us. There was a hell of a racket. It frightened the living daylights out of us. And a herd of pigs came galloping through our ambush post. No one went back to sleep again; we stayed awake for the rest of the night. I owned up about going to sleep on watch. It was probably just as well that I did because I might have done something I shouldn't have done if I'd been awake.[14]

The most remembered of all patrols was led by Second Lieutenant Peter Rogers; a band of warriors known in the annals of 161 as 'Rogers' Rangers'. Peter had some experience in ground operations in his pre-flying days and did not sidestep quickly enough when nominated to lead the 161 expeditionary force to a proposed ambush site near the Nui Thi Vais. His preparations were thorough. He consulted with 5RAR, whose AO included the site, and begged a starlight scope from SAS friends to maintain control of the action at night. Armed to the teeth and with Bruce Johnson as platoon sergeant, the patrol set off in APCs to be dropped off some distance from its objective. Murphy's Law prevailed when one of the APCs threw a tread and a long, exhausting walk ensued. As the ragged band was cautiously approaching the ambush site, one of the Rangers accidentally discharged his weapon and there wasn't much to do then but sneak around a bit and resume Plan A. As night fell the Rangers rigged Claymore mines at the ambush site and two-hour watches began. The starlight scope didn't work; the comms didn't work and it was a long night of waiting. In the morning they discovered that the Claymores had been turned so that the 'This side towards enemy' instructions were in fact pointing back at them. During the long slog back to the APC pick-up point, there was time to reflect on lessons learned as well as to appreciate the humorous side of the situation. If they could have done it again they might well have been successful. But the memories remain a treasured part of the Flight's history and no account would be complete without them.

Possum Master Five

Major Graeme Hill-Smith, AAAvn, arrived at Nui Dat on 10 June to take over as OC from Harry Benson. Hill-Smith, a Gunner before transferring to the Aviation Corps, was an experienced aviator. He qualified as an Air OP pilot after returning from a tour of duty in Malaya in 1960. He then trained on Sycamore helicopters with the Royal Australian Navy Fleet Air Arm at Nowra before completing a Sioux conversion.

After returning to Artillery duties for a period, he spent two years in the United States completing the Officers' Rotary Wing Aviators' Course and then qualifying as an instructor. Flying duties as an instructor and a maintenance test pilots' course followed before he returned to Australia to become the OC and Chief Flying Instructor of the Army Aviation training squadron. Before being posted to 161 Recce Flight as OC, he had visited Nui Dat to check the proficiency of pilots then serving under Harry Benson. Major Hill-Smith was clearly well qualified for the Possum Master role and had the forceful personality to make his mark on the Flight. He was mindful of the demands that had been placed on his predecessors as he described the operational setting and the resources he had to do the job:

> I think my 12 months was really one of stability, wholly operated from Nui Dat. Before that, in Harry Benson's period, and George Constable's, the task force had to go outside the province. They had to move around and do jobs and they were being tugged here, there and everywhere. And of course the early ones had to move from Bien Hoa to Vung Tau and then to Nui Dat and then there was the Tet Offensive.
>
> The pilots were well trained at Amberley. They knew how to fly a Bell 47 and a Cessna 180. They were competent pilots. Their training as operational pilots actually took place in Vietnam. The jobs that had to be done up there had to be taught up there. But it generally only took about a month before the fellow was competent. They were only boys, you know. They really were, the second lieutenants. I was 34. I was old, because they were only 20 or so. When I arrived I was taken out by Stan McClymont, a

second lieutenant I'd trained back in Australia, and he showed me the ropes on VRs. The things under the trees took a bit of picking out but I got the idea and found these bunkers. And having found them, I was then a reconnaissance pilot.

So I think that, flying-wise, the unit was well organised. Technically, I have to say that the maintenance people were good fellows. Starting with Captain Peter Robinson there was always a workshops commander and I don't think I ever had any serious troubles with technical back-up. The maintenance staff had become quite well established there. When I arrived, the radio and instrument people had air-conditioned workplaces and I used to have to knock on the door to be admitted. They'd say, 'Who is it?' and I'd say, 'Major Hill-Smith.' There'd be a bit of a kerfuffle in there and then I'd be allowed in.

The administration of the unit was quite different. I had a very good SSM, an infantry warrant officer. He knew what was going on. He knew what the Diggers were up to. He could tell me, and that was very important. There were things I wasn't satisfied with: the cooking was terrible and the sergeant cook wasn't up to his job. I got rid of this guy to Vung Tau and got a replacement sergeant cook from there. He had been causing trouble down there, but he couldn't do that at Nui Dat. Anyway, I got the catering sorted out and that really changed the nature of the unit. I mean, you'll remember what Napoleon said about an army marching on its stomach. It was absolutely true. Before that the pilots could come back at night after a sortie or depart early in the morning and they weren't being fed. I don't know whose fault it was but it's the OC's responsibility to make sure his troops are fed. These were the things that we got sorted out. And with my SSM, the workshop commander and so on, I thought the unit ran pretty well.

I did things that I don't regret doing and I changed some of the things that my predecessors had done because I thought they were wrong. It was a team, not just me saying 'Do this' and 'Do that', and I felt by and large that we did pretty well. In fact, what you remember from war is the good bits.[15]

Operation Camden *(29 July–30 August)*

Operation *Camden* had the dual aim of protecting an American Land Clearing Team and conducting reconnaissance-in-force operations to locate and destroy enemy main force units in the now familiar Hat Dich area. On 8 August, after heavy contacts during the preceding two days, the CO of 5RAR, 'characteristically overhead in his Possum, employed a set of Bushranger gunships to engage enemy forward defences.'[16] The enemy's 274 Regiment took heavy casualties in this action, which set the scene for what was to be a very busy operation involving some 40 contacts.

One such engagement was illustrative of the range of airborne tactical resources which could be called upon and the communications difficulties that could ensue. On 21 August, an enemy force of unknown strength was engaged and their mortar fire caused sixteen Australian casualties. While these were being evacuated by Dustoff choppers, mortar rounds continued to fall around the evacuation area. Dusk fell and made flying conditions perilous:

> Some of the aircraft in the area at this time were three Bushranger gunships, Dragon and Raider American gunships, a Jade FAC, four Dustoff choppers and a set of Black Ponies (US OV-10 Bronco ground attack aircraft). With all of these aircraft on the company net it was becoming impossible for the company commander to speak to his platoons.[17]

Fortunately, the lead Bushranger was able to assist with the coordination of the air effort. The contact was later found to be against the complete 3rd Battalion of 274 Regiment and was notable for the level of enemy aggression and persistence encountered. Once again, this strong reaction highlighted the importance to the enemy of the Hat Dich area.

For new pilots joining 161 Recce Flight and cutting their teeth on reconnaissance and direct support work, operations like *Camden* brought home the 'crowded skies' nature of flying operations in South Vietnam. For the Possums, it was dangerous enough work among the treetops if they had the airspace to themselves. During significant engagements, they usually had a senior officer aboard. They did his bidding while keeping their eyes and ears open for artillery fire and clearances, FACs, ground attack aircraft, Dustoffs, light fire teams and whoever else was after a piece of the action. Their limited radio facilities made the task even more difficult as they could not monitor all of the frequencies in use. The mental picture they carried with them was continually updated as if by random scenes from an action movie. There were inevitably near misses with other aircraft. It is testimony to their skills and powers of concentration that 161 did not lose many more aircraft and key battalion staff with them.

For the Sioux pilots in particular, there were also the routine problems of carrying passengers and their equipment in unfavourable density altitude conditions. Second Lieutenant Don Moffatt recalled one such occasion early in his tour at Nui Dat:

> If you were low, doing a bit of tricky flying, you had to have your wits about you. I'm surprised that we didn't lose more aircraft and I don't mean from being shot down, I mean from pilot error. Some of the pads we'd go into, the old Sioux was just absolutely buggered getting out. There was a mickey hair between getting over the trees and hitting the bloody things. I remember coming out of a pad and I started to overpitch, and I wasn't very experienced really when I think about it. I'm guessing but I probably had about 300 hours. So there's lots of trees and I'm starting to overpitch, and all I could think to do was to sort of tack like a fly between these trees at about five knots. I just didn't have translational lift. The bloody revs are coming back, the trees are getting bigger, it's as hot as buggery and I had this Yank major on board. Anyhow, we got out of it. As we were climbing out he said, 'That was mighty fancy flying, boy!' And I thought, 'If only you knew, mate, I'm sitting here shitting myself.' I think that was the most scared I've ever been in a bloody helicopter. I dead set didn't think we'd make it. I think with more experience I'd have aborted the take-off early. As long as your rotors are clear and the skids are level they'll take a pretty big whack.[18]

Major Hill-Smith was a stickler for flying proficiency. He spoke about the procedures he put in place to ensure that all pilots' skills were reviewed regularly:

> I didn't have a rotary wing flying instructor so I had to do all that. I had to check every helicopter pilot every three months. I'd spend an hour with each one. In fixed wing, I always had an aeroplane QFI to do the checks. In the end I trained a couple of check pilots for the helicopters, who could do the quarterly checks for me. There was nothing surreptitious about it. I just trained these fellows so that they all knew what the others might do, and if they did something they could recover from it. Autorotations, for example. The standards were pretty high, but I would enter an autorotation over the airfield, and I would pull collective at about 200 feet. And if I'd continued with that we'd have crashed. So the check pilot would have to jump in and take over, slap me on the knuckles and recover the aircraft. Frank Markcrow was one of the pilots I trained there and it all worked out very well. It left me a bit of extra time, but just as importantly showed me what these fellows could do.[19]

The night of the .50 cal

Down at the western end of the airfield was the terminal where the Caribous unloaded. It was 161's responsibility to defend the area.

Major Hill-Smith noted that it was a fairly exposed position and nobody felt comfortable about manning the bunker there at night:

> There were no supporting pits. The infantry battalion was the nearest and they were a fair way away. So I said to the deputy task force commander, 'Let's close this up. It doesn't do any good. If anyone ever got attacked down there that would be the end of them and we couldn't even come to their aid.' I suggested that we withdraw the gun to the other bunker I had half way up the airfield and man that. He said, 'Well, you'll want a decent machine gun.' Now, I wanted an M-60. We didn't have an entitlement to M-60s but we used them in the helicopters so I had a couple and another one would be very useful. And he said, 'Oh no, I'll get you a .50 cal.' I told him we couldn't handle a .50 cal as the troops weren't familiar with them. He said, 'We'll put them on a course.' So I had to send the Diggers across to learn how to use a .50 cal and they knew anyway.
>
> He rang me later to ask how they were going with the weapon. I told him they were still a bit nervous of it and that I'd still like an M-60. He said, 'I'll tell you what. Tomorrow night we'll let them fire it.' I think there were some other units that were going to do some firing as well. When the time came we got clearance to fire on a certain arc. So our .50 cal opened up, and then everyone in the task force—everyone on the perimeter—was firing. Claymore mines were being blown, the SAS was in it; it was just bedlam. Luckily it was all going outwards; I wouldn't have liked to be around if it was coming in. It was quite a night. It must have gone on for an hour. We couldn't stop them. It was a truly historic event; the only time that all of the defences at Nui Dat ever fired. So that was my .50 cal that started all that. And we had to keep it; we never got our M-60. We had to beg and steal elsewhere for those.[20]

Operations July–December 1969

The pressure on enemy forces in Phuoc Tuy was unrelenting. On its second tour from May 1969 to May 1970, 6RAR conducted fifteen operations. Operation *Lavarack*, which concluded in early July, featured 85 contacts in which 102 enemy soldiers were killed. Operation *Kingston*, conducted in the Thua Tich area from 14 September to 15 October, was one of many aimed at locating and destroying elements of D445 Battalion. This succession of operations kept the enemy forces off balance and disrupted their plans.

An aircraft accident during this period showed how easily the unexpected could happen in an environment where unusual incidents were a daily feature. On 28 October, Captain Barry Donald, with Captain Frank Markcrow as passenger, was making a routine landing at Luscombe when his Cessna lost a wheel and was extensively damaged. Fortunately, neither pilot was injured. Apparently one of the stubs on which the main wheels were mounted broke off on touchdown. The aircraft had landed on a flat tyre a few days earlier and must have damaged the stub.[21]

Other notable operations during the closing months of 1969 were *Kings Cross* and *Bondi*, conducted by 5RAR, and *Ross* and *Marsden* by 6RAR. *Kings Cross* followed on from *Camden* in the Hat Dich area, maintaining pressure on the enemy's 274 Regiment and its supporting elements. Operation *Bondi* featured a series of cordon-and-search operations in the Binh Ba area. The Possums were still maintaining 1200 flying hours each month on the full range of operational missions, and were thankful that no aircraft were lost to either enemy fire or accident during this period. As Christmas approached, there was the inevitable speculation that a new Tet Offensive might come with the New Year. Operations were therefore structured to ensure that the enemy could not consolidate in strength anywhere in Phuoc Tuy.

Arming the Sioux

The rotary wing pilots envied the firepower that their fixed wing counterparts could deliver from their rocket pods. By 1969, there was a history of attempts to turn the Sioux into an offensive weapon. In late 1967, a kit was fitted which mounted twin M-60 machine guns on the litters. Second Lieutenant Glen Duus remembered it well:

> Actually, that was a standard US Army fit from the early days. The first time we went to Bearcat, we got it up there. It had the nitrogen bottles that gave it a little bit of elevation, a little bit of azimuth. The big problem was with the reload mechanism. It wouldn't feed. We found the second problem when Spoo [Second Lieutenant Peter Spoor] used them at dark o'clock way over near the mouth of the Rung Sat. The tanks hit these sampans and one of them got away. Spoo's got this sampan lined up and he pulls the trigger and he's blinded. He was only about 100 feet off the water. Couldn't see a fucking thing. After that, we lost a lot of enthusiasm for them. Somebody told me that we returned them to the US Army. There was a

General John Tolson who wrote a monograph for the US Centre for Military History about the development of armed helicopters. And this was one of the things he mentioned; the attempts to arm the OH-13s and the fact that it didn't work too well.[22]

Despite this initial setback, it wasn't long before a new generation of pilots looked longingly at machine guns which they could visualise spitting fire from their trusty steeds. The next attempt was to mount a single M-73 on the litter. Possum Master Graeme Hill-Smith had a little problem with this fit as well:

> The M-73 was not as reliable as the M-60 as the trigger sears would break. In fact, I was down at the Light Green doing a trial with one of these, mounted on the right litter, and I started firing and the trigger sear broke. So the gun ran away. And I'm telling the sergeant with me to break the belt but he didn't. He thought I was delirious with joy as I swept through the Light Green and then out to sea and there were fishing boats out there and they were cleared. Anyway, that night an SAS patrol down there reported that a Sioux had been engaged by a heavy machine gun. In fact the Sioux was firing it. It got slower and slower but we fired 500 rounds in a burst.
>
> Later on we went to the door-mounted M-60s. They had pistol grips, the same as they used in the Iroquois. The M-60 was a very fine machine gun derived from the German MG-42 Spandau, the Second World War model. So it wasn't a totally American gun. They might have improved it a bit, I don't know. Anyway, the door-mounted gun was always an M-60.[23]

The Kiwi Possums

Major Hill-Smith was quite impressed by the proficiency of his New Zealand pilots:

> I had three of them while I was there. I had Flanagan—he was quite tenacious. And Reg Ellwood—he'd been a deer hunter in helicopters before he came into the New Zealand Army. He could fly. He was with me one night when I had a bit of trouble. And then another fellow, Mike Jamieson, came from Malaya. I only had him for a month. We got him going okay. If you knew a fellow could fly it was all right. And I would find out if they could fly because I did a lot of check flights with them.
>
> Now Bill Flanagan was a very interesting pilot. I remember writing him up for the DFC, which he got, but he was an interesting personality as well. I think he may have been part Maori, although he never mentioned it. He could do the haka magnificently and he looked like a Maori. He was

small, bald, and he acted like a Maori warrior. He wanted to go out and kill 'em all. And he was a good pilot. I recall one day when Mal Smith was doing a VR down in the Light Green and I think I must have been flying top cover for him. He said, 'I'm following a track. God, they're shooting at me!' So I said, 'Get back there and drop a smoke because I didn't see where they were shooting from.' He said, 'No. I'm getting shot at and I'm going on R & R tomorrow.' And I said, 'Well, you won't be going anywhere if you don't show me where they are.' So he went back and threw a smoke grenade and I said, 'Right, you can go back to base now.' And then Flanagan came down and took over from him. Well, Flanagan flew for the rest of the day, and he had the Kiwi's 161 Battery firing on them. He also put any number of airstrikes in there. They killed quite a few Viet Cong.[24]

The Pilatus Porter: New fixed wing capabilities

HMAS *Sydney* arrived at Vung Tau on 28 November 1969 with three Pilatus Porter aircraft aboard for service with 161 Recce Flight. The Porter was an eight place, high wing monoplane powered by a Pratt and Whitney PT6 turbine engine driving a constant speed propellor unit with reverse pitch capability. A full instrument panel, radio compass and other aids permitted limited operations by night and in bad weather. Special role fittings included two wing stations for external carriage of up to 1000 pounds of stores, an internal cargo hatch and automatic rebroadcast facilities. The rear cabin seats were removable to permit bulky cargo to be carried.

The Porter's payload under the density altitude conditions typically encountered in the hotter months in Vietnam was 800 pounds, excluding pilot and fuel, double that of the Cessna 180 and four times that of the Sioux. It thus brought a new carrying capacity to the Flight which increased operational versatility. It was not a speedy aeroplane, cruising at 105 knots for up to three hours. It had a good short take-off and landing (STOL) capability of 600 feet at sea level.[25]

The introduction of the Porter got off to a bad start. Captain John Digweed had arrived in country three days earlier to take over as 161 Workshop commander from Captain Stuart Curnow. He described his first week:

> I was very busy right from my arrival. I was met by Stuart Curnow, had one night at the Dat and then we went down to Vung Tau because the *Sydney* was in and we were unloading the Porters. The plan was to lift each aircraft

straight to Nui Dat using a Chinook. However, the first Porter was damaged in the process because the horizontal stabilisers hadn't been removed. Back in Australia they'd done all the static lift tests with the horizontal stabiliser on and it was beautiful. So they'd taken the mainplanes off, left the horizontal stabilisers on, and of course as soon as the Chinook picked it up it just sat on its tail. Once the pilot got the Chinook into translation it was all fine, but by then the bar through the back end was half way to the front end. So we had a very large repair job to do. We unloaded the other two Porters over the side onto a barge and they were assembled at Vung Tau and flown up to the Dat.[26]

New operational capabilities

The Porter enabled the Flight to carry out professional illumination missions and air photography for the first time. It also enhanced the Flight's effectiveness in the performance of other tasks including Sigint, psyops, radio rebroadcast and general hash and trash work. It was an ideal platform for firing rockets for whatever purpose and it wasn't long before that capability was exploited by the firepower-hungry Possums. Sadly, before then, the coming of the Porter also brought tragedy.

Possums down: Barry Donald and Alan Jellie

On 3 December 1969, FW section commander Captain Barry Donald was flying the first Porter night training mission, with Sioux pilot Second Lieutenant Alan Jellie in the right-hand seat. The sortie was almost finished when the aircraft took enemy ground fire and crashed near the edge of the Binh Ba rubber plantation, north of Nui Dat. The aircraft was destroyed and both pilots were killed. Back at Nui Dat, New Zealander Captain Bill Flanagan volunteered immediately to search for the aircraft in case the pilots had survived. He located the crashed aircraft with the assistance of flares and hovered near the wreckage until he was satisfied that there was nothing to be done.

Engineering Officer John Digweed recalled the night of the incident clearly. He was still in his first week. It had already been a busy and eventful one with the arrival of the Porters and the damage to the first during the unloading operation:

We got the two other Porters from Vung Tau in the air and got them up to Nui Dat. I said goodbye to Stu Curnow, and that night Barry Donald and Alan Jellie were killed. I'd gone to bed and Graeme Hill-Smith came in and woke me and said, 'We seem to have a Porter missing.' So that was a pretty long night.

I don't really know the whole story. I know that there were bullet holes in the aeroplane. Warrant Officer Don Collins went out with a crew and they had some infantry soldiers with them and they looked after it overnight. They obviously removed the bodies that night and the aeroplane sat there. Don went out next morning with the old 5-tonner with the Abbey crane on and brought the remains back. It was covered up—obviously, I had access to it—and we just looked at it, got a 'dozer out and dug a hole and buried it real quick. It didn't need to be lying around. It didn't need a Court of Inquiry to decide that it was a write-off. The fire just burned the guts out. It was not long after that we modified all of the fuel tanks. We put in the crashworthy tanks with all the foam to stop that happening.[27]

Possum Master Graeme Hill-Smith was saddened but not altogether surprised by the incident which took the lives of two popular and proficient fliers:

I'd been wondering when we were going to have a casualty. The aircraft were being shot at. I remember that Alan Jellie took a round through his shirt a while before. It took the pen and pen-holder and it didn't injure him. Aircraft were being hit all the time but nobody was being injured, at least not significantly. And I knew that there was going to be a casualty at some stage. It was a bit of a surprise that it was in a Porter. I think the aircraft had probably flown that afternoon on its first test flight, and Barry Donald had taken it up to do some training. It was the first night-flying exercise. Anyway, he got mixed up in a bit of a firefight about ten miles north of the base and yes, it was very unfortunate. I went up the next day to have a look at the aircraft and there was no doubt about the hits. It was probably the equivalent of a Bren gun—an RPD I think they called it. I don't know what he was doing. There was a post about ten miles north, and as I said they had a firefight going on, and how he got mixed up in it or why I don't know. Perhaps he was going to bring them some assistance.[28]

It was a grim ending to 1969 and once again reminded the Flight's members that tragedy could and would strike when it was least expected. Two of 161's most respected members had given their all. It was with a deep sense of loss that the Possums faced 1970.

11

Maintaining the effort:
January–December 1970

During 1970 it became evident that the US and its allies were fighting an unwinnable war. The Australian Government announced that the task force would revert to a two-battalion structure during 1971. History would show that, despite the unceasing efforts of the task force commanders and their troops, pacification could never be an outstanding success. The difficulties involved in making the South Vietnamese forces full partners in the process, while winning over a majority of the population through civic action, were beyond resolution given the Australians' limited resources.

This conclusion was perhaps not apparent as 1970 dawned, although frustration at the inconclusive nature of outcomes was always evident. The unrelenting pace of operations continued for the battalions and their supporting units, including 161 Recce Flight. The introduction of the Porter late in 1969, and the exploitation of its full capabilities, brought new dimensions to fixed wing operations in 1970, but the Sioux pilots were not so lucky. No replacement for the Sioux was then in the offing, so it was business as usual.

Operation Hammersley

The Eighth Battalion, commanded by Lieutenant Colonel K.J. O'Neill, had arrived in mid-November 1969. The New Year saw 8RAR operating along the border with Long Khanh province on Operation *Atherton* before heading to the west for Operation *Keperra* in the Nui Dinhs, and then south to the Long Hais in February on Operation *Hammersley*. The battalion's troops were indeed seeing the sights of Phuoc Tuy and experiencing much of the variety its terrain had to offer. They were well and truly blooded during *Hammersley*. This operation, conducted from 10 February to 9 March, became known as the Battle for the Long Hais.

Hammersley's initial deployment was to protect quarry operations by 17 Construction Squadron on the western side of the Long Hais. The enemy reacted strongly on the evening of 15 February, taking heavy casualties. Lieutenant Colonel O'Neill responded by stepping up ambush and reconnaissance-in-force operations with APC and tank support to minimise casualties from anti-personnel mines. Contact was soon made and it was later established that the entire enemy D445 Battalion was in the area. Australian casualties were light until 28 February, when a mine explosion killed seven soldiers and wounded many others during clearing operations supported by an engineer party. A second explosion added one killed and more wounded to the casualty list.[1]

Second Lieutenant Mal Smith, DS pilot for 8RAR, was conducting a reconnaissance over the Long Hais with an Engineer officer when he was directed to the scene of the casualties. To minimise the risk of further explosions, he hovered his aircraft with one skid on a large rock to offload his passenger. He then shuttled back and forth bringing in essential personnel and evacuating wounded soldiers. While flying these sorties he also coordinated the activities of three casualty evacuation helicopters. He was awarded the DFC for his skilful and resolute efforts.

Meanwhile, 7RAR arrived on 10 February to commence its second tour, replacing 5RAR. The latter was most appreciative of the job done by its DS pilots in their Sioux helicopters. 'This little machine was used at various times (sometimes concurrently!) for aerial reconnaissance, mini gunship, artillery observation, airborne command post, casualty evacuation, delivering urgent ammunition, delivering letters from home and eluding brigadiers. To those young Possum pilots we say "thank you!" [2]

Operation *Finschafen*, a reconnaissance and ambush operation in the eastern half of Phuoc Tuy from 9 April, brought 7RAR up to operational speed. Operations *Concrete I* and *II* followed from April through June. Meanwhile, the third of the 'fresh' battalions arrived. On 15 May 1970, 2RAR relieved 6RAR and resumed the title of ANZAC Battalion with its three rifle companies augmented by New Zealand troops in Victor and Whisky Companies. The battalion got off to a busy start on 26 May with Operation *Capricorn* in the Nui Dinhs, the sole full battalion operation of the tour with all five rifle companies deployed.

The Possums were soon called upon to demonstrate their versatility. On 2 June, Alpha Company of 2RAR requested a casualty evacuation helicopter to lift out a soldier seriously ill from a suspected snake bite. Owing to adverse weather conditions of low cloud, thunderstorm activity and reduced visibility, the evacuation helicopter, despite several attempts, was unable to locate the landing zone and returned to base. The battalion DS pilot, Second Lieutenant Dave Earley, had been monitoring the request for assistance and offered to attempt the evacuation. In conditions of almost nil visibility, he edged his aircraft up the mountainside towards the landing zone. He was guided only by radio instructions based on aircraft noise, as the securing party could not see the aircraft until it was actually hovering overhead. He took the patient on board and flew out on instruments until he could descend safely into a known clear area and continue the evacuation to Nui Dat. Lieutenant Earley had once again shown the absolute commitment to the troops on the ground that characterised 161's operations. He received an MID for his efforts that evening.

The 'oops' factor: Possum down

March 1970 brought the loss of a Sioux in unusual circumstances. The Commander's Diary noted that, on 25 March, Sioux A1-635, flown by Captain Bob Hills with Captain John Digweed as his passenger, crashed soon after departing Nui Dat. Both officers were rescued and the wreckage of the aircraft was recovered to Nui Dat where it was written off. John Digweed filled in the story behind these sparse details:

We'd taken off to mark for an airstrike and went around the tower, heading north, and I was fixing up the smokies, the white phosphorus grenades we would use. I looked over my shoulder and saw a Huey in formation. 'Can't have that,' Bob said. He rolled a few revs off to unload the head and we got through 180 degrees but the Huey was still there. So he rolled again, and he rolled off some more revs. And when we got to the bottom he only pulled one lot back. I was looking back over my shoulder watching the Iroquois, and next thing I looked forward and the bush was coming through the bubble. We bounced, and I remember seeing the tail rotor go over my head, still attached to a fair section of the tail boom. And we bounced up on top of it. There was no bubble left, of course, but I got out through the door. That seemed to be a stupid thing to have to do. I put my foot down to where the ground should be, stepped out and there was nothing there so I fell flat on my nose. I got up, went back in and started to pick up grenades and saw that Bob was out, sitting on the ground a few yards away. And I'm still picking up grenades and radios and swearing at him to get off his arse and help me. Anyway, his back was crook. The next thing I know a Huey is there and this big bloody crewie came over and tapped me on the shoulder and said, 'Can I take that off you, sir?' He took the grenades and radios and stuck them in the back of the Huey. At this time the turbocharger had started a little fire so I went in and got the extinguisher and I put that out. And the guy was saying, 'Get in the Huey, sir. Get in the effing Huey.' But I wouldn't go because I had a brand spanking new camera that I'd just bought two days before. I'd taken two shots of Lieutenant Len Machin up in the tower as we went past and I put it down to fix the grenades and I couldn't find the bloody thing. Anyway, eventually this big crewie's got this thing dangling in front of me like a carrot and saying, 'Come on, sir. Get in the aircraft.' So I got in and they took us back to the Dat.[3]

Captain Hills was taken to the field hospital Vung Tau and treated for back injuries. John Digweed was severely bruised but carried on with his duties. The Sioux was totalled. The incident was written off as an operational accident, a possibly generous outcome for Bob Hills. His OC was not noted for his tolerance of those who committed errors of technique or judgment.

Possums under fire

In mid-April the task force launched Operation *Concrete* in the eastern sector of Phuoc Tuy to continue its objective of searching out and destroying D445. The enemy battalion had been severely hit during *Hammersley* and subsequent operations. The task force commander hoped that *Concrete* might provide the opportunity for the coup de grace. The operation involved all three Australian battalions and most support units.

On 22 April, 7RAR found itself in a heavy engagement with enemy troops in eighteen bunkers. The CO, Lieutenant Colonel Ron Grey, was controlling the action from the DS chopper flown by Second Lieutenant Tom Partridge when the Sioux was hit by AK-47 fire, with rounds penetrating the seats and the main rotor blade. Luckily, neither officer was hit and Partridge recovered the aircraft safely to the fire support base. It was all in a day's work for him. The unflappable Colonel Grey retained his confidence in Possum Air and continued to spend many hours aloft managing his battalion's diverse operations.

Further proof of the Possums' skill against the enemy was soon forthcoming. On the evening of 3 May, some 60 enemy soldiers probed an ambush position southwest of Dat Do manned by troops of 8RAR's Alpha Company.[4] A substantial firefight ensued, with the enemy taking heavy casualties and six Australians wounded. The DS chopper, flown by Major Hill-Smith with Warrant Officer Don Collins as gunner, was providing fire support using a door-mounted M-60.[5] The Sioux's main rotor blade was severely damaged when the aircraft was hit by ground fire. In what was described as 'a superb display of flying skill',[6] Major Hill-Smith recovered the aircraft to the Horseshoe. He shut down the engine and found that the end of one main rotor blade had been shot off. The cap and weight were missing in action.

Concrete was successful to the extent that, by late May, enemy activities in the south of the province had been severely curtailed. However, it was not possible to plug all of the holes and D445, licking its wounds, was able to regroup in its former strongholds including the Long Hais. Meanwhile, Operation *Phoi Hop* had focused on the protection of population centres from routine infiltration by enemy troops and had achieved good results. The pacification process was proceeding as well as could be expected in light of the difficulties involved in achieving a conclusive result in Phuoc Tuy.

Porter operations and maintenance

In every operational sense, the Porter was a more versatile aircraft than its venerable predecessor. Its flare-dropping capabilities were a boon to night operations. The aircraft carried up to 28 parachute flares, each of which burned for more than three minutes with an intensity of two million candlepower. Allowing for time overlap between flares, a Porter could provide continuous illumination for about 75 minutes. The ignition height could be set from 500 feet to 14 000 feet below the aircraft, with 2500 feet above ground level being ideal for illumination. One or two crewmen in the rear compartment prepared and dropped the heavy flares through the internal hatch. If a flare failed to ignite, the parachute would not deploy and this could be unfortunate for an enemy soldier directly below.

Airframe Fitter Corporal Len Avery, who served with the Flight during 1970–71, provided a back seat description of flare operations:

> It was a demanding task. You'd have a Porter ready for a flare mission each night and, if it was called out, you'd prepare another straightaway. We could keep it up all night.
>
> Normally you'd have pilot and observer up front and in the cabin section behind was the flare rack with fourteen flares and behind where you sat there'd be spare flares so you could reload the rack in flight. The open hatch and the rack were in front of you. The procedure was to lift the flare out of the rack and ensure that the lanyard from the flare to the side of the rack was attached so the flare would be armed as it dropped out. The flare opening altitude could be reset in flight if necessary. As flare dispenser, you had a penlight torch stuck in your gob and a flare between your legs beside the open hatch and you would release the flares on the pilot's call. Reloading was a curse. You had to physically turn around and pick up this mongrel thing, which was about three feet long and weighed a fair bit, and you were usually at a steep angle of bank while you were trying to do this without falling out of the aircraft through the hole. I didn't really enjoy flying so I'd get airsick very quickly and sometimes I'd be throwing up out of the hole and then tossing the flare out behind it. By the time I finished a flare mission I was ratshit.[7]

In another role, the Porter could be equipped with a more sophisticated version of Psyops equipment. A complete module was manufactured by 161 workshops to undertake voice broadcasts and leaflet dropping missions. The equipment included a powerful (1800 watt) amplifier, a tape recorder and a leaflet dispenser. The loudspeaker unit was fixed into the internal hatchway of the Porter and the module was installed above the hatch. A selector box allowed the operator, seated in the rear cabin, to select tape, microphone, or rebroadcast of radio messages through the loudspeaker system.

Possum Master Graeme Hill-Smith recalled getting the voice gear from the RAAF's 9 Squadron for use on the Porters. It was just before Christmas 1969:

> We offered to fly it in the Porter because they weren't doing much in the Iroquois. I can remember when it arrived. An Iroquois flew right over the unit at low level and an announcement came over the voice gear that 'Possums drive Kiddie Cars!'. Then the Iroquois came round and landed and the equipment was ours. So we got it rigged up in the Porter and on Christmas Eve I said, 'Come on, Bob [Captain Bob Smith, fixed wing section commander], we'll take it down to Vung Tau and play them some Christmas carols.' So we went down there and flew over the harbour and we played this music. And bloody weapons opened up from everywhere. In fact, Vung Tau went mad that night and we got out of the place. We went and found a battalion hiding up near the May Taos and flew over them. They all came out of their bunkers and put their cigarette lighters up and they were overjoyed. But not those pricks down at Vung Tau—they tried to kill us! On the job we used to play some sort of weird Vietnamese music and stuff. We used to play it up in the hills and they were supposed to surrender because they couldn't stand it anymore. I never flew those, but Frank Markcrow and Bob Smith probably did a fair bit.[8]

The Porter was also an ideal platform for launching rockets. It could carry a fairly large payload and was usually fitted with seven rockets a side when flying top cover for Sioux VR sorties. Working on the principle that bigger is better, 19-pod launchers were 'acquired' from US friends. These gave the Porter huge firepower. The aeroplane's other attribute was that its STOL capability enabled the pilot to generate a 45-degree dive angle for launching the rockets. This technique, called a Beta approach, provided a very stable platform at a constant speed of about 100 knots in the descent. The pilot could fire one rocket after another, correcting his aim each time, until he was on target. Then he could fire for effect. A mixture of white phosphorous, high explosive and flechette (anti-personnel) rounds could be carried. A Porter with this much firepower was a fearsome machine indeed.

No account of the Porter's capabilities would be complete without noting its versatility as a resupply vehicle. Major Hill-Smith explained:

> There was a time there when some idiot cut loose and shot three sergeants at the Corps of Transport company. He got drunk at night and shot and killed three of them. As a result of this, the chiefs looked at the booze which was being drunk around the place and there was obviously too much of it and a lack of control in some areas including that one. And so the booze was stopped, except for the New Zealand Battery who got theirs from somewhere else. And I sent a Porter up to Phu Loi or somewhere and it came back full. You could fit a lot of cans of beer in a Porter. It'd come up the ramp and into the hangar and would be unloaded in a flash. Fortunately, they sorted things out and we got our beer supplies back because there'd always be problems. But to my knowledge, 161 never had any issues like that.[9]

Meanwhile, the gradual improvement on the workshops side continued. Captain John Digweed described some badly needed improvements to the Flight's maintenance control facilities in preparation for the Porters:

> When they put the new hangar in, at the end of the hangar up on a little rise they put the OC workshop's office and a decent maintenance control section [MCS]. Before that, some of the documentation that was coming back to Australia was correct but it was filthy because of the working conditions. And when you got up there you could see why. But anyway, they now had a decent MCS and so the paperwork came out well and you know how important that can be.[10]

The potential problem of carrying out Porter E (major) servicings and modifications without adequate resources was solved by the lucky circumstance that Air America, the US aircraft fleet commonly identified with clandestine operations, operated the same type of aircraft built in the United States under licence by the Fairchild Aircraft Corporation. In the usual spirit of US–Australian cooperation, Air America agreed to take on the work. John Digweed was very impressed by the combination of rapid turnaround and engineering skills offered by the company's facilities at Saigon's Tan Son Nhut airport:

> We got on well with the American forces, and with Air America. Stuart Curnow started it, and I carried it on. When we needed a modification done, we'd fly up in the afternoon and Boyd Messinger, who was the maintenance

manager, would meet us and we'd go into his office and have a cup of coffee and get rid of all the artillery off our belts into his safe and then go into town. We'd stay at Boyd's place overnight, and when we came back in the morning the modifications would be completed. We'd just do an inspection on it, and fly the aeroplane home. They did a bloody good job. They had good tradesmen. The E servicings took longer of course, but were outstanding jobs.[11]

Major Phil Calvert—Possum Master Six

When Major Phil Calvert arrived at Nui Dat on 3 June 1970 to take command of the Flight as Possum Master Six, he was no stranger to the country. In March 1967, he was attached to 1/43 ARVN Infantry Regiment as a forward observer. During several months with the South Vietnamese force, he became familiar with the tactical situation in Long Khanh, Bien Hoa and Phuoc Tuy provinces. He also gained much practical experience as an artillery forward observer.

On taking over his new command, Major Calvert found that in the two years between his first and second tours, there had been substantial changes on the provincial scene. Relatively free movement was now permitted during daylight hours; village to village, into the provincial centre and into the padi fields. Much of the security fencing had been removed from around the villages and strong points were usually manned only at night. Although the enemy was still active in Phuoc Tuy province, operations were at a lower tempo than he had experienced previously. He also found that he had inherited a sound organisation from his predecessors:

> Commanding a unit at war is no doubt the ultimate experience and test for any professional officer. To command 161 was no exception for me. My job was made easier because of the outstanding support provided by all members of the unit. It was soon obvious that the senior ranks in each area knew precisely what they must do to maintain the unit in the required state of operational readiness. They achieved their goals by virtue of complete cooperation from their subordinates who were equally well versed in their respective trades.
>
> My task was also aided by the mature behaviour of all ranks both on and off duty. This was largely attributable to the way all personnel kept themselves occupied when not on duty or resting, whether improving unit defences and general living conditions or undertaking a civic aid project which entailed restoration work on the school at, as I recall, Phuoc Loi.

> That this school had been chosen was of particular significance to me because, whilst serving with 1/43 ARVN Regiment, I had been involved with a play area project there.
>
> It would be most unfair to single out any particular element of the unit as being more effective than others because from the hygiene dutyman and batmen, through the firemen and air traffic controllers, command post and orderly room staff, maintenance crews and pilots, the professionalism and teamwork was outstanding. Notwithstanding, specific mention is due the catering element. Meals of a very high standard were always provided; sometimes very early in the day, sometimes late at night. The cooks went out of their way to obtain extra and often exotic rations, making meal time a highlight within the day's activities. I particularly recall the excellent Christmas lunch in December 1970.[12]

This testimony confirms that the prior efforts of Graeme Hill-Smith to improve the catering standards had been most successful. It is apparent also that the quality of replacement personnel via the trickle system was maintained throughout the war. New workshops faces in the first half of 1970 included Captain Bob Millar, Warrant Officer Terry Davis, Sergeant Rocky Hoare and Corporal Len Avery. Captain Reg Ellwood arrived to replace Captain Bill Flanagan as the resident New Zealand pilot. Lieutenant Terry Gygar and Sergeant Dick Yielding took over the duties of Administrative Officer and Chief Clerk respectively. Of this group, Millar, Hoare and Yielding received MIDs for their fine contributions. These and many other personnel changes proceeded smoothly in the context of an uninterrupted commitment to operations.

Notwithstanding Phil Calvert's satisfaction with the performance of his unit, he felt some disquiet about a number of issues, in particular the extent to which its intelligence output was used:

> Much valuable information was collected during low-level reconnaissance missions and it was very disappointing that the staff at task force headquarters seldom reacted positively to our intelligence input. Because of this lack of response, I found it increasingly difficult to authorise so many VR missions. Valuable aircraft hours were being consumed and pilots were being not only put to unnecessary risk but also additional strain, with in most instances no tangible end result. Had it not been for the excellent top cover provided by the FAC pilots based at Vung Tau I would have further pressured headquarters staff to reduce the intensity of such missions. There can be no doubt that the presence of the FACs was the prime reason that there were so few attacks on our helicopters.[13]

Phil felt that, in other respects, the unit's aircraft were generally well utilised but that their effectiveness could be enhanced if there was a greater understanding of 161's operational versatility. As the OC of the aviation element of the task force, he was not involved in the planning of operations. Operation Orders would be issued and he would suggest to the task force staff that unit aircraft could be employed in specific ways. His suggestions were generally accepted but he cannot recall an Operation Order actually being amended to include aviation support in addition to the standard direct support aircraft. It seems that the task force headquarters staff were set in their ways.

Home improvements—the final stage

In the 161 Recce Flight lines, the urge to live in more salubrious surroundings reached its peak during the final two years that Nui Dat was home. Long gone were the days when a floor or a decent bunk was a status symbol. Power now came from a task force grid instead of an ancient generator kept alive with skill and the occasional savage kick. Movies and visiting entertainment groups were the norm, and there had even been a memorable occasion when one of the female entertainers stripped. Life at the Dat was now much more civilised, but it was still not quite like home. Efforts to improve camp facilities therefore continued.

One project involved the procurement and installation of an above-ground swimming pool among the rubber trees. The origins of this unlikely feature remain unknown to the author, but it was probably acquired by dishonest means according to unit tradition. OC Phil Calvert recalled that the pool arrived during his tour and that not many used it but he did so regularly. It was oval in shape and about six strokes from end to end. The unit firefighters were responsible for keeping it filled. God only knows what was in it after a few months.

While each of the Messes was now quite comfortably appointed, the officers made special efforts to add a touch of class. It was now closed in with Perspex sheeting above window sill level so that an air conditioner acquired through the US logistics system could function efficiently. A consignment of rubber matting destined for the task force headquarters went missing and found a better life on the floor of the Mess. An attractive courtyard was developed, with a gravel surface and banana palms planted in strategic locations. Phil sent his pilots out to gather bamboo so that the courtyard might be enclosed in resort style and provide a haven of outdoor privacy. Captain Bob Hills added a rock pool complete with fountain and coloured lighting. Cane lounges were procured for the comfort of the officers. Phil Calvert recalled these with amusement:

> We had a reel-to-reel tape deck in the Mess which most officers used to tape music to take home. While making tapes or just relaxing in the Mess, pilots would tend not only to nod off but to fall into a deep sleep in one of the many cane lounge chairs. On numerous occasions the person concerned would wake to find himself in a bamboo cage made from as many chairs as could be stacked around and above him.[14]

A nagging problem which defied gentrification was the flaming fury latrine system. At times the stench and the niggling insects would become too much for gentlemen who had completed officer training and there would be attempts to deodorise the trenches. On one such occasion, Phil Calvert was alarmed to see two pilots helping Captain Bob Hills in the direction of the medic's tent:

> His head and light green flying suit were almost totally bright red. I naturally assumed blood resulting from a major accident in the unit lines. I hurried up to check and it transpired that Bob had been about to use the long drop when he became fed up with having certain parts of his anatomy chewed on by all manner of insects. He decided to first deliver a fatal blow to the myriad buzzing things by dropping in a red smoke grenade. The idea literally backfired as he cautiously looked through the seat to see the results of his offensive. The contents of the grenade reacted rather violently with the chemicals routinely used in the long drop and Bob wore it. Luckily he suffered no major injury but as I recall he went on R and R without eyebrows or eyelashes and with even less hair than usual.[15]

Actually, Bob Hills had been the victim of unfortunate timing. The hygiene orderly, or 'blowfly' to his peers, had dumped a can of range fuel in the long drop but had not yet ignited it. The smoke grenade saved him the trouble.

It came to pass that a porcelain toilet bowl was extracted from the ever-useful US logistics system. The officers, using their own labour and workshops expertise, built a one-hole, flushing septic toilet. The high society crapper worked a treat. It was installed near a large water tank that was topped up with hot water for showers by a choofer. This turned out to be a fatal mistake. Sergeant Paul Lidster takes up the sad tale:

> I was asked if I could have a look at this toilet's flushing mechanism because it didn't work any more. I took a look and the plastic innards, the float bowl and all, looked like a melted pretzel. 'What can you do to fix it?' they asked. 'That's easy,' I said as I flung it into the bin. 'I guess you'll have to steal another one.' What happened was that someone forgot to turn the choofer off and each time the toilet was flushed it was topped up with hotter water. Finally it was just about boiling and it cooked the crapper's intestines.[16]

Phoenix rising: The Bird Dog project

There was more going on in the unit than the gentrification program at the Officers' Mess. In the old workshops hangar, which was fairly empty after the larger hangar was built for Porter maintenance, a new aircraft was rising like Phoenix from the remains of crashed American Army Cessna O-1 Bird Dogs. Three years had passed since the Bird Dog had become a special part of 161's history in 1967, and more than two years since George Constable flew a Bird Dog on his last mission.

The initiating force in the Bird Dog rebuild project was Major Charlie Miller, an Australian Army pilot of the old school who was posted to Vietnam as a liaison officer. He noticed a crashed aircraft at Vung Tau waiting to be written off and the thought occurred to him that it might be possible for 161's workshop personnel to restore it to flying condition. Charlie Miller was an imaginative man; a lover and collector of all things aeronautical. He visualised the restored Bird Dog as a tug aircraft for the Army Gliding Club back home in Queensland.[17]

An experienced negotiator in the Ned Kelly mould, Miller was successful in securing both the wreck and the approval of the OC of 161 and the workshops officer for the rebuild to go ahead. It was understood that it was to be a 'spare time' project that would not be allowed to detract from the Flight's efficiency in fulfilling its operational and maintenance commitments. While arrangements were under way to move the remains of the Bird Dog to Nui Dat, a second fuselage section became available and was purchased for three cartons of Australian beer. On 19 August 1970, a truck carrying two misshapen pieces of metal vaguely resembling sections of a Bird Dog fuselage arrived at the 161 flight line. The project had begun.

Operation Cung Chung

As mid-1970 passed, task force operations remained focused on the interdiction of the enemy's access routes to population centres in the south of the province. Operation *Cung Chung* ('togetherness') established set areas of responsibility for each battalion. The aim was to apply as much pressure as possible to the Viet Cong attempting propaganda and liaison tasks.[18] *Cung Chung* was conducted in three phases from 12 June to 25 October, and entailed close cooperation and consultation between the Australian forces and local district headquarters regarding deployments and the participation of regional force units.

Cung Chung I produced moderately good results and *Cung Chung II* followed in early August. On 9 August, Alpha Company of 8RAR was deployed in the Long Dien sector south of Nui Dat. There was little contact until the night of 11/12 August, when an ambush position spotted about 50 enemy soldiers moving towards the village of Hoa Long. The position was relocated to cover the track used by the enemy, who duly returned along the same route when they left the village. The ambush was sprung and the surprise was total, with seventeen Viet Cong killed in the initial engagement.[19]

161 Recce Flight played a significant role in mopping up after the ambush. Despite the losses inflicted, a considerable number of the enemy escaped into the nearby countryside. Using the light of illuminating flares dropped from a Porter aircraft, Second Lieutenant Peter Bysouth flew his Sioux into the area and searched at low level in an effort to locate the escaping enemy and to guide ground troops to their locations. Approximately 300 metres from the ambush point he located two enemy soldiers hiding in a clump of bushes. He kept them illuminated with his landing light while he guided APCs by radio into the area. As the APCs approached, one enemy soldier broke from cover and ran across a padi field. Bysouth followed and illuminated

him with the result that the enemy soldier was killed by fire from the armoured vehicles.

He then returned to the clump of bushes and illuminated the remaining soldier. When the APCs arrived, six emerged from cover and surrendered. Bysouth continued searching the area until just before dawn when he was relieved by another aircraft. Not content with his night's work, he slept for a couple of hours and then went off on a low-level VR mission over the Long Hais in support of 7RAR. He took ground fire at treetop height and was hit several times. Despite control problems, he managed to fly his aircraft to the nearest fire support base where he made a successful running landing. Subsequent inspection of the aircraft revealed extensive damage to major components of the aircraft and to critical control lines. Peter Bysouth was awarded the DFC for his skill and courage on 12 August 1970.

In another notable incident on 9 November, Second Lieutenant Terry Hayes was assigned as DS pilot for 2RAR on Operation *Cung Chung III*. He was flying the CO, Lieutenant Colonel John Church, on a reconnaissance in the south western area of Phuoc Tuy when he located a fresh track. He was following it at slow speed about 20 feet above the ground when the aircraft took heavy ground fire. Colonel Church was hit and a moment later the engine failed. Hayes crash-landed the aircraft without further injury to his passenger, meanwhile transmitting on the distress frequency. A RAAF Iroquois flying some distance away heard the 'Mayday' call and radioed for another winch-fitted RAAF machine situated at Nui Dat. Colonel Church was being treated at the Field Hospital in Vung Tau within 20 minutes of the crash. Terry Hayes was uninjured. He was recognised as an effective and determined pilot throughout his tour of duty with 161 Recce Flight and received a DFC for his outstanding airmanship.

Just four days before Christmas, it was Second Lieutenant Fraser Gibson's turn to get up close and personal with the enemy. He was tasked to direct artillery fire onto a target in the Long Hais, an area in which the enemy did not hesitate to engage intruding aircraft. During the subsequent low-level damage assessment of the target, Fraser noticed another possible enemy location nearby and began a search at treetop height. The enemy objected to his presence and the aircraft took a burst of machine gun fire. The Sioux was badly damaged, but in the fine tradition of Possum pilots Fraser recovered it from the firing line without injury to himself or his passenger.

Not to be outdone, the New Zealand connection provided the news of the moment on Christmas Day. Captain Reg Ellwood was shot down by enemy ground fire while detached to the US Army 3/17 Air Cavalry. The aircraft was lost but fortunately the pilot suffered no serious injuries other than having his nose shortened by a passing bullet. Back at Nui Dat, the day was celebrated in style with the cooks making a special effort to produce a memorable meal. The cake decorations even included models of the unit's aircraft. It was as if they knew that it was to be the last Christmas at Nui Dat.

A replacement for the Sioux

Among his other reservations about 161's role and tasking, Major Phil Calvert was concerned that he was not kept in the loop when important decisions were being taken. He learned of a proposal to lease OH-58A Kiowa helicopters from the US Army in the course of a casual conversation with a US Army officer. Task force headquarters was unable to confirm or deny the proposal. He then sought confirmation from the Directorate of Army Aviation in Canberra and was advised that negotiations had been under way for some time and were being conducted by the Australian headquarters in Saigon. He was further advised that the Directorate required that the aircraft be armed and that he was to justify this requirement. When he contacted Saigon accordingly, he was informed by the Chief of Staff that all was under control and that his input was not needed because a RAAF engineer officer on the headquarters staff could provide any necessary advice. Phil was not happy:

> Despite the fact that the unit was involved in a protracted war and experience was showing, if not demanding, the need for certain changes to unit operations there was reluctance at all levels of command to confront the RAAF. It was agreed that the primary role of the unit was reconnaissance and there was no need for aircraft to be armed for this purpose. However, 161's aircraft undertook many other types of mission and it seemed logical to have the aircraft armed not only for self-preservation but more importantly to support ground forces in any possible way. But any such offensive support was considered by the RAAF to be their preserve. Their policy was

that Army aircraft would not be armed. The fact that RAAF aircraft were not always available to provide armed support on an impromptu basis was immaterial.

A further example of not confronting the RAAF was on the matter of Army pilots being trained and operating as Forward Air Controllers. Because the enemy tended to operate in areas of dense vegetation, the American FACs found it difficult to locate targets and thus could not mark them accurately for strike aircraft. Their problems were compounded by not being permitted to fly below 1500 feet. Accordingly, in the task force area of responsibility, 161's helicopters carried out low-level target identification and marking and returned for bomb damage assessment and further marking as required. It would have been far simpler for 161's pilots, who were totally familiar with airstrike procedures, to undertake the entire mission. In practice, they did undertake such missions when, from time to time, American strike aircraft reported in their area with weapon loads available for opportunity targets and there was no FAC available.[20]

Phil Calvert was not alone in his reservations about the role played by the RAAF in the negotiations to lease the Kiowas. His successor would be similarly taken aback. In the meantime, 1971 beckoned and it was operations as usual.

12

The final challenge:
January–September 1971

At Nui Dat, 1971 did not begin as the year of change and withdrawal it later became. Pacification operations continued in what was now a well-established routine. There was perhaps an expectation that Australia's involvement in South Vietnam might end soon because the size of the task force had been scaled down, but the only certainty was that there was still a job to be done. For 161's pilots and maintenance crews, the endless daily round of operations and aircraft maintenance continued. In his monthly summary, Possum Master Phil Calvert noted that January, his last full month as OC, was relatively quiet with 1101 hours flown. There was the usual speculation that Tet, which fell on 26 January, might see the enemy make another concerted effort. But once again the threat failed to materialise.

Possum Master Seven: Major Neil Harden

Major Neil Harden took over the duties of OC on 11 February. Little was necessary in terms of handover-takeover as he had spent time with the Flight during 1970 preparing a Training and Information Letter on 161's functions and procedures. Phil Calvert, who was awarded an MID which he attributed to the efforts of the entire

Flight, went home knowing that the unit was in experienced and knowledgeable hands. Captain Bob Hills also returned to Australia. His place as operations officer was taken by the unit liaison officer, Lieutenant Digby Mackworth.

The new Possum Master was the last of a distinguished group of OCs. Like all except the first, Major Paul Lipscombe, he started his career in artillery. His aviation career commenced with Air OP pilot training in 1954. Several years of experience in artillery in Australia and Malaya followed before a staff appointment as SO3 (Air) at Army Office. He then completed fixed wing instructor training in Britain and gained experience as an instructor there. From 1962 to 1967 he served at Amberley, first as senior flying instructor (fixed wing) and then as OC Training Flight. He attended Staff College in 1967 and then spent two years on the Australian Army staff in Washington DC. During this posting, he completed rotary wing instructor training at Fort Rucker before returning to 1 Aviation Regiment and a short time later to the command of 161. He was respected as both a confident leader and an aviator. His professionalism demanded the best from others, and he was not one to suffer fools gladly. 'You didn't fuck with Major Neil,' recalled rotary wing pilot Captain Tub Matheson. Some of the pilots he commanded still refer to him affectionately as 'Boss'.

February brought another special event: the last flight of the Cessna 180 in South Vietnam. The honour fell to Lieutenant Dennis Coffey on 14 February. Flanked by three Porters, he flew over the task force area so that all might salute the Cessna for a job well done. This aircraft type had clocked up 11 169 sorties in South Vietnam for a total of 16 150 hours.[1] Its replacement, the Porter, had proven its worth and within six months the Flight would achieve another quantum leap in operational capability when the trusty Sioux was replaced by OH-58A Kiowas leased from the US Army.

Close encounter

The rotation of battalions and flow of operations continued, with 7RAR and 2RAR finishing their second tours in March and June respectively. They were replaced by 3RAR and 4RAR. In the field, the *Cung Chung* series of operations continued, to be followed by Operation *Phoi Hop* from 1 February to 2 May.

On 31 March, Alpha Company of 3RAR engaged an estimated enemy force of two companies in a four-hour contact in the Xuyen Moc area. Second Lieutenant Fraser Gibson was flying DS for the battalion with the CO, Lieutenant Colonel Peter Scott, as passenger when a platoon called for maximum fire support to extract itself from a dangerous situation. To mark its location, the platoon requested that additional smoke grenades be dropped into its position. Ground fire damaged the Sioux's engine and cockpit as Fraser went in for the drop. He recovered the aircraft to a safe area and both he and Colonel Scott escaped injury. The Sioux was airlifted to Nui Dat for repair. For his actions during this contact, and for his skill in recovering his aircraft after taking ground fire in the Long Hais a few months earlier, Fraser was awarded the DFC.

Developments at Possum Manor

Life at Luscombe Field went on, with old hands leaving and replacements marching in to take up their duties without any thought of an abbreviated tour. On 17 March, Captain Rowan Monteith arrived to take over as rotary wing section commander. His early memories and impressions were reminiscent of many arrivals:

> We had the Husky Chucks, I think they called them, the tracked American 155mm guns that were based at Nui Dat. I think that someone used to organise one of their harassment and interdiction night shoots over the top of 161 every time a new pilot came in. I was having a drink in the Mess that night when the 155s fired straight over the top of us and I was on the floor saying, 'What in the bloody Hell was that?' while the rest continued drinking. As an introduction to the country it was a bit scary.
>
> Terry Gygar—now Professor of Law at Bond University—was the Admin Officer. I shared a tent with him, opposite Neil Harden's tent, and we started our life there. I spent some time then with Ken Cairns and I think Terry Hayes, flying with Terry and with Fraser Gibson to familiarise myself with the area and all of the different tasks before taking over. Ken was staying on as second in command, so that was a help during my takeover period. I fell into the routine of things quite simply; the daily VRs and support for the battalions and sometimes the tracks or the tanks. The

only time that things changed a bit was when there was a bigger operation on; like the deployment of the task force headquarters and the whole lot to Courtenay Hill, north of Nui Dat.

There was humour as well. At 1ATF we used to have the Ready Reaction Force. The Flight often had to provide troops for it. When the alarm went off because the bad guys were on the wire, suddenly all these APCs would appear down in front of the hangar, and Terry Gygar would go down with his troop of 'infantry'; his trained killers. They called them 'Gygar's Guerillas'. They'd all charge off down to the APCs and go off to attack the bad guys when they broke through the wire. Better to let the bad guys in, I think.[2]

The day after Rowan Monteith's arrival, he was no longer the new kid on the block. Lieutenant Grant Steel, the last of the New Zealand pilots posted to 161, arrived to replace Captain Reg Ellwood. Grant would later distinguish himself, but for the moment he was just another fledgling to be mentored like all new arrivals. Major Harden, like his predecessors, checked out his new pilots very carefully before cutting them loose:

> I would not clear a pilot, fixed or rotary, to fly alone in country until he had been there at least a couple of weeks, and I did a dual check. And that wasn't a flying check only, but primarily an 'in country' check. When a new pilot came in, we'd brief him on all of the ops things and show him the maps and then we'd send him out with his section commander as a passenger. And then he'd go out with a VR pilot and sit there. When the section commander felt that he was ready for an 'in country' check, I'd fly with him. Now, I knocked back two pilots the first time. I sent them back until I was satisfied that they were ready to go out on their own. As far as VRs were concerned, they didn't get to be a good VR pilot for two to three months whether they were experienced pilots or not. Some of them became very good at it. I remember that Second Lieutenant John Sonneveld came back one day and said, 'I reckon that somewhere between 25 and 35 people passed over that track within the last 24 hours.' And everybody said, 'Come on, now.' When the infantry arrived they found 30 people had gone over that track about 18 hours before his recce.[3]

The new Possum Master's experience and thoughtfulness as an OC was evident in his description of a new element he introduced to the nightly briefing:

> After dinner, we'd have our normal ops briefing and I introduced a 'This is a silly thing I did today' feature. Basically, if somebody made a mistake, get

up and tell everyone so we don't make the same mistake again. All of the pilots used to get up and say what they'd done and I think that was good. I had to lead it once. I did a terrible thing. I was doing a forced landing with Ian Sinnott and I thought, 'no problems with this', and I actually feathered the prop. We nearly ran off the end of the strip by the time we touched down. So I said, 'This is the stupid thing I did today.' The talk was also used to alert people, like 'Watch out for this area' or 'There's a new track here'. So we had a good interchange of ideas and the engineers used to talk about their problems as well.[4]

Neil Harden recalled that he didn't have any problem with the tasking of 161. He felt that he had the right number of pilots. The routine of ten days on and a day off was hard on the pilots when they first got there, but was accepted by all and after a while didn't seem to be so tiring. There didn't seem to be any morale problems or bad feelings about the length of the tour. The Flight was functioning well.

The Bunny II project

In the old hangar, the rebuild of the Bird Dog continued. Airframe Fitter Corporal Len Avery was part of the team:

I was fortunate enough to work on the rebuild for the majority of the time and to be in country when it was test flown in May 1971. Wally Nelson, an engine fitter who was in country with me, was one of the prime movers on the job. And Laurie Wood, another airframe fitter, was the one who created the colour scheme for the aircraft. I think at some stages during the project we treated it as a bit of a joke. After all, we were literally creating an aircraft from scrap. There were many days when we didn't think that it could ever fly, given what we started with. But we progressed under the guidance of Sergeant Bob Zitzlesberger. That was his second tour and he was a brilliant fitter. He got an MID for his work during his first tour. He was very creative and very clear in his directions on how to build this thing. I mean, we were just airframe fitters and engine fitters and an aircraft's an aircraft. If you needed to replace the skin, you replaced the skin. You just replaced whatever was needed: the instruments, the engine, whatever. But we had no proper jigs for alignment or anything like that. We used bits of scrap timber and metal; whatever was to hand.

The availability of spares was quite good once you established contacts at the respective bases. We made up a shopping list of what we needed: new wings and an engine and we tried to change as many flight controls as we could. We had to get all of the instruments. Radios weren't a problem. Then we had to get all new cables, pulleys and that sort of stuff. To gain extra knowledge I spent some time up at Phu Loi, talking to maintenance people and doing some training on the aircraft.[5]

As news of the project spread there were donations from many sources. The pilots were keen and scrounged parts during their travels. Major components like mainplanes, undercarriage and engine were harder to come by and it must be said that there was an element of lying and cheating involved in their procurement. The engine posed a particularly difficult problem. However, as luck would have it, a brand new engine was discovered in a hangar at Vung Tau. The hangar had been taken over by an American squadron flying OV-10 'Bronco' aircraft and they didn't have a use for the engine. They did however need a vehicle for a detachment in the Delta country. Their people there needed a vehicle for recreational use. The ever-alert Major Charlie Miller became aware that the RAAF at Vung Tau were in the process of writing off a Holden staff car. A complicated and totally dishonest process began which saw the Holden restored to operational condition, except for a windscreen, and presented to the Americans in exchange for the new engine.[6]

With the major components in place, the Bird Dog was quickly completed. It was named Bunny II after an aircraft owned by Hugh Hefner of *Playboy* magazine fame. The idea was that the men of Army Aviation would have as much fun with it as Hefner reportedly did with his Playboy Bunnies. The challenge now was to prepare Bunny II for flight. Three-time Vietnam veteran Sergeant Paul Lidster became involved in the project during his final tour:

> They asked me if I'd ever worked on Bird Dogs and I told them that when we were down at Vungers there were two of them stationed next to us on the field. There was only one 'all trades' Yank with them and the two pilots. So we did a few jobs for them on the Bird Dogs. The guys at Nui Dat said, 'Can you rig it?' Len Avery already had the manual so we did all the flight control rigging. I got a crew chief to come down and check it. He looked at it and checked all the figures and said, 'Let's go. Let's try her out.' We said, 'Hang on. We haven't lockwired in the turnbuckles or anything.' He said, 'Goddam. You gonna do all that, are you?'
>
> Anyway, we got it all locked up and it was ready to go and we got a pilot down, Warrant Officer Charlie Brewster. He checked her out and took her up by himself. We had a bottle of champagne there and he was

> gone for a fair while. We were starting to get a bit worried when he called up and said he was on his way back. He landed and we cracked the champagne and slapped each other on the back and all that. And Brewster turned round and said, 'Hey. Who rigged this ship?' I said, 'I did.' He said, 'Goddam, man. I've been flying these things for a hundred years and this is the first one that when I put her into the stall she just kept going and going and in the end I had to turn her around. It would not stall. I've never seen that in a Bird Dog.'[7]

Len Avery recalled that the Bird Dog's reluctance to stall was primarily a weight and balance problem as radios which were normally fitted were not in place for the test flight. So the remedy was simple.

Air Traffic Controller Sergeant Bill Hudnott was in the tower for the first flight and cleared Bunny II for take-off on 9 May 1971:

> Everybody, including those who were airborne at the time, wanted to see the Bird Dog fly. They admired Charlie Brewster, who was one of the true legends. It was a really moving moment to see this little blue aeroplane, the Bird Dog, sitting on the end of my runway, and all of the other pilots wishing him well up there and just going around in slow circles to watch. His preflight was slow and careful and then he took off and he said, 'This is beautiful.' It was a pretty good moment.[8]

Today, Bunny II resides in the Army Aviation Museum at Oakey in Queensland. It is a treasured reminder of that time and of the men who flew and maintained the little aeroplanes borrowed from the Americans. More importantly, it epitomises the 'can do' spirit that made possible the consistently excellent performance of the Flight throughout its service in South Vietnam.

The Kiowas: Upgrading the RW capability

During July and August, the leased OH-58A Kiowa light observation helicopters replaced the workhorse Siouxs. Possum Master Neil Harden recalled that the introduction of the eight turbine-powered Kiowas went very smoothly. He was ably assisted by 161's maintenance engineer, Captain Fred Barlow. During the changeover period, there were no accidents or reduction in support for task force operations; a remarkable but expected performance. An American training team at Vung Tau conducted pilot conversions and technical training for the fitters and storemen. Warrant Officer Bob Bell, an instrument fitter, remembered that the Americans were somewhat surprised at the expertise of the Australians:

> They did their maintenance in a different way from us. They did about six weeks of training to qualify as a crew chief who could carry out 'all trades' servicing at the basic level. When we went to the 5th Aviation Detachment for training, after two days the sergeant there said, 'You guys know more about the aircraft than I do.' It was embarrassing for the poor bloke. At the end of the first week, we had an objective test and I think our lowest score was 93 per cent. So from then on they said, 'What can we employ you as?' We fixed up the odd thing and they thought we were very nice people.[9]

The first three aircraft were delivered shortly after the first pilots and maintenance crews completed training. When a pilot had completed the Kiowa conversion course, he did not fly the Sioux again in South Vietnam. As the QFI, Major Harden was the exception to this rule. The Siouxs were progressively withdrawn from service and returned to Australia. The OC reflected on his impressions at the time:

> It helped that we had some excellent maintenance people there. Len Avery was there then. We had a really good bunch of fellows. If you look at some of the statistics of the aircraft serviceability rate in Vietnam—100 per cent, 98 per cent—you could not in any way match it. It was unbelievable. I think the morale of the Flight was very, very high.
>
> I suppose my biggest bitch, and I had this fight with the task force Chief of Staff when I arrived, was that they refused to accept the American offer of putting miniguns on the Kiowas. That, I think, was wrong. It was part of the fit. The decision was made in Saigon. When I came in, I was introduced and I asked why. The Chief of Staff said, 'Well, we don't see the necessity' and I said, 'Who's we?' He said, 'Well, the Air Force commander and me.' And I said, 'Well, I'm disgusted that nobody thought to ask the Army Aviation commander.' I don't know whether I'd have left the armament on every aircraft, but I'd certainly put it on all the VR aircraft. Mind you, it's a hell of a thing when it goes off. It throws you about 15 degrees to one side. I fired the minigun in the Hughes model. I did an instructors' course on the Hughes with the Americans and part of that included two days firing on the range with this minigun. Three thousand rounds a minute. It makes a hell of a noise, just like paper tearing. As soon as you press the button you've got to whack in a bloody great bootful of anti-torque pedal.[10]

There were of course some teething problems with the Kiowa, but luckily these were fairly minor. Fraser Gibson carried out a precautionary landing when his 'Transmission Oil Hot' warning light illuminated. The landing area was secured by APCs from A Squadron, 3 Cavalry while Warrant Officer Bob Bell was flown out to investigate and rectify the fault. A few days later John Sonneveld put his aircraft down when his 'Transmission Oil Hot' and 'Transmission Oil Pressure' warning lights illuminated. Captain Fred Barlow was flown in to check the fault and determined that the aircraft could be flown back to Nui Dat. Investigation showed that the illumination of warning lights had been due to system malfunctions rather than component failures.

There were design shortcomings as well. The Kiowa had not been built for operations in a rough environment. Captain Tub Matheson remembered some of the problems which ensued from the aircraft's 'soft' design:

> The Australian Army had made the decision to buy the Kiowa. I was around when they looked at the SA-341, the OH-6 and all of the others and they chose the Kiowa. But then they said, 'Right. Part of the deal is that it's got to be manufactured in Australia, and another part is that we're going to lease eight of them from the US Army to give us experience.' Well, it certainly did that. We gained a whole bunch of experience with that machine. Lieutenant Mick Reynolds penned a very good report. I'd like to get my hands on it, not just for history purposes but also to see the recommendations that we guys in 161 made and what was actually incorporated into the Australian aircraft. One of them, definitely, was high skids. The low skids we had on the OH-58s in Vietnam were a menace. When you clear bush with a machete you tend to take the upwards swipe. You get a small bush and cut the stem on an angle, like maybe the size of a pencil or a bit bigger. It would go straight through the skin of a Kiowa landing on it, and if moisture got into the honeycomb through the hole then you could get delamination very quickly. So we said that high skids were a must. I remember too that we had trouble with people, with their weapons going into the honeycomb. We got around that with that high density rubber that you put on instrument fitters' benches. That was put on all the floors, and it's still in Army Kiowas today.[11]

Rotary wing commander Captain Rowan Monteith recalled an incident which highlighted just how careful pilots and passengers in the Kiowa had to be:

We were new to the aircraft and there were lots of things we didn't know. I remember a guy declaring an emergency and coming back with major noise from the aircraft. He thought that he had a rough-running engine and that everything was turning to worms. But he got the thing back on the ground and it turned out that what he had was a rough-running seat belt. Some infantry type had gotten out of the back and left the seat belt hanging outside. The noise the pilot heard was the flailing of the seat belt along the side of the aircraft, which did a tremendous amount of damage. It was in that kind of soft core area. And then of course the rough-running seat belt became a major thing and we had to change the rules a bit about people hopping in and out of the aircraft because you really had to check that the door was closed and the belt was inside.[12]

Kiowas on operations

The first three Kiowas went into operational service on 28 July 1971 after being painted with Australian markings. Initial operations were in direct support of task force Operation *Iron Fox* from 28 July to 5 August. The increase in operational effectiveness was immediately evident. Major Neil Harden commented that the aircraft could be used for SAS insertions. 'We'd send two aircraft out for a six or seven man patrol. We'd get in tactically, drop them off and go.'[13]

Captain Tub Matheson added his thoughts on the new machine:

The big thing, apart from its power, was its ability to get around in a hurry. If a job occurred up at Courtenay, you could be up there in probably ten minutes. In the Sioux it was a cut lunch and a compass. Another thing was radio relay. The Kiowa could do it automatically. I spent quite a few hours sitting up there purely to provide an airborne radio relay facility in support of particular operations. It was a good pilot's aircraft but, as with any other new machine, you had to learn new procedures. I remember that John Sonneveld, back in our early days with the Kiowa, scared the shit out of himself. He was working with 4RAR. He had a panic departure, I think it was off Courtenay itself, and he hadn't got the throttle fully opened as he pulled pitch. The rotor RPM drooped and if it wasn't for the fact that he had 300 feet of hill he would have crashed. I guess it just hadn't been knocked into us hard enough to 'Ensure throttle fully open'. With the old Sioux, you played the throttle. But with a turbine helicopter, it's 'full open'. There are some differences now with the newer models, like the Bell 407, and as an instructor you have to check very carefully the procedures for the aircraft you're flying. You just have to be so careful or you can do a lot of damage. But if you've been properly trained—and we were properly trained in the Army—you can fly anything. If you use correct technique, you don't get found out.[14]

In addition to its all round capabilities, one of the Kiowa's features that impressed Rowan Monteith was that it offered more protection for the driver:

> The Kiowa made a big difference. We were able to do a lot more and you just felt safer. I know that sounds silly, but we had armour-plated seats. I mean, we had always been issued with chicken plate. It was a huge thing that sat in this vest you were supposed to wear. No one wore them because they were so uncomfortable. We used to sit on them; put them under the seat in case the family jewels were damaged. But the Kiowas were pretty safe aircraft and we felt more comfortable.
>
> Our operations changed a lot, although we still did the same things. We still did the VRs, we still did support, but it made it a lot easier for the battalion commanders. They could now go out on a recce and take their battery commander and intelligence officer with them. So from the battalion commander's point of view the change was quite dramatic. And we had more capacity for resupply, things like that.[15]

Fixed wing operations: Supporting the broader effort

Liaison and administrative support remained an important feature of 161's operations, and included support for the Australian Army Training Team. The advisors on the team worked with the South Vietnamese and Allied forces at locations as widely separated as the Mekong Delta area in the south and Pleiku in the north. Each element of the team was visited once a month. Major Harden described a fairly adventurous trip:

> John McGhie and I were flying a Porter up to Pleiku. We had to drop some information or mail into Wayne Shannon, an infantry warrant officer advisor attached to the Korean Division. We had to call him up on a frequency at some distance out from Pleiku, and I'll never forget his call sign: Gentle Reaper 31. We landed on a strip out there, and Wayne came up in a Jeep and we gave him the mail and we took off. We were a fair way north then, and I think we might have circled for a bit on the way in. Anyway, by the time we got airborne again we were down a little on our fuel reserves into Pleiku. So we called up and they said, 'Negative landing, we're under mortar attack.' I said, 'What do you reckon, John?' and he

replied, 'Well, we can't hang around too long.' So we called back minimum fuel, and we landed on the end of the strip that was away from where the mortars were coming in. That was an interesting little exercise.[16]

Major Harden had a much more unnerving experience while flying a voice mission over the Long Hais:

I was flying and the operator was chieu-hoing[17] away and, the next minute, there was some bugger outside hitting the aircraft with this bloody great hammer. I was lucky, of course. We had been hit by three rounds along the aircraft. It sounded like a lot more. And I just declared a Mayday because I didn't know what had been hit, control cables or whatever. I just about glided into Vung Tau and landed there and we checked the aircraft all over and next day flew it back to Nui Dat.[18]

The life of a Porter pilot was a busy one. Apart from the OC, who was dual qualified, there were four fixed wing pilots for the four Porter aircraft. The daily routine always included a courier run around Phuoc Tuy and American bases outside the province such as Bien Hoa and Bearcat. This early morning task incorporated a low-level reconnaissance of the of roads system to check for sabotage overnight or other signs of enemy activity. On return from this task the pilot would be allocated to other routine daytime missions: top cover for VRs (161 relied much less on the Jades by 1971), Sigint sorties, liaison tasks into Tan Son Nhut and a plethora of others. An eight-hour flying day was not unusual.

Possum down—Captain Rowan Monteith

On 26 April, Rowan Monteith carried out a successful emergency landing after his top cover Jade pilot warned that he was leaving a trail of smoke:

A round took out an oil line that runs up to the top of the Sioux's transmission and suddenly the engine oil was being pumped all over the outside of the engine and the aircraft was bathed in smoke and flames. I can remember the Jade, I think it was a guy called Larry Sorena, said to me, 'Hey, Possum, y'all are trailing smoke.' We were right up to the north in jungle country, about 15 or 20 klicks from the nearest friendlies. I put the aircraft down on a logging track and used the extinguisher to spray foam on the fire and then ran off into the jungle and hid. Larry brought a pair of Phantoms down on top of me, doing low passes at literally nothing feet. It was quite reassuring that I had a hell of a lot of fire support available to me. I remember being, you know, alert, and cocking my weapon in anger or perhaps in anticipation. I left the aircraft because I thought that the bad guys were going to come looking for it. I had my little URG-10 radio. I was talking to the FAC but I didn't want to make a lot of noise so it was a bit silly because I was whispering into this thing. It was dead still and quiet and it seemed at the time like ants marching by were like battalions coming through the jungle.

A lot of things had been set in train because Larry had given a Mayday call on my behalf as I went into the trees and disappeared from sight. I was on the ground for about 40 minutes before Digby Mackworth came up in a Sioux and pulled me out of there. Tanks came up, from Xuyen Moc I think, to secure the aircraft and the area while Warrant Officer Terry Davis was flown out to fix the aircraft. I was still at Luscombe having a nervous cigarette when it was ready, and there was no one else available so I had to go back out to pick up the aircraft. Four tanks were parked around it, each loaded with canister and pointing out in a different direction. So I felt a whole lot more comfortable flying it out.[19]

Behind the operations

When Captain Fred Barlow, RAEME, took over from Captain Bob Millar as OIC Workshop in April 1971, he had a hard act to follow but did it well. Bob Millar had made a professional contribution and was awarded an MID for his leadership in maintaining three types of aircraft at very high standards of serviceability and availability.

On the fixed wing side, Lieutenant John Howard arrived to replace Lieutenant Dennis Coffey as section commander. At that stage, the Porters were racking up 420 hours each month, with the lion's share of that total on reconnaissance and Sigint missions. John Howard saw in the commencement of night VR missions with illumination provided by Porter flare drops. This too had its dangerous side. The aim was always to overlap the illumination periods but inevitably there were flare failures. It was scary for the Sioux pilot down in the weeds when everything went black because his night vision had been shot to pieces by the light of the flares.

Operations and other serious business aside, April was notable for an ANZAC Day celebration with American friends from the 3/17 Air

Cavalry. This unit had welcomed many rotary wing Possums to its ranks to gain flying experience on its various helicopters. Possum Master Neil Harden recalled the brief interlude with pleasure:

> We hadn't heard from them for a long, long time. Then one of our guys heard their call sign again and found out they'd been 'elsewhere'. He told them we were having a bit of a function on Anzac Day if they'd like to drop in to say g'day. On Anzac Day, they arrived. I'm not talking about two or three choppers, but the whole outfit. Their commander said, 'We're just out of ops. I've had my unit in ops for five weeks or more and we've taken something like 15 per cent pilot casualties and I'm giving them a day off to come to the 161 party.' So you can imagine what it was like. We had something like four Iroquois, two or three Cobras, a couple of Kiowas lined up on the strip—all fully gunned up! And they had a good time! It really made our day.[20]

May was marked by a visit from Possum Master One, Paul Lipscombe, who was then chief flying instructor at 1 Aviation Regiment. He spent nine days completing the annual recategorisation of all 161 pilots. Much had changed since he led his small band with four aircraft to Bien Hoa in 1965. The Flight was now routinely achieving 1200 hours a month with its twelve aircraft. The camp facilities were more resort-like than his own had been, with the Officers' Mess sporting its new fountain. Sergeant Geoff Deacon recalled the building and christening of this fine feature:

> Captain Bob Hills was the main driver. His idea was you could sit around it on your chairs at night and have a beer at the fountain. It was a proper job, cement with rock edges and all. In the middle of it they put this pipe up with up a .50 cal shell on top with some holes drilled in it. So when you turned on the water the little spout thing would go off. When they finally finished it was a good excuse for a piss-up so there was a grand opening. Most of the pilots had been around Vietnam a bit and had friends in other units. On the big day a variety of aircraft rolled up bringing both men and women. And they were having a whale of a time leading up to the opening ceremony.
>
> The water supply for this fountain was the old American water trailer that we acquired years earlier courtesy of Harold Holt. I think it was just casually towed out of Vung Tau and arrived at 161, where we painted out the big star on the side. Anyway, they parked this water trailer up top by the Sergeants' Mess so gravity feed would provide a bit of head pressure. Without naming names, there was a certain Quartermaster—his initials were Derek Sims—and a certain airframe sergeant named Rocky Hoare who acquired

THE FINAL CHALLENGE: JANUARY–SEPTEMBER 1971

this drum of detergent and went up and put it in the water trailer. So everyone's crowded around the Officers' Mess listening to this opening speech and they turned on the tap and nothing but all of these bubbles shot out of it. This created a bit of angst among the officers but everyone else there thought it was a top bloody joke. So they kind of laughed it off and the party went on. But when the visitors left they started looking for who might have done it. For some reason they thought I was involved. Now I had been involved in some things but I didn't physically put in the detergent. I got the blame anyway, along with Rocky Hoare and Derek Sims. The officers just came over to us and grabbed us and dragged us down and threw us into this bloody fountain. Then we had a beer and all was forgiven.[21]

There were times too when fun was had in the most unexpected circumstances. For example, procedures for 'stand to' situations were well established but sometimes all didn't go as planned. Radio Sergeant Brian Reardon told of one such occasion:

There was a stand to and we'd had this new air trafficker, Sergeant Les Idiens, come in from Australia. Whenever there was a stand to, the duty air trafficker had to take the phone off the bar and bring it up to our bunker area and hook it up to a phone line to the CP. So 'stand to' is called and Les grabs the phone and we head for the bunker. He'd been an infantry section corporal on his first tour and he'd been shot at, so he took all this very seriously. The rest of us were old hands and we were not expecting much to happen. Anyway, Les hooks up the phone and he's ringing and ringing and getting nowhere and next thing the CP sent up a runner to see why we hadn't checked in. They decided there must be a break in the line and they'd fix it next day. About five minutes later the 'all clear' goes and soon after the lights come back on. We saw straightaway what had happened. Some bugger had got a bit of telephone cable and strung it up between two rubber trees alongside the bunker and hung his washing on it. Les is hooked up to this and he's ringing the shit out of this bloke's washing! Well, when we saw this I just cracked and I was absolutely pissing myself laughing and rolling on the ground. It was the funniest thing. If Les had had a gun in his hand I was dead then![22]

The last battalion

Late in May 2RAR went home on HMAS *Sydney*. To mark the occasion, Lieutenants Digby Mackworth and Fraser Gibson flew past in two Siouxs. The OC accompanied them in a loudspeaker-equipped Porter and played the regimental march as the ship departed. By this time, 4RAR/NZ, the last battalion to serve in Vietnam, had settled in and commenced operations. The Eighth had not been replaced on the completion of its tour in November 1970, so only 3RAR and 4RAR remained to cover the TAOR previously shared by three battalions. The pressure was relentless. Intelligence had indicated a substantial build-up of enemy forces on Phuoc Tuy's northern border with Long Khanh province. Cross-border operations were notoriously difficult, involving complex clearance formalities with South Vietnamese military and civil authorities as well as the more routine coordination requirements between Australian and American forces.[23] The Fourth had arrived at a demanding time.

Operation *Overlord* in June was a search-and-destroy operation aimed at disrupting enemy activities in the Suoi Nhac area, ten kilometres southeast of the American base at Black Horse. This was the suspected key build-up area for enemy forces. The Third was also involved in *Overlord*, driving enemy forces from the north onto 4RAR's blocking position parallel to and south of the border with Long Khanh. On the evening of 8 June, a Porter flareship crewed by Lieutenants John McGhie and John Howard illuminated an area from which the noise of enemy movement could be heard. However, the ground forces detected nothing. On 12 June, an APC was ambushed and the detonation of Claymore mines it was carrying killed seven Australians. Captain Rowan Monteith was quickly on the scene:

> Early morning, I was flying in support of the task force and a group of vehicles left a night position. As they came out into a clearing just south of the Courtenay rubber, a rocket-propelled grenade was fired at the rear vehicle and they got a sympathetic detonation of all of their Claymores on top. It killed seven troops. I flew there at once and spoke to the vehicle commander. The belly plate had been blown off the rear vehicle. The driver had been decapitated. The commander was sitting on top of the vehicle and had been blown away. And the mini-team, the engineers, had been sitting on top instead of inside as they were wont to do. All but one of them were killed as well. And the problem was, they weren't all there. They were scattered about. So for the first little while I hovered around and it was in a large, open sort of kunai grass patch and I was saying 'There's a piece here, there's a bit there' as we were trying to put things together. Then the Air Force arrived and wouldn't land until the area was secure. It wasn't anything to do with the pilots involved but their SOPs were so particular that they weren't allowed to land in a contact area until it was secured. I told them I'd been in and no one was shooting and there were wounded to extract

but they wouldn't land until more infantry arrived. It was those restrictive procedures that made them look bad sometimes, because most of their drivers were fine. But for us it was different. You went in whether they were shooting at you or not. In the Army, that was part of the deal. That was your job. So those differences between RAAF and Army sometimes led to a personal side and created difficulties.[24]

The Possums flew 365 hours in support of *Overlord*. OC Neil Harden's diary noted an increase in the number and variety of tasks such as command and control, radio relay, map and artillery spotting. After *Overlord*, 4RAR's command post was established permanently on Courtenay Hill as that area had become the centre of operations. Operation *Hermit Park* followed. On 22 June Lieutenants Smokey Dawson and Ian Sinnott carried out flare drops over A Squadron, 3 Cavalry who had sprung an ambush and required light for a sweep through to collect enemy bodies.

Operations *Iron Fox* and *North Ward* continued the harassment of enemy forces in the north. The latter was in progress on 18 August when the Australian Prime Minister, William McMahon, announced that the task force would cease operations in Phuoc Tuy in October. First out would be 3RAR on 6 October, with 4RAR, less Delta Company, following on 8 December. Delta Company would remain for three months to secure 1ALSG at Vung Tau. A detachment of 161's Kiowas would also remain.

Operation Ivanhoe (18 September–2 October 1971)

Operation *Ivanhoe* was perhaps the defining point of 4RAR's second tour. People sniffer missions flown by 161 Recce Flight during *North Ward* had indicated the presence of an enemy force, thought to be part of 33 North Vietnamese Army Regiment, north of the task force area to the east of Nui Le. A reconnaissance by 161 on 10 September found new tracks leading into Phuoc Tuy from Long Khanh province. *Ivanhoe* was mounted to find and confront the enemy regiment. On 21 September, 4RAR was involved in a number of heavy contacts with the enemy in the area east of Route 2 in the northern half of Phuoc Tuy province.

The engagement escalated as Delta Company's 11 Platoon, led by Second Lieutenant Gary McKay, came under attack from a huge bunker network. McKay was severely wounded in the ensuing firefight and was awarded the Military Cross for his courage under fire. It was a rough day and night for the soldiers on the ground. However, McKay had a friend and classmate from Scheyville on the scene. DS pilot Second Lieutenant John Sonneveld flew more than eleven hours in his Kiowa, delivering urgently required ammunition. When it became obvious that a large enemy force was involved, he continued his reconnaissance operations at treetop height to locate the enemy and guide other elements of the battalion to their positions. He was awarded the DFC for his skill and daring during this last major engagement with the enemy in Phuoc Tuy.

A time to plan

The announcement of the withdrawal of the task force brought in the end phase for the units involved. Suddenly, there was a sense of relief that the long and inconclusive campaign would soon be over. Operations would continue, but plans for going home also had to be put in place. For the supporting units like 161, leaving Nui Dat was not a simple exercise. Back in the land of the round eyes, there were embittered men who worshipped the gods of Accountancy and Inventory. To these soulless misfits, the possession of an extra spare tyre was a crime. After more than six years of begging, borrowing, souveniring and stealing, 161 had a lot more than that. A Bird Dog, for starters.

13

The end phase:
August 1971–March 1972

Major Neil Harden's diary notes for August 1971 relate that 'the unit has been warned for a move to Vung Tau in late September and is required to be operational by 6 October. Preparation is well under way, together with preparation for the move back to Australia sometime in December.'[1] The moves and accounting compliance requirements called for drastic measures. The OC thoughtfully appointed Captain Tub Matheson as stocktake officer. Tub was not a stocktake enthusiast but complied with his instructions at least some of the time:

> When the word came that we were pulling out we went from wartime to peacetime accounting, which pissed me right off because I was stocktake officer and couldn't go flying much. Every time I did the boss would come up on channel, 'Possum Four, this is Niner! Get back on the ground, Matheson. Have you finished the stocktake?'[2]

Radio Sergeant Brian Reardon remembered the stocktake well because he had a large surplus of radios provided by the ever-generous US maintenance system:

> The OC came in this day doing his checks and he got around to ARC-51 BX UHF radios. He said to me, 'How many 51 BXs have you got?' I said, 'Well, how many do you want?' I threw off this cover and there were heaps,

and he dressed me down and read me the riot act! Of course, I had just carried on the tradition. There were already too many when I first went there. To make it worse I'd just sent a troop down to Vung Tau to change a chassis over and I knew full well he was going to come back with a new radio under his arm. I'm thinking, 'DJ, please don't come in while the boss is here.' Next thing, bang, the door opens. And he comes in and drops it on the bench. The boss just looked at it, looked at me, swore and went out. And he's never let me forget it![3]

The purge went on for weeks. Excess items and contraband were disposed of in everything from the flaming furies to the South China Sea. Sad times had indeed fallen on 161.

Return to Vung Tau

On 13 September, Captain Rowan Monteith led the advance party to Vung Tau to establish accommodation and working areas. The Flight's headquarters and orderly room were allocated space in the 2 Advanced Ordnance Depot car park and accommodation for all ranks was organised in that unit's lines. The operational element and workshops were set up adjacent to the RAAF Caribou squadron at the airfield. Rowan remembered the new living area only too well:

> The Engineers gave us this area and we built this row of tents and sand-bagged them. We worked like drovers' dogs for about ten days. On the afternoon we finished, Vung Tau was hit by the mother of all storms. Next day all you could see were the tops of the tents. It turned out that, unbeknown to us, although surely the Engineers must have known better, this was a sort of catchment area for the whole bloody Vung Tau Army base. It was just a huge flood. The whole thing was destroyed, so we had to pull it down and rebuild it. It became a great joke; poor silly bloody Monteith who'd built all these tents where there was ten feet of water whenever it rained.
>
> Everything was bodgie built. We set up operations in an old Conex on the airfield. These large containers were reasonably useful; we had air conditioners in the windows and that sort of thing. We scraped and stole. We moved our admin side into one of those big 40 x 20 tents. From then things went on pretty much as normal. Working conditions weren't great. There was an embargo on road movement at Vung Tau during curfew hours, so a duty officer, CP staff, night standby pilots and duty maintenance crew had to sleep on the airfield. We were still doing a lot of operations, although our VRs were now much closer in, around the Rung Sat area and between

Vung Tau and Baria, and that swampy area up towards the Nui Thi Vais. And we still patrolled the Long Hais out to the east. From there it just tailed down slowly.[4]

On 1 October, control of the 161 command net was passed to the new CP at Vung Tau and the main body departed from Nui Dat. Four days later, the Flight's area at Nui Dat was handed over to 4RAR. The rear party, commanded by Captain Tub Matheson, moved to Vung Tau by road. There was more than a little sadness at the fate of the task force area that had been home for so long. Rowan Monteith described the scene:

> The saddest thing was the destruction of Nui Dat. We left it as a going concern; all of the tents and fittings and hangars and buildings. The Vietnamese came in and just tore the place apart. I can remember flying over it in the last months and it was just a pile of foundations. All of the buildings and the hangars were gone. It was all for sale on the Baria market.[5]

Operations from Vung Tau

On 6 October, 3RAR sailed on HMAS *Sydney*. Three Kiowas, flown by Neil Harden, Mick Reynolds and Blue Wright, together with a voice-equipped Porter flown by John McGhie, made a formation flypast to farewell and serenade the battalion. One of the fun things about voice operations was the occasional opportunity to reduce the grunts to tears to assist in their emotional rehabilitation.

The phased withdrawal of Australian forces from Nui Dat continued. The Flight flew numerous VR and people sniffer missions, but there was little contact with the enemy. On 7 November, Lieutenant Grant Steel flew the last DS task in South Vietnam as 4RAR ceased operations. On the same day, Major Neil Harden with Lieutenants Mick Reynolds and Creagh Mecham provided continuous top cover for convoys from Nui Dat to Vung Tau from dawn until the move was completed in mid-afternoon.

The daily routine of first light recces and administrative support tasks continued from Vung Tau. On 26 October, Second Lieutenant John McGhie was flying the Army Training Team pay run when he was hit by ground fire:

I was trying to get into one of the bases, Dong Tam, and the weather was not conducive to getting in there and so I'd gone under some cloud and I was probably at 500 feet, the wrong height to be. I still remember the Clang! Clang! Clang! as the aeroplane was hit. A warrant officer on the Training Team was in the back of the aircraft and this hole suddenly appeared in the cabin above his head. He said, 'Excuse me! I think we've been hit.' The engine stopped at that point and I did the approved pilot emergency thing which was 'Turn off everything that was ON and turn on everything that was OFF'. One of the rounds had actually cut the fuel line which was only about as big as your little finger. We think that the electric fuel pump actually pumped the fuel across the hole. So the engine was sucking on one side and the pump was blowing from the other side and the guys at the base then saw me coming because there was a huge plume of fuel behind the aeroplane. It was just pissing out everywhere.

I got the thing down and then I had to try to get it fixed. That was my first and only experience of trying to use the American Army telephone system in Vietnam. They still used the old field phones and you'd wind the ringer thing and get the switchboard. Then you'd have to go around the whole switchboard circuit to eventually get to your unit. But each time you started to make progress there'd be a 'click!' and the line was gone. So after a while I wandered back out to the aircraft and called on the FM radio and by chance managed to talk to a helicopter that was flying quite high in the Nui Dat area. I told him I had a problem, and an hour or two later a helicopter turned up with some maintenance guys and we tore up the floor, found the hole in the fuel line and covered it with a bit of plastic pipe. We patched up a few holes in the tail and fuselage and I flew the thing home.

An interesting bit was that the guy who was sitting in the right-hand front seat in the cabin was very, very lucky that day because I'd picked up mail from the Training Team people at one of the bases. It was quite heavy, so instead of chucking it right behind the back seats I stacked it behind my seat so that it was up against a firm bulkhead. And this round had come up through the fuselage, through the fuel line, through the floor and into these mailbags. It rattled around and fell on the floor. It would have hit this guy in the side of the head if not for the bags. I gave him the bullet. I said it was his since it had his name on it.[6]

Ground fire incidents actually increased markedly after the move to Vung Tau. On 15 November, Lieutenant Grant Steel was flying a reconnaissance mission north of Long Son Island when he located an occupied enemy camp. Before he could report this information, he was engaged by several automatic weapons and his aircraft was badly damaged by at least a dozen rounds. He nursed the aircraft along until he could land in a relatively safe area. Neither he nor his passenger was injured, although Neil Harden recalled that the latter had a lucky escape:

> When I was talking to this new ordnance officer—it was his first day in country and he probably arrived a bit late to see if he could help with the withdrawal or to clean up some of the mess—I said, 'Have you checked your pistol holster?' He said 'Why?' I said, 'Well, you seem to have a tear in your magazine pouch on the side of your holster and there's a black mark.' He pulled it out and there was a bullet lodged in the magazine and half of the bullets inside were distorted and leaking. He never even knew he'd been hit.[7]

Grant Steel distinguished himself during his tour with 161. He had previously served in Vietnam as an infantry platoon commander during 4RAR's first tour. His detailed knowledge of both the terrain and the difficulties faced by the soldiers on the ground fitted him well for the duties of a direct support pilot. He was awarded the DFC for his outstanding service, and in particular the skills he demonstrated when his aircraft was shot down. He had carried on the tradition of notable contributions by NZ Army pilots to 161's operations. On 10 November, he and John McGhie flew the last Kiowa and Porter document runs. Other than the major accident to Grant's Kiowa, the remainder of November's operations were relatively trouble free. The OC's diary summarised the operational situation:

> With the withdrawal of all Australian forces from Nui Dat on 7 November 1971, the unit has experienced a considerable drop in flying hours, particularly on the rotary wing side. The task force is now concerning itself only with the areas immediately to the north and northwest of Vung Tau and concentrated VRs in these areas are continuing. There has been a marked increase in the number of liaison flights to the Saigon and Long Binh areas. The document runs carried out by rotary wing aircraft for many years have now ceased with the Liaison Officers being brought back in. The first light road recces only cover the road between Vung Tau and Baria. Plans for four Kiowas to remain behind until March 1972 are now complete and Captain Tub Matheson will command the small detachment left behind. Accommodation for this element will be at Vung Tau airfield, using the space vacated by 9 Squadron which leaves early in December.[8]

Last out of Luscombe

Sergeant Mike Croker joined Sergeants Les Idiens and Bill Hudnott at Nui Dat in August 1971. When 161 moved to Vung Tau, the three air traffic controllers stayed behind with the firemen to run the airfield until operations ceased. Early in November orders came through to deactivate the tower. Les and Mike went out to Vung Tau on the last road convoy, while Bill Hudnott stayed for another day that he won't forget:

> On 7 November, I sat in a lounge chair at the end of the runway with a PRC-77 radio controlling the final chalks as we pulled out to Vung Tau. I was real cocky because I had been in Nui Dat with the Americans the day it opened in '66 and I was the last Possum to leave in '71. Then, as the last aircraft was coming to pick me up, the SAS blew up a heap of mine detonator cord. The pilot saw the explosion and refused to land as he thought it was Charlie incoming. I didn't know what it was and rolled onto the ground trying to keep as low a profile as I could and even a lounge chair was too high! He finally came and took me away from all that. The last Possum had left the Dat.[9]

The main body goes home

On 8 November, the Flight was advised that its main body would depart South Vietnam on 23 December. The advance party, commanded by Captain Rowan Monteith, left on 9 December with the bulk of the Flight's equipment and stores. Lieutenant Mick Reynolds assumed Rowan's duties as second in command.

The fixed wing pilots continued 'shush' missions and liaison tasks until the three remaining Porters were withdrawn from service on 13 December and prepared for shipment to Australia in January 1972. Since their introduction in December 1969, the Porters had racked up 6987 sorties for a total of 8053 flying hours.[10] The decision to return the Porters by ship was a disappointment for the OC and his pilots, who wanted to fly them home. John McGhie had been nominated to examine the viability of this option:

> The only problem was that there were a couple of long over-water legs; one from South Vietnam to Malaysia and another from Kupang to Darwin.

We needed the ferry kit that had been used by Pilatus to fly them out to Australia from Switzerland. It was a very simple thing, just three 44 gallon drums in a wooden rack that sat in the fuselage with a fuel pump on it. We were going to do it in pairs; take two aircraft back and then return with the kits to take the other two home. But it didn't happen. We didn't get the necessary approvals.[11]

Instead of finalising details for an interesting ferry trip through the Far East, John McGhie found himself with a much less glamorous job to wind up his Vietnam experience:

> I finished flying part way through December 1971. I think the boss said I was getting a bit twitchy, which I probably was because I realised I'd survived that far. I think when you first went there, you never even thought about the survival question, but as you got closer to going home you'd begin to think that, having survived that far, it'd be a pity to not make it.
>
> Neil Harden gave me the job of Unit Packing Officer. There were all these shipping containers on the parade ground at Vung Tau. So I filled them up. We had a big collection of captured weapons, but were only allowed to take back two weapons for each Mess. So I loaded all these extra weapons in a Porter and flew out over the South China Sea and splashed them.[12]

Meanwhile, Rowan Monteith arrived at the 1 Aviation Regiment base at Oakey, and set about winding up the Flight:

> We had Hell's own trouble because we had to bring the Bird Dog home. It came disguised as a crate of spares. And there were other problems. It looked as if containers had been opened and stuff taken. Luckily, Tub Matheson was still in country and I was sending signals to him saying 'We need 20 Land Rover tyres' or whatever. So he started collecting the odd things we needed. We had problems too where there was extra gear that someone had put into the containers. I remember Staff Polkinghorne and myself sitting down at the back of the shed at Oakey one day and we cut the blades off 200 M-16 bayonets.
>
> It was just stupid. We had to get rid of all sorts of stuff that was usable, or was memorabilia, or whatever. There was a theory that if you brought something home that wasn't Australian kit that you couldn't maintain it. So what? Use it until it breaks and then throw it away. You might get years out of it. However, the powers above me made those decisions and I had to follow them. So we unloaded the Conexes, brought stuff to charge; everything had to have paperwork. Stuff that was a dime a dozen in Vietnam was suddenly accountable. And serial numbers didn't match up because we had

swapped and acquired so much kit. 'But where's the one you were issued with?' they'd say. It was crazy. It was a very difficult task to wind it up.

In the end we solved the problems and there was lots of regimental property that was held in trust for a while because we didn't want to lose the identity of 161; things that some people thought we shouldn't have. There was a lot of Viet Cong stuff that had been collected and so forth. Eventually, 171 Flight down in Sydney was redesignated 161 and a lot of gear was sent to them. And now, 161 Squadron is in Darwin and they have a special room dedicated to the collection. The various OCs have done a lot since to preserve and add to it.[13]

The main body of 161 flew to Tan Son Nhut early on 23 December and departed by Defence charter. The traditional cheer of relief would no doubt have been heard as the QANTAS Freedom Bird rotated off the runway and headed south. Only Tub Matheson's rearguard party remained. A long and vital chapter in the history of Army Aviation was almost over.

The final four

It was lonely at Vung Tau after the main body of 161 left, in particular because it was Christmas. Nevertheless, there was plenty to keep Tub Matheson and his men busy:

> The detachment continues to fly the majority of its liaison missions between Vung Tau, Saigon and Long Binh. Reconnaissance tasks, which until 21 January were confined to the first light recce of Route 15 between Vung Tau and Baria, have now increased. Other commitments permitting, the unit now carries out three coastal recce missions per week for the Third Coastal Zone Intelligence Office. Even from our task force-imposed minimum altitude of 1500 feet above ground, pilots are detecting numerous movements of persons and small craft in non-civilian access areas. The aircraft have continually taken ground fire, however, no hits have been recorded. On separate occasions Captain Matheson and Lieutenants Triplett and Mecham have carried out AOP tasks using Vietnamese artillery. Due to extreme ranges, the language problem and apparently non-calibrated weapons, results have been mediocre.
>
> During the last week of the month, The Australian Army Training Team headquarters moved from Free World Headquarters in Saigon to Van Kiep and experienced communication difficulties between Van Kiep, Vung Tau and Saigon. For this reason, the unit commenced a twice-daily courier

Maj Graeme Hill–Smith, Capt Barry Donald (KIA 3 December 1969) and friends, Nui Dat, 1969.
Photograph courtesy 161 Association.

2Lt Alan Jellie, KIA 3 December 1969, Nui Dat.
Photograph courtesy 161 Association.

Sgt 'Rocky' Hoare and Lt Terry Ellis, Nui Dat, 1969.
Photograph: Rocky Hoare.

Team Rockets, Nui Dat, 1971. L-R Lt Digby Mackworth (RW pilot),
Cfn Kevin Thrush, Cpl Bill Wright (Engines), Cfn Blue Nicklin (Airframes),
Cpl Russell Gordon (Radio), Sgt David Payne (Ops), Cpl Laurie Wood (Airframes),
Cfn Bruce Cairnes (Electrical), Sgt Brian Reardon (Radio).
Photograph courtesy 161 Association.

Fitters loading rockets into 19-pod launchers on Porter, Nui Dat, 1970.
Photograph: Fred Reus.

Cfn Fred Hardidge with Sioux with M–40 grenade launcher fitted, 1970.
Photograph: Fred Reus.

Maj Phil Calvert (right) and Sioux pilot 2Lt Peter Bysouth with the Honorary Colonel of the Australian Army Aviation Corps, Federal Minister for National Development Mr Reginald Swartz, Nui Dat, 1970.
Photograph: Phil Calvert.

Maj Neil Harden and Lt John McGhie with WO Wayne Shannon, AATTV and Allied soldiers, Pleiku area, 1971.
Photograph: Neil Harden.

Pilot's view of Luscombe Field, circa 1970. The 161 flight line and revetments are left of the Runway 28 threshold, with the 161 hangars and unit area opposite the flight line at the edge of the rubber plantation.
Photograph: Bruno Kwas.

Airframe fitter Cpl Len Avery with the shell of Bunny II, Nui Dat, 1970.
Photograph: Len Avery.

Bunny II in flight, Nui Dat, 1971.
Photograph: Bob Carroll.

In safe hands. Luscombe crash crew, Sgt Geoff Moller and firies.
Photograph: Geoff Moller.

Luscombe Tower and Fire section, Nui Dat, 1971.
Photograph: Jim Sneesby.

Kiowas on flight line at Nui Dat, September 1971.
Photograph: Bob Carroll.

Lt Mick Reynolds with Kiowa, 1971.
Photograph courtesy 161 Association.

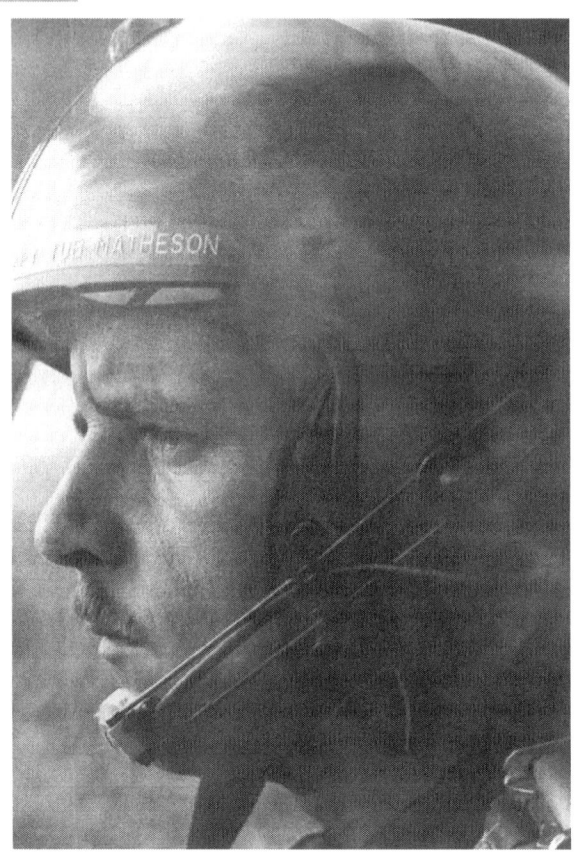

Capt Tub Matheson,
Nui Dat, 1971.
*Photograph courtesy
161 Association.*

Laurie Woods, Bob Zitzlesberger and Len Avery, Nui Dat, 1971.
Photograph: Len Avery.

Relaxing in the OR's Sundowner Club, Nui Dat 1971. L–R John Goritchan, Alan Murray, Wally Nelson, Fred Bower, Gary Nicklin, Ron Hodges.
Photograph: Len Avery.

End phase: return to Vung Tau, 1971.
Photograph courtesy 161 Association.

Preparing Porters for return to Australia, Vung Tau, December 1971.
Photograph courtesy 161 Association.

service between the three locations carrying personnel as well as private and official mail. Due to the scaling down of American Army aircraft numbers, training team members have frequently used the unit's aircraft for liaison between the various training bases in Phuoc Tuy province.[14]

The detachment was required to provide two of its four aircraft daily in support of the Australian task force. The workshop, led by Sergeant Phil Watson, produced a serviceability rate of 82 per cent. It was becoming increasingly difficult to obtain Kiowa spares at short notice through US Army sources, so to maintain a high rate of availability it was often necessary to swap components among aircraft. Sergeant Watson and his troops did a fine job until the end.

Operations continued through February, with a large increase in flying hours due to an increased requirement for liaison runs between Vung Tau, Saigon and Long Binh. On 14 February, the telephone links between Free World in Saigon and Vung Tau were greatly reduced and the twice daily courier task was increased to four missions. Each pilot flew in excess of 130 hours for the month, and on most sorties the aircraft carried maximum weight. An RA Signals member travelled on each flight to handle the large amount of classified material being carried. The Flight had maintained its prodigious flying effort to the last.

On 29 February the detachment flew numerous liaison tasks between the task force and HMAS *Sydney*. The last operational sortie was flown by Tub Matheson, who carried his detachment's heavy baggage to Free World at 2100 hours. Two days later he and his pilots flew the detachment's four Kiowas to Saigon, painted out the 'red rats' and handed them over to the American Army. During the short period the Kiowas had been in service with 161, their pilots had flown 3766 sorties for a total of 3534 flying hours.[15]

It was time to go home. Many valuable lessons had been learned from the aspects of both operations and maintenance, and many very good friends had been made. Perhaps the finest tribute to the Possums was that paid by the Fourth Battalion:

> Ever keen, the 'Red Barons' John, Digby, Terry, Fraser, Tom, Blue Wright, Mick and Kiwi Grant [ex 4RAR/NZ platoon commander], were usually found in the Intelligence Section terminal . . . fabricating plots to log even more hours in support of the Fourth. No task was ever too big, or too small, for them to successfully complete on our behalf. Typically, our direct support

Kiowa was airborne for eleven hours, twenty minutes on 21 September 1971, dropping in much-needed ammunition to Delta Company.

Possum grew up in South Vietnam. The pilots were remarkable young men. There was always a swashbuckling aspect about them, heightened by their sky blue berets, the Aviation Corps wings surmounted by the crowned lion on their breast, and the inevitable 9mm pistol, worn, for convenience sake, in a shoulder holster. They were invariably cheerful and no task was ever too difficult or too much trouble. And they were, besides, immensely courageous.[16]

On 4 March 1972, Tub Matheson led his party home to Australia. The adventures of the Possums in South Vietnam were over, but their story would not be forgotten by the soldiers on the ground they had served so well.

Epilogue

The spirit and tradition of 161 Recce Flight lives on in another incarnation: that of 161 Reconnaissance Squadron based in Darwin. This unit has experienced active service in support of UN forces in East Timor and has served in other regional areas. Looking to the future, new aircraft like the Tiger armed reconnaissance helicopter will ensure that Australia's forces can continue to perform with distinction on their own or in operations with its allies. Yet perhaps there is still a role for slow and trusty steeds like those of the Vietnam era. Not every task needs a super machine with terrifying firepower. Sometimes an illegal rocket pod, a homemade grenade launcher or a detergent bomb is just the ticket.

Today, there is little sign of 161's long presence at Nui Dat. A few houses are scattered along the site of Luscombe field, with a small school across the way built with the assistance of Australian veterans. Rubber is processed where once stood the control tower. Not much is left of the runway, just patches of cracked asphalt with weeds poking through. We might never have been there. But I like to think that, on a quiet night, a keen listener might hear some ghostly echoes of the past; muffled laughter and a song, perhaps, and the clang of a dropped spanner or the cough of a cold engine starting up for a night recce. And in the treetops, against the backdrop of the stars, it might just be possible to make out the silhouette of a possum, patiently waiting and watching for movement below.

Appendix 1

161 Reconnaissance Flight/161 (Independent) Reconnaissance Flight:
Nominal Roll 1965–72

Note: This unit roll is complete according to the records of the 161 Recce Association. The author apologises for any inadvertent omissions. The roll does not include personnel who were attached to the unit for duty or administrative purposes as these records are incomplete. To those who contributed to 161's role but were not on posted strength, the author and the Association extend appreciation for and acknowledgment of your efforts.

Adams, RS, Cpl, 69–70
Ahern, BE, Pte, 71
Aird, D, 2Lt, 69–70
Alcorn, R, Cpl, 69–70
Alderson, GP, Spr, 69–70
Alexander, RM, L/Cpl, 68–69
Allen, JG, Cfn, 70
Allman, JR, Sgt, 66–67
Alsop, K, Sgt, 68–69
Ambler, DJ, Pte, 67–68
Amos, AJ, Cfn, 68
Anderson, GL, Tpr, 68–69
Andrews, RK, Pte, 67–68
Angus, DR, Cfn, 69–70

Arkinstall, NG, Cfn, 68–69
Arnold, JL, Pte, 68–69
Arnold, RT, L/Bdr, 71
Arnott, TW, Cfn, 67–68
Ashley, CA, Pte, 69
Askew, RW, 2Lt, 66–67
Avern, GH, Cpl, 65–66
Avery, L, Cpl, 70–71
Baker, DJ, Pte, 67–68
Baker, PF, Cpl, 68–69
Baldacchino, V, Gnr, 68–69
Bale, J, Cfn, 69–70
Bambridge, GJ, Pte, 68–69

Bamford, KG, Pte, 71
Banks, PL, Cpl, 69–70
Bank-Smith, SR, Gnr, 69–70
Banner, CH, Cfn, 70–71
Barlow, FC, Capt, 71
Barnes, H, WO2, 70–71
Barron, CJ, 2Lt, 66–67
Bartos, JC, Sgt, 69
Barwell, GR, 2Lt, 71
Baryla, S, Cpl, 71
Bass, RA, SSgt, 68–69
Baxter, RS, WO2, 68–69
Bean, BL, Cpl, 66
Bell, DJ, 2Lt, 70–71

Appendix 1: Nominal Roll

Bell, K, LAC, 65–66
Bell, RV, WO2, 71
Benes, A, Sgt, 69–70
Benfield, FH, Cpl, 70–71
Benjamin, GV, Sgt, 69–70
Bennett, NR, Cfn, 66
Bennett, S, Sgt, 68–69
Benson, HA, Maj, 68–69
Betts, RG, Cpl, 67–68
Bevan, RJ, Cpl, 67–68
Bevans, ET, Cfn, 69–70
Bishop, RC, Bdr, 70–71
Black, JW, Cpl, 65–66
Blair, TH, L/Cpl, 65–66
Blakey, J, Pte, 65–66
Blanchette, BR, Spr, 69–70
Blissett, PM, Cpl, 67–68
Blunden, BR, Pte, 68
Boland, MD, Capt, 67–68
Bonser, DH, Bdr, 69–70
Booby, DJ, Cfn, 71
Bootes, PH, Sgt, 66–67
Boothroyd, RP, Cpl, 69–70
Bostock, NL, Bdr, 68–69
Bostock, WJ, Pte, 67–68
Bower, FE, L/Cpl, 70–71
Bracken, IW, Cfn, 68–69
Britnell, OE, Cfn, 68–69
Brooker, E, Capt, 68–69
Brookes, BW, Spr, 71
Brooks, JC, Cfn, 67–68
Brophy, MP, Pte, 69–70
Brown, BA, Pte, 69–70
Brown, DF, Sgt, 67–68, 70–71
Brown, DF, Sgt, 70–71
Brown, JA, Cpl, 66–67
Brown, NJ, Cpl, 70–71
Bruce, BG, L/Cpl, 68–69
Brundle, NA, Pte, 68–69
Bryan, J, L/Cpl, 71
Buckley, HJ, Pte, 69–70

Budd, DN, Cfn, 65–66, Cpl, 68
Bultitude, KG, Cfn, 70–71
Burgess, A, Sgt, 67
Burow, DJ, Cpl, 68
Butterworth, M, Pte, 66
Butterworth, NJ, Gnr, 70–71
Byng, M, Cpl, 66–67
Bysouth, PA, 2Lt, 69–70
Cairnes, BW, Cfn, 70–71
Cairney, V, Cfn, 67–68
Cairns, KR, Capt, 70–71
Calder, B, Cpl, 69–70
Callaghan, MR, Spr, 67
Calvert, PJ, Maj, 70–71
Cameron, HJ, Cpl, 68–69
Campbell, CJ, WO2, 66–67
Campbell, GS, Pte, 68–69
Campbell, JD, Capt, 66–67
Cardow, DK, Tpr, 68–69
Carpenter, WG, Cfn, 68–69
Carroll, RJ, Cpl, 71–72
Carter, GH, Pte, 71
Carter, RC, Cfn, 67–68
Castle, ED, Cfn, 68–69
Champion, BP, Pte, 67–68
Chandler, DW, Cpl, 66–67
Channells, GC, Pte, 67
Chapman, TJ, Pte, 68–69
Charles, SR, Cfn, 69–70
Christgoergl, HG, Cpl, 68–69
Chumak, V, Pte, 69–70
Clark, BV, Pte, 71
Clark, PJ, Cpl, 69–70
Clarke, JC, Cfn, 66–67
Clarke, N, Sgt, 71
Cochran, PL, Sgt, 69

Cockerell, D, 2Lt, 65–66
Cocking, CD, Cpl, 69–70
Coffey, CS, Tpr, 70
Coffey, DB, 2Lt, 70–71
Coggan, JL, Capt, 67–68
Coker, RJ, Sgt, 69–70
Colclough, RK, 2Lt, 67–68
Coleman, NR, Cpl, 68–69
Collin, DJ, Cfn, 70–71
Collins, DA, WO1/Lt, 69–70
Collins, JP, Pte, 71
Conroy, MF, Tpr, 69–70
Consalvo, PJ, Cpl, 68–69
Constable, GA, Maj, 67–68, KIA 23.5.68
Conyers, GC, Pte, 71
Coombs, R, L/Cpl, 65–66
Corbett, GC, Pte, 66–67
Corkery, MA, Cpl, 70–71
Courtney, CE, Cfn, 67–69
Cousins, KL, Pte, 67–68
Crawford, RI, Cfn, 67–68
Crawford, RJ, Cpl, 69–70
Croker, MH, Sgt, 71
Crook, CD, Pte, 65–66
Crook, JF, Cpl, 65–66
Crook, PL, 2Lt, 68–69
Cross, GL, Spr, 70–71
Crotty, IR, Gnr, 69–70
Croxford, JF, Pte, 68–69
Csibi, L, Cfn, 70–71
Cummings, PG, Cpl, 65–66
Cupitt, KH, Cfn, 67–68
Curnow, FS, Capt, 68–69
Custance, JS, Sgt, 68–69
Daniels, RR, Cpl, 71
Darts, CB, Cfn, 70–71
Davidson, GE, Cpl, 70–71

Davies, W, 2Lt, 66
Davis, PC, Sgt, 70–71
Davis, TG, WO2, 70–71
Dawber, LS, Sgt, 65–66
Dawson, DB, Lt, 70–71
De Loryn, PB, Cpl, 71
Deacon, GS, Cpl, 67–68, Sgt, 69–70
Dean, GJ, Cpl, 70–71
Dick, BJ, 2Lt, 69–70
Dickson, NJ, 2Lt, 68–69
Digance, RD, Cpl, 69–70
Digweed, JF, Capt, 69–70
Diss, IS, Cpl, 68–69
Dobrowolski, S, Pte, 67–68
Docen, RA, Pte, 67–68
Dodd, PS, Cfn, 67–68
Dodds, KL, Sgt, 67–68
Donald, BC, Capt, 68, 69, KIA 3.12.69
Donnelly, FP, Bdr, 66–67
Dover, D, Cpl, 71
Downey, AW, L/Cpl, 67–68
Downing, DJ, Cpl, 70–71
Doyle, LG, Maj, 66–67
Doyle, RD, Pte, 65–66
Driffield, MC, Tpr, 70
Driver, ED, Lt, 69–70
Drummond, IG, Pte, 68–69
Dupree, AL, Cpl, 71
Duus, GM, 2Lt, 67–68
Dyson, JB, L/Cpl, 66–67
Earley, DH, 2Lt, 69–70
Ebner, CE, Sgt, 65–66
Edie, LR, Cfn, 71
Edwards, FE, Cpl, 68–69
Egan, PR, Cfn, 70–71
Ehsman, PJ, Cpl, 69–70
Einam, KA, FSgt, 68
Elek, J, Sgt, 71
Elledge, MC, Cfn, 68–69

Ellis, BW, L/Cpl, 69–70
Ellis, J, Sgt, 66–67
Ellis, RJ, L/Cpl 68, Cpl 70–71
Ellis, TR, Lt, 68–69
Ellwood, R, Lt, 70–71
Elson, KT, Sgt, 66–67
Engleby, GJ, Sgt, 67–68
Ettridge, DT, 2Lt, 65–66
Fagan, WH, Cpl, 66
Farbridge, GW, Pte, 66–67
Farrell, JP, Cfn, 68–69
Fellenberg, RF, Cpl, 67–68
Feltham, RG, Pte, 67–68
Ferluga, RM, Cpl, 70
Finnigan, FT, Pte, Sep 65, Sep 66
Fisher, Terry, W, Pte, 70–71
Flanagan, WB, Capt, 69–70
Fleming, RJ, Cfn, 67–68
Florian, DG, Cfn, 69–70
Ford, GJ, Cpl, 68
Forrest, BJ, Capt, 67–68
Foulkes, TC, Spr, 69–70
Foyle, GR, Cpl, 71–72
Fraser, MR, Cfn, 66–67
Fritsch, AJ, 2Lt, 66–67
Frost, WR, 2Lt, 68–69
Gallagher, WA, L/Cpl, 69–70
Gallasch, BM, Pte, 69–70
Gardner, RH, Cpl, 70–71
Garrett, MA, Cfn, 70–71
Garton, PL, 2Lt, 67–68
Gaze, RJ, Pte, 66–67
Gepp, FA, Sgt, 69
Gerard, DE, 2Lt, 68–69
Gibb, TN, SSgt, 69–70
Gibbons, JE, Cpl, 68–69
Gibson, FM, 2Lt, 70–71

Gibson, HJ, Sgt, 65–66
Gibson, KJ, Cfn, 69–70
Gibson, LJ, Pte, 69–70
Giles, SC, Cfn, 68–69
Gill, AG, Cpl, 69–70
Gillies, EJ, Pte, 71
Gilligan, TJ, Cpl, 67–68
Ginman, P, Sgt, 67
Gissane, GJ, Cpl, 69–70
Goldspink, RD, 2Lt, 66–67
Good, SR, Cpl, 69–70
Gordon, CJ, Cpl, 68–69
Gordon, RW, Cpl, 70–71
Goritchan, JJ, Cfn, 70–71
Graham, RJ, Cfn, 71
Green, JD, Sgt, 67–68
Greenbury, PJ, Cpl, 67–68
Gregory, RL, Cfn, 71
Griffiths, AA, Gnr, 68–69
Grimmer, RG, Sgt, 71
Grosvenor, FL, Cpl, 71
Guild, JA, Lt, 65–66
Guivarra, TW, 2Lt, 66–67
Gygar, TJ, Lt, 70–71
Hailes, PL, L/Cpl, 67–68
Ham, CN, Pte, 68–69
Hambly, SH, Cfn, 71
Hamilton-Smith, NW, Cfn, 70–71
Hancock, RG, Pte, 66–67
Hand, DJ, Pte, 68–69
Hansford, RF, Cfn, 68–69
Harden, NH, Maj, 71
Hardidge, FR, Cfn, 69–70
Harding, DJ, Cpl, 67–68
Harris, AL, Sgt, 66–67
Harris, GJ, Cpl, 70–71
Harrison, WN, Sgt, 69–70
Hart, PT, Sgt, 70–71
Hart, RJ, Bdr, 65–66
Harvey, GE, Gnr, 70
Harvey, JE, Gnr, 71
Hatton, JB, Pte, 67–68

Hawkins, PJ, Pte, 68–69
Hayes, TJ, 2Lt, 70–71
Hayne, J, Sgt, 69–70
Haynes, W, Cpl, 69–70
Hayward, E, Gnr, 68–69
Healey, TC, Sgt, 71
Heapy, WJ, Cpl, 69–70, 71
Heard, MD, Pte, 70–71
Hehir, BA, Pte, 68–69
Henderson, JV, L/Cpl, 70–71
Hendrie, RT, Pte, 68–69
Henry, PE, Pte, 67
Hepburn, GG, Cpl, 67–68
Herbig, KF, Pte, 70
Heritage, NE, WO1, 70
Heron, WA, 2Lt, 67–68
Hesse, TF, Grn, 66–67
Hewitt, PR, Pte, 70–71
Higginbottom, AJ, Sgt, 65–66
Hills, C, Cpl, 67–68
Hills, RC, Capt, 70–71
Hill-Smith, G, Maj, 69–70
Hilton, BE, Cpl, 67–68
Hindmarch, DG, Cfn, 71
Hoare, RE, Cpl, 68–69, Sgt, 70–71
Hobbs, RW, Bdr, 70
Hobbs, SV, Cpl, 67–68
Hodges, RW, Cfn, 70–71
Hodgkinson, RE, Cpl, 66–67
Holland, R, Pte, 65–66
Howard, JF, Lt, 71
Hudnott, WJ, Sgt, 70–71
Hughes, JN, Pte, 70–71
Humby, JA, Cpl, 68–69
Humby, RJ, Cpl, 68
Humphrey, RC, Cpl, 65–66
Humphreys, BL, Cpl, 65
Humphreys, JA, Cpl, 69–70, 71

Hutchinson, KD, Cfn, 69–70
Hutchinson, R, Lt, 67–68
Hutchison, RP, Pte, 65–66
Hyde, L, Cpl, 69–70
Hyde, WF, Trp, 68–69
Ible, AG, Cfn, 67–68
Idiens, LJ, Sgt, 71–72
Iwanko, JJ, Cpl, 68–69
Jakeman, WD, Sgt, 67–68
Jameson, DG, Sgt, 68–69
Jeffrey, ML, Cfn, 71–72
Jellie, AD, 2Lt, 69, KIA 3.12.69
Jenkins, DJ, L/Cpl, 66–67
Jewell, JL, Sgt, 66–67
Jobling, CD, Cpl, 68–69
Jobling, TE, Sgt, 69–70
Jogar, J, Pte, 71
Johns, RA, Pte, 67–68
Johnson, BA, Cpl, 68–69
Johnston, DT, Pte, 71
Jones, AE, Sgt, 69–70
Jones, RA, Cfn, 71
Jones, RJ, Sgt, 67–68
Jordan, JS, Cpl, 66–67
Jorgensen, KJ, Pte, 71
Juckett, GC, Pte, 69
Justice, M, Cpl, 66–67
Keane, OW, Sgt, 71
Keating, DA, Pte, 66–67
Keevers, NE, Cpl, 70–71
Keith, DJ, Bdr, 69–70
Kemp, KC, Cfn, 71
Kendall, DL, Cpl, 67
Kennett, DW, Sgt, 66–67
Kerr, AG, 2Lt, 69–70
Kerr, KD, LAC, 66–67
Kerrison, LF, Pte, 69–70
Kibblewhite, IC, Pte, 70–71
Kippax, PW, Cpl, 68–69
Klas, MJ, L/Cpl, 70–71
Klass, E, Cpl, 67–68

Knight, RB, Capt, 66–67
Korczak, J, Pte, 70–71
Korn, B, Gnr, 69–70
Kowalenko, J, Pte, 67–68
Krause, GR, L/Cpl, 66–67, Sgt, 69–70
Kuczynski, JJ, Pte, 69–70
Kwas, B, Cfn, 68–69
Kwaterski, LJ, Cfn, 70–71
Lafferty, MB, Pte, 70–71
Lamb, J, Cfn, 70–71
Lamond, PR, Gnr, 69–70
Langridge, CW, Sgt, 67–68
Lanza, A, Cpl, 66–67
Lappin, MH, Cpl, 69–70
Larney, L, F/Sgt, 65–66
Laughlin, HC, Pte, 68–69
Lee, RW, Sgt, 70–71
Leech, JL, Pte, 71
Leslie, RG, Bdr, 71
Leslie, RJ, Pte, 69–70
Levy, DL, Bdr, 69–70
Levy, PM, Cpl, 66–67
Lewis, GJ, Cpl, 66–67
Lewis, J, Spr, 70–71
Lewis, KH, Sgt, 69–70
Liddle, HL, Sgt, 68–69
Lidster, PA, Cfn, 66–67, Sgt, 69–70, 71
Lindgren, EE, Cfn, 66–67
Lindsay, DR, L/Cpl, 69–70
Lipscombe, PD, Maj, 65–66
List, RL, Pte, 67–68
Little, AR, Cpl, 67
Little, RC, Cfn, 66–67
Livingstone, MR, Pte, 71–72
Lockwood, DL, Cpl, 70
Lojkin, N, Cpl, 71
Loneragan, MJ, Cfn, 68–69

Longland, GN, 2Lt, 69–70
Loughlin, BP, Gnr, 69
Lourensen, AJ, L/Cpl, 67–68
Love, DD, Tpr, 70–71
Lydiate, AL, Sgt, 69–70
Lyon, JB, Pte, 67–68
Macdonald, IM, Cpl, 65–66
Macdonald, RA, Spr, 68–69
Machell, JM, Cfn, 68–69
Machin, LA, Lt, 69–70
Mackenzie, IM, Cfn, 66–67
Mackworth, DJ, Lt, 70–71
Maley, CG, WO2, 67–68
Manfield, DM, Cpl, 68
Mangioni, PJ, Pte, 70–71
Markcrow, FJ, Capt, 69–70
Marr, LG, Sgt, 65
Marrs, DJ, Cpl, 69–70
Marsden, JC, 2Lt, 71
Martin, CL, Cfn, 71
Martin, RF, Pte, 66–67
Mason, LA, Cfn, 68
Mateer, BJ, Sgt, 65–66
Matheson, HM, Capt, 71–72
Matthews, JJ, Pte, 67
Matthews, RP, WO2, 70–71
Maudsley, WN, Cfn, 69–70
McCarthy, LC, Pte, 66–67
McClymont, JS, 2Lt, 68–69
McFadzen, IT, L/Cpl, 68–69
McFarlane, GF, Cfn, 67–68
McFerran, DG, 2Lt, 67–68

McGhie, JJ, 2Lt, 70–71
McGregor, RJ, Sgt, 68–69
McLachlan, GN, L/Bdr, 70–71
McLean, R, Cfn, 65–66
McMillan, RI, L/Cpl, 70–71
McVie, IR, WO2, 67–68
Mecham, DC, 2Lt, 71–72
Meehan, MJ, 2Lt, 66–67
Meiklejohn, AG, L/Cpl, 66–67
Meldrum, A, Pte, 71
Menear, PD, Cpl, 65–66
Menzies, D, Sgt, 67–68
Meredith, RL, Cpl, 69
Mikelsons, AI, Cpl, 68–69
Millar, RM, Capt, 70–71
Miller, PJ, Pte, 70–71
Mitchell, FS, Cfn, 67–68
Mitchell, LC, Cfn, 67–68
Mitka, J, Pte, 71–72
Moffatt, DL, 2Lt, 68
Molinaro, LF, L/Bdr, 70–71
Moller, GR, Sgt, 68–69
Monk, GL, Cpl, 67–68
Monteith, GD, 2Lt, 69–70
Monteith, RE, Capt, 71
Moore, JW, Cfn, 68–69
Moore, SJ, Pte, 67–68
Morero, MJ, WO1, 71
Morgan, CA, Bdr, 68–69
Morris, RG, Cpl, 68–69
Moss, KJ, Cpl, 69–70
Muir, PA, 2Lt, 68–69
Mullens, PJ, Cfn, 69–70
Muller, WR, Pte, 66–67
Mundy, PW, Tpr, 69–70
Murphy, AJ, Cfn, 71
Murray, A, Cfn, 70–71
Murton, KR, L/Cpl, 71–72
Muscat, PR, Bdr, 70–71

Musgrove, DR, Sgt, 71
Mussared, LE, Gnr, 68–69
Myall, BC, Pte, 66–67
Napier, JC, L/Cpl, 69–70
Naudi, L, Gnr, 69–70
Nelson, WJ, Cpl, 70–71
New, RA, Sgt, 66–67
Nichol, H, WO2, 66–67
Nicholls, GJ, Tpr, 70
Nicklin, GD, Cfn, 70–71
Nickols, JA, Cfn, 65–66
Nilon, LMl, Cfn, 69–70
Nixon, J, Cfn, 68–69
Nockolds, HF, Cpl, 68–69
Nolan, PE, Cpl/Sgt, 67–68
Noormets, IJ, Pte, 70–71
Nurse, MR, Pte, 70–71
O'Brien, DW, Cfn, 65–66
O'Brien, MF, Pte, 69–70
O'Brien, P, Lt, 67–68
O'Brien, TW, Cfn, 69–70
O'Bryan, DJ, Pte, 68–69
O'Connor, RL, Pte, 67
O'Loughlin, BK, Cpl, 70–71
O'Mara, TM, Pte, 66–67
O'Reilly, JP, Cfn, 67
O'Sullivan, TS, Lt, 69–70
Ockwell, LW, Cpl, 71
Oliphant, RH, Cpl, 66–67
Olivieri, VP, Cfn, 67–68
Opdam, J, Cpl, 70–71
Oredat, A, Cfn, 68–69
Orreal, RK, Sgt, 69
Otago, M, Sgt, 66–67
Ott, LA, Cfn, 68–69
Ovens, RJ, Sgt, 68–69
Owens, JA, Cfn, 69–70
Pacey, IF, Pte, 67–68
Page, DJ, Sgt, 69–71
Pankowski, SA, Cpl, 68–69
Parkes, KB, Cfn, 69–70

Partridge, TR, 2Lt, 69–70
Pascoe, RN, Cfn, 69–70
Patterson, D, Cpl, 66–67
Paxton, CD, Gnr, 71
Payne, DJ, Sgt, 70–71
Peacock, KL, Lt, 67–68
Pearce, LB, Pte, 70–71
Pearce, RF, Spr, 68
Pearce, RR, Gnr, 69–70
Pearson, BG, Pte, 65–66
Pearson, SK, 2Lt, 70–71
Peel, ER, Cpl, 66–67
Perry, RG, Spr, 70–71
Petersen, AT, Pte, 71
Petherick-Collins, MD, Cpl, 67–68
Petty, RA, Cfn, 70–71
Phillips, AE, Cpl, 66–67
Phillips, DN, Cpl, 67–68
Phillips, LR, Cpl, 70–71
Phillips, TP, WO2, 66–67
Pike, GR, Cfn, 66–67
Pinch, NA, Pte, 68
Pinker, IR, L/Cpl, 71
Pinkham, NR, Capt, 65–66
Piper, GW, Cfn, 66–67
Piscopo, J, Pte, 71
Pitham, TD, Sgt, 69
Pittorino, FP, Pte, 70
Polkinghorne, KB, SSgt, 71
Porter, RA, Pte, 68–69
Potocnik, P, Pte, 67–68
Potter, ER, L/Cpl, 66–67
Potts, LD, Cpl, –68
Powell, RJ, Cpl, 68
Powell, RJ, Pte, 71
Power, JC, Cfn, 66–67
Priestland, JC, Cpl, 71
Pring, DC, Gnr, 68
Prior, BJ, Spr, 68–69
Pugh, C, Cfn, 70–71
Pukallus, LS, L/Cpl, 65–66

Pullen, WD, Cpl, 71
Purvis, JA, Lt, 65–66
Pyle, AD, Cpl, 67–68
Quee, BM, WO2, 67–68
Ragg, MV, Pte, 67–68
Railton, RB, Lt, 68–69
Raison, KC, Cpl, 65–66
Ramsay, E, F/Sgt, 66–67
Rankin, JF, Pte, 66–67
Rasmussen, JT, Cpl, 69–70
Rawling, WJ, Cpl, 65–66
Reardon, BT, Sgt, 70–71
Reddin, WD, Cfn, 69–70
Reid, IV, Capt, 67
Reid, RF, Cpl, 68–69
Reid, SG, Pte, 71
Reimer, WR, Gnr, 69–70
Reus, PA, Cpl, 69–70
Reynolds, MC, Lt, 71
Reynolds, OC, Cfn, 65–66
Rich, RS, 2Lt, 66
Richards, JR, L/Cpl, 68–69
Richards, WJ, Spr, 70–71
Richardson, IT, Cpl, 69–70
Ritchie, RD, Cpl, 71
Roberts, JT, Cpl, 69–70
Roberts, PJ, Capt, 67–68
Robertson, KW, Sgt, 65–66
Robinson, AJ, Bdr, 69–70
Robinson, PM, Capt, 67
Rogers, PH, 2Lt, 68–69
Rolfe, DS, Cpl, 70–71
Rollason, BD, Cpl, 69–70
Rook, GS, Pte, 70–71
Ross, DW, Gnr, 71
Ross, JW, L/Cpl, 71
Rowe, KL, 2Lt, 68–69
Rowe, RA, Cpl, 70–71
Ruming, GR, Cpl, 71
Rupe, LL, Cfn, 71–72

Rutten, JH, Pte, 70–71
Ruttley, J, Pte, 66–67
Ryan, JO, Sgt, 67–68
Salmon, VT, 2Lt, 66–67
Salter, CG, Pte, 66–67
Sargent, AL, Pte, 70–71
Satchell, AC, L/Cpl, 69–70
Saunders, RA, L/Cpl, 71
Sawtell, JF, Gnr, 70–71
Scafe, CO, WO2, 65–66
Scammell, PE, Gnr, 68–69
Scott, CW, 2Lt, 66–67
Scott, DB, Cfn, 69–70
Scott, KW, WO2, 68–69
Scroggie, TE, Cfn, 67–68
Scully, CH, Pte, 69–70
Sedgers, AJ, Lt, 69–70
Seeley, GM, Sgt, 70
Sell, QL, Tpr, 66–67
Sharp, PJ, Pte, 67–68
Shearer, DH, Cfn, 67–68
Shepherd, RK, Cpl, 66–67
Sheppard, KW, Cpl, 67–68
Sherman, AE, Cpl, 66–67
Shier, CH, Bdr, 69–70
Shine, RJ, Gnr, 71
Simpson, DA, L/Cpl, 68–69
Sims, DB, WO2, 70–71
Sinnott, IR, 2Lt, 70–71
Sitarz, M, Pte, 65–66
Skinner, BW, Cpl, 69–70
Skinner, MJ, Gnr, 70–71
Small, GS, Gnr, 70–71
Smith, AV, WO2, 69–70
Smith, BJ, Capt, 65–66
Smith, CA, Cpl, 65–66
Smith, GM, Cpl, 68–69
Smith, MR, 2Lt, 69–70
Smith, RF, Capt, 69–70
Smith, RH, Cpl, 67–68

Smith, RJ, Cpl, 66–67
Smith, RK, Cfn, 69–70
Smythe, CA, Cfn, 67–68
Sneesby, JH, Spr, 70
Solomon, JH, Sgt, 66–67
Sonneveld, MJ, 2Lt, 70–71
South, RH, Cpl, 69–70
Sparham, ES, Pte, 68
Sparke, TB, Spr, 70–71
Sparrow, MJ, Cfn, 66–67
Spilsbury, BF, Sgt, 70–71
Spoor, PB, 2Lt, 67–68
Stace, L, Cpl, 69
Stead, JR, Cfn, 70–71
Steel, EG, Lt, 71
Steele, KJ, Cpl, 66–67
Stein, JM, Pte, 68–69
Stevens, PN, 2Lt, 68–69
Stevens, RJ, Sgt, 68–69
Stewart, KC, Gnr, 68–69
Stewart, KM, Cfn, 67
Stockley, JW, Pte, 69–70
Stower, KG, Cfn, 71
Suiter, WD, Pte, 67–68
Sullivan, J, Sgt, 66–67
Summers, FA, Cfn, 68–69
Sutcliffe, RJ, Pte, 69
Swain, MS, F/Sgt, 67–68
Szymanski, WJ, Pte, 68
Taylor, JA, Cpl, 67–68
Tessmer, HR, Tpr, 67
Thompson, RP, Sgt, 65–66
Thomson, RW, 2Lt, 68–69
Thorpe, RW, Cpl, 65–66
Thrush, KM, Cfn, 70–71
Thurlow, GG, Tpr, 71
Tibballs, CF, Pte, 71–72
Tickle, DR, Cpl, 71
Timmins, CP, Sgt, 66–67
Timson, GS, Cfn, 67–68
Tippet, RK, 2Lt, 68
Tizzard, SK, 2Lt, 68

Tonkin, AR, Gnr, 69–70
Townsend, GH, Cpl, 70–71
Townsend, HJ, Cpl, 70–71
Traverse, B, Cpl, 71
Treble, DL, Cfn, 69–70
Trick, DJ, 2Lt, 67–68
Triplett, TS, 2Lt, 71–72
Turl, AR, Sgt, 71
Turner, DR, Pte, 66–67
Turner, GJ, L/Cpl, 68
Underwood, RJ, Cfn, 71–72
Van Aken, RC, Sgt, 68–69
Verkys, RJ, Cfn, 70–71
Viney, P, Pte, 65–66
Von Meunchhausen, H, Lt, 65–66
Wall, BJ, Pte, 66–67
Wallace, BJ, Pte, 66–67
Wallder, MR, Sgt, 68–69
Walsh, MJ, Bdr, 71
Ward, DH, Sgt, 67–68, 70–71
Wark, TF, Capt, 69–70
Waterfield, DC, Pte, 69–70
Watson, NR, Cpl, 70–71
Watson, P, Cfn, 67–68, Sgt, 71–72
Watson, RT, Pte, 71
Weaver, BM, 2Lt, 66–67
Webster, MC, Capt, 66–67
Webster, SM, WO2, 68
Weertman, AR, Pte, 67–68
Welbourn, AP, Spr, 68
Welch, PE, Cpl, 71
Weston, NE, Gnr, 67–68
Wheelahan, KA, Pte, 68–69
Whitcher, BC, Cpl, 66–67

White, MM, Pte, 70–71
White, RK, Cfn, 66–67
Whybrow, NJ, Cfn, 71
Wiggins, LA, Pte, 70
Wilkins, PW, Cfn, 71–72
Wilkins, WJ, Sgt, 68–69
Williams, AC, SSgt, 70–71
Williams, AP, Pte, 68–69
Williams, CJ, Pte, 66–67
Williams, EM, Cpl, 67–68
Williams, PG, Cpl, 67–68
Williams, RC, Cfn, 66–67
Willis, HR, Cfn, 66–67
Willis, OH, Sgt, 68
Wilmer, Q, Pte, 69–70
Wilson, AW, Cpl, 68–69
Wilson, EJ, Cpl, 65–66
Wilson, J, SSgt, 67–68
Wilson, LR, Cpl, 66–67
Windberg, W, Cfn, 68–69
Winterton, TA, Cpl, 65–66
Wood, HG, LAC, 66–67
Wood, LR, Cpl, 70–71
Woodley, TR, Capt, 68–69
Woods, NH, Cpl, 66
Woodward, RC, Pte, 69–70
Wools-Cobb, SA, Sgt, 66–67
Wright, GC, 2Lt, 70–71
Wright, JT, Capt, 66–67
Wright, JS, Cpl, 71
Wright, JW, Pte, 71
Wright, WC, Cpl, 70–71
Xanthopoulos, G, Cfn, 69–70
Yielding, RA, Sgt, 70–71
Young, GJ, Sgt, 69–70
Young, RA, Sgt, 67–68
Zeilstra, JC, Pte, 70–71
Zitzlesberger, R, Cpl, 67–68, Sgt, 70–71

Appendix 2

Honours and awards

Member of the Order of the British Empire (MBE)
340180 Captain Peter Mervyn Robinson RAEME

Distinguished Flying Cross (DFC)
25516 Major Henry Arthur Benson RAA
25621 Major Lawrence Gerard Doyle RAA
28356 Major Graeme Hill-Smith AAAvn
18548 Captain James Douglas Campbell RAEME
235246 Captain John Leslie Coggan RAA
39875 Captain William Bevil Flanagan NZAAC
39545 Lieutenant Terence John Hayes AAAvn
17699 Lieutenant Colin Walter Scott RAINF
30799 Lieutenant Edwin Grant Steel NZAAC
2243939 Second Lieutenant Peter Alexander Bysouth AAAvn
39548 Second Lieutenant Fraser Maxwell Gibson AAAvn
1200956 Second Lieutenant Peter Harry Rogers AAAvn
44101 Second Lieutenant Malcolm Roy Smith AAAvn
3112007 Second Lieutenant Michael John Sonneveld AAAvn

Queen's Commendation for Brave Conduct
213017 Second Lieutenant Robert William Askew RAEME

Mention in Despatches (MID)
235149 Major Philip John Calvert AAAvn
27240 Major Neil Hilton Harden AAAvn
235266 Captain Robert Malcolm Millar RAEME
1200935 Captain Rowan Edmond Monteith AAAvn
11509 Captain Bevan John Smith RAE
37498 Captain John Trevor Wright RAINF

51727 Lieutenant Ross Hutchinson RAA
1200008 Second Lieutenant Charles John Barron RAASC
1200953 Second Lieutenant David Herbert Earley AAAvn
216990 Second Lieutenant Thomas William Guivarra RAA
216990 Second Lieutenant Phillip Norman Stevens AAAvn
42857 Staff Sergeant Robert Arthur Young RAAMC
64358 Sergeant Rockleigh Edward Hoare RAEME
A11639 Sergeant Douglas William Kennett RAAF
1200565 Sergeant Richard Anthony Yielding RAASC
38498 Sergeant Robert Zitzlesberger RAEME

Vietnam 'End of War List'

On 3 June 1998, the Vietnam 'End of War List' was announced by the Australian Government. Five members of 161 Reconnaissance Flight and 161 (Independent) Reconnaissance Flight were honoured.

Medal for Gallantry (MG)
11509 Captain Bevan John Smith RAE

Distinguished Service Medal (DSM)
29745 Captain Barry Creig Donald (posthumous) AAAvn
37498 Captain John Trevor Wright RAINF

1200008 Second Lieutenant Charles John Barron RAASC
216990 Second Lieutenant Phillip Norman Stevens AAAvn

Allied Honours and Awards

A number of awards were presented to members of 161 Reconnaissance Flight and 161 (Independent) Reconnaissance Flight by both the United States and the South Vietnamese. There are known omissions from the following list of recipients. Some members of the Flight did not receive any official document with their award; hence there is no official record of the event.

Distinguished Flying Cross (United States)
235246 Captain John Leslie Coggan RAA

The Gallantry Cross, with Gold Star (Vietnam)
61106 Major Paul Lipscombe RAASC

The Gallantry Cross, with Bronze Star (Vietnam)
61106 Major Paul Lipscombe RAASC

The Bronze Star for Meritorious Service (United States)
37980 Captain Fred Barlow RAEME

The Army Commendation Medal for Service (United States)
215225 Second Lieutenant Steve Tizzard AAAvn

United States Army Meritorious Unit Commendation

On 4 July 1991, 161 Reconnaissance Squadron was awarded the United States Army Meritorious Unit Commendation (MUC) for the services of 161 Reconnaissance Flight as part of the 1RAR Battalion Group in South Vietnam during 1965–66. All military personnel who served with units of the 1RAR Group, attached to the 173rd Airborne Brigade (Separate), United States Army, during the period of 5 May 1965 to 16 May 1966 are entitled to the award. The Australian and New Zealand forces of 1RAR Group were: 1RAR; 1APC Troop, 3 Cavalry Regiment, RAAC; 105 Field Battery, RAA; 161 Field Battery, RNZA; 3 Field Troop, RAE; 1 Australian Logistics Support Company, RAASC; and 161 Reconnaissance Flight.

The Commendation was presented by Lieutenant General W.S. Carpenter, Jr., General Officer Commanding ROK/US forces Korea after considerable effort by the veterans of the first tour in achieving recognition of 1RAR Group's considerable achievements. The Commendation consists of the Citation, a streamer for attachment to the Colours and the individual MUC decoration. The decoration is to be worn by veterans of the tour in perpetuity and members of 161 Reconnaissance Squadron while serving in the unit.

The following members of 161 Reconnaissance Flight qualified for the MUC:

61007 Major Paul Lipscombe RAASC

335138 Captain Neville Pinkham RAAC

11509 Captain Bevan Smith RAE

O313248 Flight Lieutenant Donald Tidd RAAF
235224 Lieutenant John Guild RAINF
213816 Lieutenant John Purvis RAASC
15508 Lieutenant Holger von Meunchhausen RAAC
243041 Second Lieutenant Donald Cockerell RAEME
43088 Second Lieutenant Donald Ettridge RAASC
1967 Warrant Officer Charles Scafe RAINF
A1770 Flight Sergeant Lloyd Larney RAAF
37722 Sergeant Laurie Dawber RAAOC
14264 Sergeant Clement Ebner RAINF
15219 Sergeant Jack Ellis RAEME
12423 Sergeant Harold Gibson RAAMC
A576 Sergeant Allan Higginbottom RAAF
A3260 Sergeant Les Marr RAAF
15224 Sergeant Brian Mateer RAINF
A2772 Sergeant Mervyn Otago RAAF
15676 Sergeant Kevin Robertson RAINF
A13660 Sergeant Raymond Thompson RAAF
310973 Corporal George Avern RAAOC
243108 Corporal Barry Bean RAEME
A19208 Corporal John Black RAAF
58683 Corporal Maxwell Byng RAEME
A42637 Corporal James Crook RAAF
213447 Corporal Philip Cummings RAAOC
58727 Corporal Kenneth Elson RAEME
A13197 Corporal Richard Humphrey RAAF
A15765 Corporal Benjamin Humphreys RAAF
16082 Corporal James Jordan RAEME
342753 Corporal Ian MacDonald RAEME
A219443 Corporal Peter Menear RAAF
A217613 Corporal Donald Patterson RAAF
16715 Corporal Kelvin Raison RAAC
214122 Corporal William Rawlings RAEME
14832 Corporal Charles Smith AACC
A216966 Corporal Ralph Thorp RAAF
A15767 Corporal Eardley Wilson RAAF
11456 Corporal Trevor Winterton RAEME
14413 Lance Corporal Thomas Blair RAEME
3842 Lance Corporal Ronald Coombs RAINF
16684 Lance Corporal Lyall Pukallus RAEME
2410879 Bombardier Robert Hart RAA
342813 Craftsman Neil Bennett RAEME
243192 Craftsman Derek Budd RAEME
58750 Craftsman Robert Hodgkinson RAEME
43140 Craftsman Ronald McLean RAEME
18645 Craftsman John Nickols RAEME
342821 Craftsman David O'Brien RAEME
243094 Craftsman Owen Reynolds RAEME
243200 Craftsman Robert White RAEME
342872 Craftsman Herbert Willis RAEME
A110529 LAC Keith Bell RAAF
A13534 LAC Harry Wood RAAF
311406 Private John Blakey RAINF
14871 Private Cecil Crook AACC
16928 Private Robert Doyle RAINF
16894 Private Francis Finnigan RAINF

210474 Private Reginald Holland RAASC
215724 Private Robert Hutchison RAINF
215026 Private Leslie McCarthy AACC
120007 Private Bevan Pearson RAINF
18772 Private Mitchell Sitarz RAASC
15857 Private Philip Viney RAASC

Glossary of terms and acronyms

NUMERICAL DESIGNATIONS
1ALSG   First Australian Logistic Support Group
1ATF   First Australian Task Force
161 Bty   161 Battery (RNZA) at Nui Dat
2IC   Second in Command
1RAR   First Battalion, The Royal Australian Regiment (and 2RAR, 3RAR, etc)

AIRCRAFT
B-52   US strategic heavy bomber
Bronco   US OV-10 ground attack aircraft
Bushranger   RAAF Iroquois gunship
Caribou De Havilland Canada   Tactical transport aircraft
Cessna 180   Light observation/liaison aircraft used by 161 Recce Flight
Cessna O-1 'Bird Dog'   Forward air control (FAC) aircraft
Cessna O-2   Twin-engined FAC aircraft
Cayuse OH-6   Light observation helicopter
Chinook Boeing Vertol CH-47   Medium lift helicopter
C-47 Dakota   Military designation for Douglas DC-3 transport aircraft
Hercules   Lockheed C-130 tactical transport aircraft
Huey   Bell UH-1 series Iroquois utility helicopter
Huey Cobra   US helicopter gunship
OH-58A Kiowa   Light observation helicopter used by 161 Recce Flight
Otter   Light tactical transport aircraft
Phantom F-4   US fighter/ground attack aircraft

GLOSSARY OF TERMS AND ACRONYMS

Porter   Pilatus Porter light observation and liaison aircraft; replacement for 161 Recce Flight's Cessna 180 fixed wing aircraft

Sioux   Bell 47G series of light observation helicopters; US Army designation OH-13

Super Sabre F-100   US fighter/ground attack aircraft

Skycrane   Sikorsky heavy lift helicopter

Wallaby   RAAF Caribou aircraft

A

AAAvn   Australian Army Aviation Corps
AATTV   Australian Army Training Team Vietnam
A Sqn 3 Cav   A Squadron, 3 Cavalry Regiment
AGL   Above ground level
AHQ   Army Headquarters
ALO   Air Liaison Officer
AO   Area of Operation
AOR   Area of Responsibility
AOP   Air Observation Post
APC   M-113 Armoured Personnel Carrier
ARC   54 VHF/FM aircraft radio transceiver
Arty   Artillery
ARDF   Airborne Radio Direction Finding
ARVN   Army of the Republic of South Vietnam
ATC   Air Traffic Control
AWCC   Artillery Warning Control Centre

B

BDA   Bomb damage assessment

C

Casevac   Casualty evacuation
CO   Commanding Officer
CSM   Company Sergeant Major
CP   Command Post

D

DFC   Distinguished Flying Cross
DS   Direct Support
Dustoff   US casualty evacuation helicopter (acronym for 'dedicated, untiring service to our fighting forces')
DZ   Drop Zone

E

Eagle Farm   Helicopter landing pad at Nui Dat

F
FAC Forward Air Controller
FFR Fitted For Radio
Fire Trail One of a network of trails cleared through jungle areas of South Vietnam by Allied engineers to facilitate access by air or ground
FM Frequency Modulation (as distinct from Amplitude Modulation)
FO Forward Observer (artillery or mortar fire)
FSB Fire Support Base (a forward location for Artillery and command/defensive elements to bring a battalion AO within range of artillery support)

G
GSE Ground Support Equipment (used for aircraft maintenance)
GSO General Staff Officer

H
H & I Harassment and Interdiction
HE High Explosive
HORSESHOE Fire Support Base location south of Nui Dat
Hotel Pad Helicopter landing pad at the Horseshoe

I
IO Intelligence Officer
Int Intelligence

K
Kangaroo Control Artillery Warning Control Centre, Nui Dat
KIA Killed in Action
KVA Kilo-Volt-Amperes. (A measure of the capacity of an electricity generating set to provide power to users. A 5 KVA generator is quite small; 35 KVA is quite large.)

L
LFT Light Fire Team, comprising two helicopter gunships
LO Liaison Officer
LZ Landing Zone

M
Medevac Medical evacuation
MID Mentioned in Dispatches (recognition of outstanding service)
MO Medical Officer
M-60 7.62mm general purpose machine gun

N
Nasho Australian national serviceman
NCO Non Commissioned Officer

Nui Vietnamese for 'hill'
NVA North Vietnamese Army

O
OC Officer Commanding
OCS Officer Cadet School, Portsea, Victoria
OTU Officer Training Unit, Scheyville, NSW

P
Pax Aircraft passenger(s)
PF Popular Forces (South Vietnamese militia)
POL Petrol, oils and lubricants stores
Possum Call sign for 161 Recce Flight pilots
Psyops Psychological Warfare Operations
PRC-25 Manpack VHF/FM radio communications set

Q
QFI Qualified Flying Instructor
QM Quartermaster
Q Store Quartermaster's store—unit equipment store

R
RAA Royal Australian Artillery
RAAC Royal Australian Armoured Corps
RAAOC Royal Australian Army Ordnance Corps
RAASC Royal Australian Army Service Corps
RAE Royal Australian Engineers
RAEME Royal Australian Electrical and Mechanical Engineers
RAR Royal Australian Regiment
RAAF Royal Australian Air Force
RCL Recoilless Rifle
Recce Reconnaissance
RF Regional Force (South Vietnamese militia)
RMO Regimental Medical Officer
RNZIR Royal New Zealand Infantry Regiment
RPG Rocket-propelled grenade
RSM Regimental Sergeant Major
RW Rotary Wing
R & C Rest and convalescence
R & R Rest and recreation

S
SAS Special Air Service
SLR 7.62mm self-loading rifle; standard issue for Australian riflemen

Song Vietnamese for river
SOPs Standard Operating Procedures
SPAT Self-Propelled Anti-Tank gun
Sqn Squadron
SSM Squadron Sergeant Major
SUNRAY Radio appointment title for Commander
Suoi Vietnamese for creek or stream
Swan A trip with no apparent operational purpose

T
TAOR Tactical Area of Operational Responsibility
TOC Tactical Operations Centre

U
UHF Ultra High Frequency
U/S Unserviceable
USAF United States Air Force
USMACV US Military Assistance Command Vietnam

V
VC Viet Cong
VHF Very High Frequency
VR Visual reconnaissance

W
WP White phosphorus (grenade or rocket)

Notes

Prologue
1 Bevan Smith, interview, 19 November 2004.
2 Air Staff Directive 235, circa 1960.
3 'Viet Cong' is derived from 'Vietnam Cong San', meaning 'Vietnamese Communist'.

1 161 Reconnaissance Flight: Formation and deployment
1 Australian Army practice is to designate commanders (up to the rank of major) of minor units as Officers Commanding (OCs). Higher ranking officers commanding larger units (e.g. battalions) are Commanding Officers (COs).
2 Cessna O-1 'Bird Dog' light aircraft of the 19th Tactical Air Support Squadron were used for Forward Air Control (FAC) operations.
3 Contraction of 'Aviation' and 'Electronics'; a general reference to aircraft communications–electronics systems.
4 Paul Lipscombe, interview, 5 January 2005.
5 The Army's senior non-commissioned rank is Warrant Officer (WO). There are two classes, WO1 and WO2, with WO1 the senior.
6 Jim Crook, interview, 23 March 2005.
7 Paul Lipscombe, op. cit.
8 DUKW was an amphibious vehicle used by the Australian Army in the 1960s.
9 Jim Crook, op. cit.
10 A technical procedure carried out to recalibrate an aircraft's compass after significant events. For aircraft arriving in Vietnam, a compass swing was necessary because of the significant change in magnetic deviation at the new location.

11 Ultra High Frequency communications radios for use with Air Traffic Control facilities.
  12 Very High Frequency communications radios, also for use with Air Traffic Control.
  13 Bevan Smith, interview, 19 November 2004.

2 Bien Hoa: Fitting in
  1 Ryan drones are high altitude unmanned vehicles equipped with electronics that made them appear larger (like a U-2) to attract enemy fire. The drone could intercept and relay fusing signals from the Russian SA-2 Surface-to-Air Missiles (SAMs), the primary air defence weapons used by the Soviets and their client states at that time.
  2 Specialist unit for the collection of Signals Intelligence (Sigint).
  3 A US unit equipped with air droppable 'Scorpion' armoured personnel carriers mounting 90-mm anti-tank guns.
  4 Paul Lipscombe, interview, 5 January 2005.
  5 Lloyd Larney, interview, 14 February 2005.
  6 Jim Crook, interview, 23 March 2005.
  7 C. Coulthard-Clark, *The RAAF in Vietnam: Australian Air Involvement in the Vietnam War 1962–1975*, Allen & Unwin in association with the Australian War Memorial, Sydney, 1995, pp. 65–70.
  8 ibid., p. 69.
  9 Paul Lipscombe, op. cit.
  10 Laurie Dawber, 'Reccelections', 161 Recce Association records, 2 November 1993.
  11 Jim Crook, op. cit.
  12 Lloyd Larney, op. cit.

3 Learning the ropes: October 1965–May 1966
  1 I.G. McNeill, *To Long Tan: The Australian Army and the Vietnam War 1950–66*, Allen & Unwin in association with the Australian War Memorial, Sydney, 1993, p. 118.
  2 Corps Tactical Zone (CTZ): geographical area of responsibility of an ARVN Corps. South Vietnam was divided into four CTZs numbered I, II, III and IV. III CTZ covered a large area to the north, east and south of Saigon which included War Zone D, Bien Hoa and Phuoc Tuy province.
  3 Major Neil Harden, *Training and Information Letter 1/71*, 1 Aviation Regiment, p. 4–2.
  4 Paul Lipscombe, Interview, 5 January 2005.
  5 An area over which a commander is allotted primary tactical responsibility for an indefinite period and in which he can conduct operations on a continuing basis.
  6 War Zone D was one of four designated zones of Viet Cong activity in South Vietnam.
  7 Paul Lipscombe, op. cit.

8   Bell UH-1 utility helicopter.
9   Bevan Smith, interview, 19 November 2004.
10 ibid.
11 Paul Lipscombe, op. cit.
12 McNeill, *To Long Tan*, p. 140.
13 ibid, pp. 147–8.
14 Jim Crook, interview, 23 March 2005.
15 Bevan Smith, op. cit.
16 ibid.
17 Perforated Steel Planking (PSP)—lengths of metal planking perforated to reduce weight—was used to permit operations of vehicles over boggy ground and to make hardstandings and airstrips for air operations and maintenance in wet areas.
18 Bevan Smith, op. cit.
19 McNeill, *To Long Tan*, pp. 167–69.
20 Douglas C-47 Dakota transport aircraft.
21 Acronym for Tactical Air Navigation equipment. Airborne TACAN equipment provides distance and bearing information for pilots approaching or departing an airfield equipped with a TACAN facility.
22 Paul Lipscombe, op. cit.
23 ibid.
24 McNeill, *To Long Tan*, p. 243.
25 An abbreviated form of 'medical evacuation'. Similarly, 'casevac' is shorthand for 'casualty evacuation'. Also see Glossary.
26 Bevan Smith, op. cit.
27 ibid.

4   The 1st Australian Task Force

1   I.G. McNeill, *To Long Tan: The Australian Army and the Vietnam War 1950–66*, Allen & Unwin in association with the Australian War Memorial, Sydney, 1993, p. 196.
2   R.J. O'Neill, *Vietnam Task: The 5th Battalion, Royal Australian Regiment 1966/67*, Cassell Australia, Sydney, 1995, pp. 14–15.
3   ibid., p. 15.
4   ibid., p. 16.
5   McNeill, *To Long Tan*, p. 244.
6   ibid., p. 252.
7   ibid., p. 254.
8   Paul Lipscombe, interview, 5 January 2005.
9   One of many US Army ranks designating people with specialist skills, in this case a plant operator in the Corps of Engineers.
10 Dick Knight, 'Reccelections', 161 Recce Association records, 1995.
11 Paul Lidster, interview, 31 March 2005.
12 Felix Mitchell, interview, 23 March 2005.
13 Jack Jewell, interview, 26 February 2005.

14 Felix Mitchell, op. cit.
15 Paul Lidster, op. cit.
16 Dick Knight, op. cit.
17 ibid.

5 Vung Tau: May 1966–March 1967

1 I.G. McNeill, *To Long Tan: The Australian Army and the Vietnam War 1950–66*, Allen & Unwin in association with the Australian War Memorial, Sydney, 1993, p. 261.
2 ibid., p. 262.
3 Paul Lipscombe, interview, 5 January 2005.
4 McNeill, *To Long Tan*, p. 285.
5 ibid., pp. 307–310.
6 Laurie Doyle, interview, 21 September 2004.
7 McNeill, *To Long Tan*, p. 380.
8 ibid., p. 381.
9 ibid., p. 429.
10 ibid., p. 384.
11 ibid., p. 385.
12 R.J. O'Neill, *Vietnam Task: The 5th Battalion, Royal Australian Regiment 1966/67*, Cassell Australia, Sydney, 1995, p. 131.
13 ibid., p. 145.
14 An American acronym for a casualty evacuation helicopter.
15 O'Neill, *Vietnam Task*, pp. 145–7.
16 MID citation, Second Lieutenant Charles 'Chic' Barron.
17 100-hourly servicings.
18 1200-hourly servicings.
19 Resupply missions.
20 Laurie Doyle, op. cit.
21 ibid.
22 I.G. McNeill and A.K. Ekins, *On the Offensive: The Australian Army in the Vietnam War 1967–68*, Allen & Unwin in association with the Australian War Memorial, Sydney, 2003, p. 69.
23 ibid., p. 74.
24 ibid., p. 106.
25 ibid., p. 119.

6 Relocation to Nui Dat

1 Laurie Doyle, interview, 21 September 2004.
2 ibid.
3 Geoff Deacon, interview, 6 December 2004.
4 Felix Mitchell, interview, 23 March 2005.
5 ibid.
6 Peter Robinson, 'Reccelections', 161 Recce Association records, 23 September 1993.

7 D.J. Dennis, *One Day at a Time: A Vietnam Diary*, University of Queensland Press, Queensland, 1992, p. 13.
8 Vietnamese currency.
9 Dennis, *One Day at a Time*, p. 14.
10 Slang for GSO2 (Air), the staff officer responsible for tasking 161.
11 Dennis, *One Day at a Time*, p. 14.
12 Jack Jewell, interview, 26 February 2005.
13 A check to ensure that search-and-rescue operations were initiated if an aircraft did not return at the scheduled time.
14 Peter Blissett, 'Reccelections', 161 Recce Association records, undated.
15 Laurie Doyle, interview, 21 September 2004.
16 ibid.
17 MID citation, Lieutenant Tom Guivarra.
18 I.G. McNeill and A.K. Ekins, *On the Offensive: The Australian Army in the Vietnam War 1967–68*, Allen & Unwin in association with the Australian War Memorial, Sydney, 2003, p. 56.
19 ibid., p. 56.
20 Bernie Forrest, interview, 7 March 2005.
21 Laurie Doyle, op. cit.
22 MID citation, Staff Sergeant Bob Young.

7 Nui Dat: March–December 1967

1 I.G. McNeill and A.K. Ekins, *On the Offensive: The Australian Army in the Vietnam War 1967–68*, Allen & Unwin in association with the Australian War Memorial, Sydney, 2003, pp. 32–3.
2 ibid., p. 35.
3 ibid., p. 80.
4 R.J. O'Neill, *Vietnam Task: The 5th Battalion, Royal Australian Regiment 1966/67*, Cassell Australia, Sydney, 1995, p. 231.
5 Captain Jim Campbell, *Pilots' Notes*, Nui Dat, 1967, 161 Recce Association records.
6 Laurie Doyle, interview, 21 September 2004.
7 ibid.
8 Ross Hutchinson, *Forays*, Journal of the Australian Army Aviation Association, vol. 1, No. 12, April 2000, p. 20.
9 John 'Skeeta' Ryan, interview, 21 September 2004.
10 Ross Hutchinson, op. cit., p. 20.
11 ibid., p. 20.
12 McNeill and Ekins, *On the Offensive*, p. 187.
13 ibid., p. 203.
14 ibid., p. 203.
15 DFC citation, Lieutenant Colin Scott.
16 Don Dennis, 'Profile: Major George Alfred Constable', *Forays*, Journal of the Australian Army Aviation Association, vol. 1, No. 12, April 2000.
17 McNeill and Ekins, *On the Offensive*, p. 223.

18 ibid., p. 237.
19 Victor Company, RNZIR, 'The return', www.vcoy67.org.nz'/green.htm. Accessed 11 June 2005.
20 Don Dennis, op. cit., pp. 7–8.
21 McNeill and Ekins, *On the Offensive*, p. 245.
22 ibid., p. 265.
23 ibid., p. 249.
24 ibid., p. 257.
25 ibid., p. 257.
26 John 'Skeeta' Ryan, op. cit.
27 Peter Robinson, 'Reccelections', 161 Recce Association records, 23 September 1993.
28 Bernie Forrest, interview, 7 March 2005.
29 Glen Duus, interview, 1 September 2005.
30 D.J. Dennis, *One Day at a Time: A Vietnam Diary*, University of Queensland Press, Queensland, 1992, pp. 76–8.
31 Bernie Forrest, op. cit.
32 Paul Lidster, interview, 31 March 2005.
33 Felix Mitchell, interview, 23 March 2005.

8 The Tet Offensive: January–July 1968

1 I.G. McNeill and A.K. Ekins, *On the Offensive: The Australian Army in the Vietnam War 1967–68*, Allen & Unwin in association with the Australian War Memorial, Sydney, 2003, p. 287.
2 ibid., p. 290.
3 Glen Duus, interview, 1 September 2005.
4 McNeill and Ekins, *On the Offensive*, p. 293.
5 Ground Controlled Approach (GCA); a radar-assisted approach for landing in conditions of poor visibility.
6 Glen Duus, op. cit.
7 McNeill and Ekins, *On the Offensive*, p. 297.
8 MID citation, Lieutenant Ross Hutchinson, nd.
9 Bernie Forrest, interview, 7 March 2005.
10 McNeill and Ekins, *On the Offensive*, p. 299.
11 ibid., p. 303.
12 ibid., p. 304.
13 ibid., p. 327.
14 ibid., p. 339.
15 ibid. pp. 331–2.
16 Glen Duus, op. cit.
17 K.E. Newman (ed.), *The ANZAC Battalion: 2RAR/NZ*, John Burridge Military Antiques, Swanbourne, 1995, p. 71.
18 McNeill and Ekins, *On the Offensive*, p. 347.
19 ibid., p. 349.

NOTES   227

20 ibid., p. 372.
21 Glen Duus, op. cit.
22 From records kept by Lt Col (Rtd) Tub Matheson, the first Army pilot posted to the Directorate of Air Force Safety.
23 Major Harry Benson did in fact investigate the circumstances surrounding the crash but was unable to obtain sufficient evidence to reach a firm conclusion.
24 Bernie Forrest, op. cit.
25 Don Moffatt, interview, 9 February 2005.
26 McNeill and Ekins, *On the Offensive*, p. 383.
27 ibid., p. 389.
28 ibid., p. 389.
29 Harry Benson, interview, 7 February 2005.
30 Peter Rogers, correspondence, 5 November 2005.
31 Harry Benson, op. cit.
32 ibid.
33 Don Moffatt, op. cit.
34 L. McAulay, *The Fighting First: Combat Operations in Vietnam 1968–69, The First Battalion, The Royal Australian Regiment*, Allen & Unwin, Sydney, 1991, p. 118.
35 ibid., pp. 127–8.
36 On 26 February 1967, 161 Recce Flight was visited by Lt Col L.W. Wright MBE RNZA, Director Army Aviation. This may have led to New Zealand's involvement in the Flight.
37 Ted Brooker, interview, 6 January 2005.
38 R. Donnelly, *The Scheyville Experience: The Officer Training Unit, Scheyville, 1965–1973*, University of Queensland Press, Queensland, 2001, p. 166.
39 H.M. 'Tub' Matheson, interview, 6 February 2005.

9 The aftermath: August 1968–February 1969

1 G. McNeill and A.K. Ekins, *On the Offensive: The Australian Army in the Vietnam War 1967–68*, Allen & Unwin in association with the Australian War Memorial, Sydney, 2003, p. 405.
2 ibid., p. 405.
3 Don Moffatt, interview, 9 February 2005.
4 Harry Benson, interview, 7 February 2005.
5 Operation which seeks to trap the enemy between an attacking force and a blocking force.
6 L. McAulay, *The Fighting First: Combat Operations in Vietnam 1968–69, The First Battalion, The Royal Australian Regiment*, Allen & Unwin, Sydney, 1991, p. 157.
7 ibid., p. 157.
8 Don Moffatt, op. cit.
9 Peter Rogers, interview with Gary McKay, 23 May 2001.
10 Ted Brooker, interview, 6 January 2005.
11 McAulay, *The Fighting First*, pp. 234–5.
12 Peter Rogers, op. cit.

13 ibid.
14 CS gas is a type of tear gas. It is actually a white solid powder, usually mixed with a dispersal agent such as methylene chloride which carries the particles through the air. The physical effects (coughing, burning in the nose, extreme teariness, pain and breathing difficulties) are felt almost immediately after contact. The antidote is fresh air. While CS gas causes severe discomfort, its effects are rarely fatal.
15 Bernie Forrest, interview, 7 March 2005.
16 ibid.
17 Ted Brooker, op. cit.
18 ibid.
19 M.R. Battle, *The Year of the Tigers: The Second Tour of 5th Battalion, The Royal Australian Regiment in South Vietnam, 1969–70*, John Burridge Military Antiques, Swanbourne, Western Australia, 1987, p. 47.

10 Pacification: March–December 1969

1 DFC citation, Major Harry Benson.
2 Harry Benson, interview, 7 February 2005.
3 The Ready Reaction Force comprised an infantry company with supporting elements including APCs and a tank troop. The force was on 30 minutes' notice to react to a threat to a population centre anywhere in Phuoc Tuy province.
4 M.R. Battle, *The Year of the Tigers: The Second Tour of 5th Battalion, The Royal Australian Regiment in South Vietnam, 1969–70*, John Burridge Military Antiques, Swanbourne, Western Australia, 1987, p. 51.
5 ibid., p. 57.
6 Barry Skinner, interview, 8 December 2004.
7 ibid.
8 Mike Croker, 'Reccelections', 161 Recce Association records, April 1994.
9 Bill Richards, 'Reccelections', 161 Recce Association records, undated.
10 John Custance, correspondence, 15 October 2005.
11 Bill Hudnott, interview, 14 February 2005.
12 Paul Lidster, interview, 31 March 2005.
13 Harry Benson, interview, 7 February 2005.
14 Barry Skinner, op. cit.
15 Graeme Hill-Smith, interview, 6 January 2005.
16 Battle, *The Year of the Tigers*, p. 66.
17 ibid., p. 67.
18 Don Moffatt, interview, 9 February 2005.
19 Graeme Hill-Smith, op. cit.
20 ibid.
21 Warren Heapy, 'Reccelections', 161 Recce Association records, undated.
22 Glen Duus, interview, 1 September 2005.
23 Graeme Hill-Smith, interview, 6 January 2005.
24 ibid.

25 Major Neil Harden, *Training and Information Letter 1/71*, 1 Aviation Regiment, January 1971.
26 John Digweed, interview, 6 December 2004.
27 ibid.
28 Graeme Hill-Smith, op. cit.

11 Maintaining the effort: January–December 1970
1 A. Clunies-Ross (ed.), *The Grey Eight in Vietnam: The History of Eighth Battalion The Royal Australian Regiment November 1969–November 1970*, John Burridge Military Antiques, Swanbourne, Western Australia, 1989, p. 121.
2 M.R. Battle, *The Year of the Tigers: The Second Tour of 5th Battalion, The Royal Australian Regiment in South Vietnam, 1969–70*, John Burridge Military Antiques, Swanbourne, Western Australia, 1987, p. 96.
3 John Digweed, interview, 6 December 2004.
4 Clunies-Ross, *The Grey Eight in Vietnam*, p. 78.
5 The door-mounted M60 machine gun was part of 161's ongoing efforts to arm its helicopters. To become a gunner was a source of pride and entailed quite rigorous training.
6 DFC Citation, Major Graeme Hill-Smith.
7 Len Avery, interview, 20 September 2004.
8 Graeme Hill-Smith, interview, 6 January 2005.
9 ibid.
10 John Digweed, op. cit.
11 ibid.
12 Phil Calvert, 'Reccelections', 161 Recce Association records, 4 June 2000.
13 ibid.
14 ibid.
15 ibid.
16 Paul Lidster, interview, 31 March 2005.
17 'Bird Dog; the bits and pieces aeroplane', *Aircraft Magazine*, February 1991, p. 48.
18 Clunies-Ross, *The Grey Eight in Vietnam*, p. 83.
19 ibid., p. 103.
20 Phil Calvert, op. cit.

12 The final challenge: January–September 1971
1 Statistics courtesy of Len Avery, 161 Recce Association.
2 Rowan Monteith, interview, 19 November 2004.
3 Neil Harden, interview, 11 October 2004.
4 ibid.
5 Len Avery, interview, 20 September 2004.
6 'Bird Dog; the bits and pieces aeroplane', *Aircraft Magazine*, February 1991, p. 49.
7 Paul Lidster, interview, 31 March 2005.
8 Bill Hudnott, interview, 14 February 2005.
9 Bob Bell, interview, 7 December 2004.

10 Neil Harden, op. cit.
11 H.R. 'Tub' Matheson, interview, 6 February 2005.
12 Rowan Monteith, op. cit.
13 Neil Harden, op. cit.
14 Tub Matheson, op. cit.
15 Rowan Monteith, op. cit.
16 Neil Harden, op. cit.
17 Calling on enemy troops to surrender.
18 Neil Harden, op. cit.
19 Rowan Monteith, op. cit.
20 Neil Harden, op. cit.
21 Geoff Deacon, interview, 6 December 2004.
22 Brian Reardon, interview, 21 September 2004
23 J. Taylor, *Last Out: 4RAR/NZ (ANZAC) Battalion's second tour in Vietnam*, Allen & Unwin, Sydney, 2001, p. 165.
24 Rowan Monteith, op. cit.

13 The end phase: August 1971–March 1972
1 Commander's Diary, 161 (Indep) Recce Flight, August 1971.
2 H.R. 'Tub' Matheson, interview, 6 February 2005.
3 Brian Reardon, interview, 21 September 2004.
4 Rowan Monteith, interview, 19 November 2004.
5 ibid.
6 John McGhie, interview, 7 December 2004.
7 Neil Harden, interview, 11 October 2004.
8 Commander's Diary, 161 (Indep) Recce Flight, November 1971.
9 Bill Hudnott, interview, 14 February 2005.
10 Statistics courtesy of Len Avery, 161 Recce Association.
11 John McGhie, op. cit.
12 ibid.
13 Rowan Monteith, op. cit.
14 Commander's Diary, 161 (Indep) Recce Flight, January 1972.
15 Statistics courtesy of Len Avery, 161 Recce Association.
16 J. Taylor, *Last Out: 4RAR/NZ (ANZAC) Battalion's second tour in Vietnam*, Allen & Unwin, Sydney, 2001, pp. 107–8.

Bibliography

Books

Battle, M.R., *The Year of the Tigers: The Second Tour of 5th Battalion, The Royal Australian Regiment in South Vietnam, 1969–70,* John Burridge Military Antiques, Swanbourne, Western Australia, 1987

Clunies-Ross, A. (ed.), *The Grey Eight in Vietnam: The History of Eighth Battalion The Royal Australian Regiment November 1969–November 1970,* John Burridge Military Antiques, Swanbourne, Western Australia, 1989

Coulthard-Clark, C., *The RAAF in Vietnam: Australian Air Involvement in the Vietnam War 1962–1975,* Allen & Unwin in association with the Australian War Memorial, Sydney, 1995

Dennis, D.J., *One Day at a Time: A Vietnam Diary,* University of Queensland Press, 1992

Donnelly, R., *The Scheyville Experience: The Officer Training Unit, Scheyville, 1965–1973,* University of Queensland Press, 2001

McAulay, L., *The Fighting First: Combat Operations in Vietnam 1968–69, The First Battalion, The Royal Australian Regiment,* Allen & Unwin, Sydney, 1991

McNeill, I.G., *To Long Tan: The Australian Army and the Vietnam War 1950–66,* Allen & Unwin in association with the Australian War Memorial, Sydney, 1993

McNeill, I.G. and Ekins, A.K., *On the Offensive: The Australian Army in the Vietnam War 1967–68,* Allen & Unwin in association with the Australian War Memorial, Sydney, 2003

Newman, K.E. (ed.), *The ANZAC Battalion: 2RAR/NZ,* John Burridge Military Antiques, Swanbourne, 1995

O'Neill, R.J., *Vietnam Task: The 5th Battalion, Royal Australian Regiment 1966/67,* Cassell Australia, Sydney, 1995

Taylor, J., *Last Out: 4RAR/NZ (ANZAC) Battalion's second tour in Vietnam,* Allen & Unwin, Sydney, 2001

Interviews by the Author (ex-161 Recce Flight personnel)
Avery, L, 20 September 2004
Bell, R, 7 December 2004
Benson, H, 7 February 2005
Brooker, E, 6 January 2004
Crook, J, 23 March 2005
Deacon, G, 6 December 2004
Digweed, J, 6 December 2004
Doyle, L, 21 September 2004
Duus, G, 1 September 2005
Forrest, B, 7 March 2005
Harden, N, 11 October 2004
Hill-Smith, G, 6 January 2005
Hudnott, W, 14 February 2005
Jewell, J, 26 February 2005
Larney, L, 14 February 2005
Lidster, P, 31 March 2005
Lipscombe, P, 5 January 2005
Matheson, H, 6 February 2005
McGhie, J, 7 December 2004
Mitchell, F, 23 March 2005
Moffatt, D, 9 February 2005
Monteith, R, 19 November 2004
Reardon, B, 21 September 2004
Ryan, J, 21 September 2004
Skinner, B, 8 December 2004
Smith, B, 19 November 2004

Other Interviews
Rogers, P. by G. McKay, 23 May 2001

Unpublished Government Records
Major Neil Harden, *Training and Information Letter 1/71*, 1 Aviation Regiment
161 Recce Flight Commanders' Diaries, 1965–72

Private Records
161 Recce Association (courtesy Len Avery, OAM)

Index

1 Aust Fd Hosp, 203
1 Base Ordnance Depot, 16
1 CA Unit: role, 83; in Operation *Ainslie*, 92
1 Fd Sqn, RAE, 54, 70
1ALSG: 40, 45, 106, 191; Comp Ord Depot, 46; 2AOD, 194
1ATF: xxii, 23, 39– 41 *passim*, 63 Australian Govt decision to augment, 94–5; map, 69; map, deployment on Operation Coburg, 107; organisation and operational control, 39–40; perimeter defences, 58, 80, 151–2 *see also* Line Alpha and Line Bravo; selection of Nui Dat base area, 42–4; TAOR, 39, US operational and logistics support, 40
1RAR: xxii, 4, 10, 11, 24, 26, 32: 1RAR Gp, 20, 29; second tour, 113, 122, 128, 130, 132, 139; BCoy, 117
1st Armd Regt, C Sqn, 95
2RAR: 88, 90, 105, 107; second tour, 160, 176, 189
3 Cav Regt, 1 Tp A Sqn, 105
3RAR: 110, 113, 117; second tour, 176, 177, 190, 191, 195
4RAR: 128; second tour, 176, 184, 190–2 *passim*, 195, 201; D Coy, 191
5RAR: 42, 50, 52, 59, 61, 65, 86, 88, 111; second tour, 139, 140, 147, 149, 153, 159; D Coy, 140–1
6RAR: 42, 44, 55–6, 59, 62, 65, 86–7, 88; second tour, 139, 140, 152, 153, 160
7RAR: 88, 90, 92, 105, 107, 111; second tour, 159–60, 161–2, 172, 176
8RAR, 159, 162, 171, 190
9RAR, 139
16 Army Light Aircraft Sqn, 3, 15, 57
17 Const Sqn, RAE, 159
18 NS Trg Bn, 4
102 Fd Bty, 113
104 Sig Sqn, 76
105 Fd Bty, 11
161 Recce Flight/161(Independent) Recce Flight, *throughout*: deployment to Bien Hoa, xxiii, 6–9 *passim*; Estab and Eqpt Tables, 5; formation, 3–9 *passim*; living and maint. facilities at Bien Hoa, 11–14; loan of Cessna O-1 Bird Dog aircraft, 97; optimising role, 87–8; relationships with US flying units, 64; relocation to Nui Dat, 68–74; relocation to Vung Tau (1966), 45–9 *passim*; second relocation to Vung Tau (1971), 193–5;

upgrade to 161 (Independent) Recce Flight, xxiii, 35, 45; departure from SVN, 198–202 *passim*
176 AD Coy, 46
547 Signals Troop, 56, 78

AATTV: deployment, xxii; support ops by 161 Recce Flight, 185, 195–6
Abrams, Creighton, Gen., 126
Adelaide, xix
Agent Orange, 30
AHQ, 5
aid projects *see* civic action
Air America, 165
Air Observation Post (AOP), xvii, 3, 23, 67, 87, 91, 148, 176
air traffic control: establishment of facilities at Luscombe Field, 74–7 *passim*; control of Nui Dat airspace, 143, 145; Fire section, 144; first Luscombe Tower, 76–7, 144; second Luscombe Tower, 143–4
airborne radio communications, xvii: UHF problems, 9, 22
airborne radio direction finding: at Bien Hoa, 23; sigint ops with 547 Sig Tp, 79, 105, 187
aircraft losses/major incidents: Cessna 180, Capt. Donald, 153; Cessna 180, 2Lt. Driver, 140; Cessna 180, Lt. Tizzard, 79; Cessna O-1 Bird Dog, Maj. Constable (KIA), 115–17; Cessna O-1 Bird Dog, Lt. Guivarra, 97–8; Kiowa, Lt. Steel, 196–7; Pilatus Porter, Capt. Donald/2Lt. Jellie, (both KIA), 156; Sioux, Capt. Brooker, 135–6; Sioux, 2Lt. Colclough, 98–9; Sioux, 2Lt. Davies, 59; Sioux, 2Lt. Hutchinson, 89; Sioux, Capt. Hills, 160–1; Sioux, Lt. O'Brien, 98; Sioux, 2Lt. Weaver, 96
aircraft maintenance: at Bearcat and Coral, 118; at Bien Hoa, 15–16, 31; at Nui Dat, 70–3 *passim*, 95–7 *passim*,141–2, 149, 175, 181–2; at Vung Tau, 47–9 *passim*; 'D' Servicings, 63; 'E' Servicings (Cessna), 63, (Porter), 165–6; effects of increased flying hours during 1966, 63; expansion of facilities at Nui Dat, 141–2, 165; rebuild of crashed Sioux, 89; recovery and repair of crashed Cessna O-1 Bird Dog, 98; serviceability rates in Vietnam, 182; US helicopter repair ship USS *Corpus Christi Bay*, 96–7, 112
airfield construction, Nui Dat *see* Luscombe Field
Allman, James, Sgt., *see* photo sections

Amberley RAAF Base, xxiii, 3, 4, 6, 45, 123, 124, 176
An Ngai, 68
ANZAC Battalion: first, 2RAR/NZ, 89; 123
Ap Ngai Giao, 122
Ap Suoi Nghe, 92
APC M-113 see also 3 Cav Regt, 11, 29, 65, 110, 140, 147, 159, 172, 178; fatal incident, 122; D & E Platoon incident, 190
Army of the Republic of (South) Vietnam (ARVN), xxi, xxii, 27, 34, 86, 111, 128: Corps Tactical Zones, 20, III CTZ, 39, 113; map, 21; operations in Phuoc Tuy, 58, 110; units, 1/43 Inf Regt, 166
Artillery Warning and Control Centre, Nui Dat see Kangaroo Control
artillery observation, xix
ARVN see Army of the Republic of (South) Vietnam
Asia, xxi, xxii
Askew, Robert, 2Lt., 59, 60–1, awarded Queen's Commendation for Brave Conduct, 74, see also photo sections
ATC see air traffic control
Australian Army see individual formations, units and bases
Australian Army Aviation: 118; achieves Corps status, 122–3; brief history, xviii–xx; Directorate of, 173; 1 Army Avn Coy, xviii; 1 Avn Regt, 176, formation, 91; Oakey, 199; 16 ALA, 3, 15, 57, formation, xix; 16 AOP Flight, xviii; 57; 161 Recce Flight, *throughout*, see 161 Recce Flight; roles, xix; Museum, 181; 161 Sqn Darwin, 200, 203
Australian Flying Corps, xviii
Australian Government: announces withdrawal of forces, 158; background to involvement in South Vietnam, xx–xxii *passim*; cessation of operations, 191; commitment of forces, xxii; Embassy, Washington, D.C., 118, 176; increase in forces to Brigade-level task force, 31, 94–5
Automatic Personnel Detector (people sniffer), 129–30, 191, 195
Avern, George, Cpl., 16
Avery, Len, Cpl., xvi, 124, 163, 167, 179–80, 181, 182, see also photo sections
AWCC see Kangaroo Control

B-52 bomber airstrikes, 111
Balmoral see Battles, see also fire support bases
Bankstown Airport, xviii
Bao Di, Emperor, xxi
Baria (Phuoc Le), 41, 42, 68, 109, 195
Barlow, Frederick, Capt., 181, 183, 187
Barron, Charles, 2Lt., awarded MID 61; 62, 87, 88, see photo
Battle Efficiency (BE) courses, 5, 119
Battle, Michael, Capt., 141

battlefield surveillance, xix
Battles: Balmoral, 117–18, 118, 121; Binh Ba, 140–1; Coral, 113–15, 118; Long Hais, 159; Long Tan, 118; Nui Le, 191–2
Baxter, Ronald, Sgt., 143, 144
Bean, Basil, Cpl., 35
Bearcat airfield, 107, 118, 135
Bell 47G-2A helicopter, xix
Bell 47G-3B1 helicopter see Sioux
Bell AH-1G Huey Cobra helicopter gunship, 64,123, 86, 150
Bell UH-1 Iroquois helicopter see Iroquois helicopters
Bell OH-58A Kiowa helicopter see Kiowa
Bell, Keith, LAC., 32, 34, 35, see also photo sections
Bell, Robert, WO2., 182, 183
Bennett, Neil, Cfn., 35
Bennett, Philip, Lt Col., 113, 129, 132
Benson, Harold, Maj., 118–20, 125, 127, 129, awarded DFC 139–40, 146, 148, see also photo sections
Bevans, Edward, Cfn., 143
Bien Hoa air base: xxii, xxiii, 4, 8, 9, 10, 14, 15–16, 17, 18, 19, 20, 24, 35, 40, 46, 68, 78, 88, 105, 106, 109, 113, 124; arrival of 161 Recce Flight, 9; establishing camp, 11–13 *passim*; map, 12; Province, 121, 136
Big Daddy see also US Army 54th Avn Coy, Vung Tau, 63–4; detachment and training of 161 Recce Flight pilots, 63–4
Binh Ba rubber plantation: 32, 40, 52, 65, 68, 153; Battle of, 140–1; Operation *Abilene*, 31–2; site of fatal crash, 156
Binh Gia, 59
Binh Tuy Province, 26, 40
Bird Dog (Cessna O-1) light observation aircraft: 5, 30, 121, 128; accident at Black Horse, 98; fatal crash, 115–17; on loan to 161 Recce Flight, 97; rebuild project (Bunny II), 170–1, 179–81
Black Horse airfield, 97–8, 140, 190
Black, John, LAC., 7, 8, 13, 35, see also photo sections
Blissett, Peter, Cpl., 77
Boland, Michael, Capt., 106, 141
Bootes, Peter, Sgt., 48, see also photo sections
Borneo, 4
Bower, Frederick, LCpl., see photo sections
Brewster, Charles, WO., 180–1
Brisbane, 5, 16
Bristol Freighter, 123
Britain: xxii; 94, 176; British Army, 4, 118; 1 Commando Bde, 4
Bronco OV-10A aircraft, 150, 180
Brooker, Edwin, Capt., 123, 127, 131, 135–6
Brown, David, Sgt., 77
Buck, John, Capt., 64
Byng, Max, Cpl., 35
Bysouth, Peter, 2Lt., awarded DFC 171–2, see also photo sections

Index

C-47 Dakota transport aircraft/gunship, 10, 30
C-123 Provider transport aircraft: 13; aerial spraying of defoliant, 30
C-130 Hercules transport aircraft, 8, 10, 13, 30, 40, 123
C-141 Starlifter transport aircraft, 13
Cairns, Kenneth, Capt., 177
Cairnes, Bruce, Cfn., *see* photo sections
Calvert, Philip, Maj.: 166–9 *passim*, 173–4; awarded MID 175–6
Cambodia, xxi
Campbell, Colin, WO2., 48
Campbell, James, Capt., awarded DFC 65, 86, 88, *see also* photo sections
Cape, Timothy, Maj Gen., 6, *see also* photo sections
Caribou aircraft, 30, 141, 151
casualty evacuation (casevac): xx, 161 Recce Flight Sioux, 60–1, 65, 88, 110, 160; by Dustoff Iroquois, 60, 89, 99, 150
Cat Lo, 49
Cayuse OH-6 helicopter, 64, 128
Centurion tanks, deployment: 95; FSB Coral, 115; Balmoral 117; Binh Ba, 140; Long Hais, 159
Cessna 180 fixed wing aircraft: *throughout*; last flight in Vietnam, 176
Cessna O-1 FAC aircraft *see* Bird Dog
Cessna O-2 FAC aircraft, 128, 136
Channells, Gary, Pte., 73, *see also* photo sections
Chiang Kai-Shek, xxi
China, xxi
Chinook helicopter, 29, 53, 72, 79, 99, 119, 128, 134, 156
Church, John, Lt Col., 172
Citizens' Military Force, xviii
civic action: 65, 92; 161 Recce Flight involvement, 83; after Tet offensive, 110
Cockerell, Donald, 2Lt., 22, 52, 56
Coffey, Dennis, 2Lt., 176, 187
Coggan, John, Capt.: awarded DFC 110; 117, 127, *see also* photo sections
Colclough, Roger, 2Lt.: crash 98–9, 127
Cold War, xxi
Collins, Donald, WO1., 157, 162
command and control: xix; 1ATF, 39; at Bien Hoa, 20; *see also* flying operations
command post: 161 facilities at Vung Tau, (1966) 48, (1971) 195; Intelligence Register, 75, 80; Nui Dat, 74–6
Constable, George, Maj.: 91–4, 97, 99, 101, 106, 112, 118, 119, 148, 170; KIA 115–17; *see also* photo sections
Coombs, Ronald, LCpl., 18, 28
Coral *see* Battles; *see also* fire support bases
counterinsurgency doctrine: 126; ops, 58, 83, 126
Courtenay (rubber): 32, 40, 68, 82, 190; Hill as base for operations in 1971, 184
Crane, Richard, Capt., 122
Croker, Michael, Sgt., 143, 198

Crook, Cecil, Pte., 18
Crook, James, Cpl., 6–7, 8, 13–14, 17, 27, 35, *see also* photo sections
CS gas, 134
Cu Chi, 29
Curnow, Stuart, Capt., 141–2, 155, 157
Custance, John, Sgt., 144

D445 Local Force Battalion *see* Viet Cong
Da Nang, xxii
Dat Do, 65, 68, 86, 110, 140, 162
Davies, William, 2Lt., 59
Davis, Terry, WO2., 167, 187
Dawber, Lawrence, Sgt., 15–16
Deacon, Geoffrey, Cpl., 71, Sgt. 188, *see also* photo sections
Deloach, John, Maj., 55
Dennis, Donald, 75, 76, 77, 91, 94, 98, 112, 121, 127, *see also* photo sections; *see also* Trick, Donald, 2Lt.
density altitude: Cessna accident at Black Horse, 140; effect on aircraft performance, 22; effect on Porter safe payload, 155; incident with Sioux, 150–1
detachment: of fixed wing pilots to US 54th Avn Coy, 63; of helicopter pilots to US flying units, 64, 128
Dien Bien Phu, xx
Digweed, John, Capt., 155–6, 160–1, 165
direct support (DS) operations: *throughout*; enhanced capabilities with introduction of Kiowa, 173–4, 181, 184; Operation *Ivanhoe*, 191–2; Operation *Portsea*, 86; Operation *Renmark*; 65; pilot reports, 87; pilot's role and responsibilities, 23, 119–20, 129; versatility of role, 130–1
Domino Theory, xxi
Donald, Barry, Capt.: 127; Cessna crash 153; Porter crash KIA, 156–7, *see also* photo sections
Dong Tam, 196
Doyle, Lawrence, Maj., 57, 63–4, 67, 70, 78, 80–1, 88, 91, 128, *see also* photo sections
Driver, Errol, 2Lt., crash, 140,
DS *see* direct support
Duc My, 52
Dustoff *see* casualty evacuation
Duus, Glen, 2Lt., 98, 106–7, 112, 114, 122, 123, 127, 153

Earley, David, 2Lt., awarded MID, 160
East Timor, 203
Ebner, Clem, Sgt., 32, 34
Einam, Keith, FSgt., 142
Ellis, Jack, Sgt., 48, 72, *see also* photo sections
Ellis, Terrence, Lt., *see* photo sections
Ellwood, Reginald, Capt., 154, 167, 173, 178
Elson, Kenneth, Cpl., 35
Essex-Clark, John, Maj., map 12, 33
Ettridge, Donald, 2Lt., 8, 22

F-4 Phantom USAF FGA aircraft, 11, 16, 64
F-100 USAF FGA aircraft, 9, 11, 49, 99, 132–4
FAC *see* forward air control
Fellenberg, Raymond 'Chuck', Cpl., 95
fire support bases: Andersen, 107; Balmoral, 117–18, 121; Battle of Coral, 113–15; Coral, 121; Harrison, 107; Horseshoe, 86, 100, 111, 162
First Indochina War, xx, xxi
First World War, xvii, xviii
Flanagan, William, Capt., 154–5, 156, 167
flying operations, 161 Recce Flight: *throughout*; 1ATF procedures, 76,83, 86; command and control at Bien Hoa, 24; courier services, 24, 25, 78, 186; direct support helicopter ops *see* direct support; in support of 1 RAR at Bien Hoa, 24–29 *passim*; in support of 1ATF in Phuoc Tuy, 121–23; in support of final ops Vung Tau, 197–201 *passim*; in support of task force admin reqts, 78; increased flying hrs 1967–68, 63; intelligence contribution, 75, 80; mission procedures, 22–4; operational constraints, 20–2; near misses, 30, 150; pilot proficiency checks, 151, 178, 188; Porter ops, 163-5; tasking at Bien Hoa, 26; psyops *see* psychological warfare operations; VR *see* visual reconnaissance;
forced landings: Cessna 180, Lt. Tizzard, 79; Porter, Maj. Harden, 186; Porter, 2Lt. McGhie, 195–6; Sioux, Lt. Askew, 59; Sioux, Maj. Benson, 140; Sioux, 2Lt. Bysouth, 172; Sioux, 2Lt. Gibson, 177; Sioux, 2Lt. Hayes, 172; Sioux, Maj. Hill-Smith, 162; Sioux, Capt. Monteith, 186–7; Sioux, 2Lt. Partridge, 162; Sioux, 2Lt. Rich, 53
Forrest, Bernard 'Father', Capt., 82, 97, 99–100, 106, 108, 115, 127, 134, *see also* photo sections
forward air control (FAC) operations: 75, 98–9, 186; call sign Jade, 128, 150; case for Army pilots conducting FAC ops, 174; co-op with 161 Recce Flight, 64; direction of air strikes, 64, 132–4; top cover operations with 161 Recce Flight pilots, 128, 167
France, xx, xxi
Fritsch, Adam, 2Lt., *see also* photo sections
FSB *see* fire support bases

Gardner, Reginald, Lt. Col., 112
Garton, Peter, 2Lt., 127, *see also* photo sections
Gibson, Fraser, 2Lt.: 172, 183, 189 awarded DFC 177
Glendinning, Duncan, Maj., 45
Goldspink, Ross, 2Lt., 87, 96, *see also* photo sections
Graham, Stuart, Brig., 74, 85–86, 95
Green, John, Sgt., *see* photo sections
Gordon, Russell, Cpl., *see* photo sections
Goritchan, John, Cfn., *see* photo sections

Grey, Ronald, Lt Col., 162
Guild, John, Lt., 22, 25, 28, *see also* photo sections
Guivarra, Thomas, 2Lt.: xv, 78; awarded MID 81, 87; crash 97–8, *see also* photo sections
Gygar, Terry, Lt.: 167, 177; Gygar's Guerillas, 178

Hammett, Anthony, Maj., 115
harassment and interdiction (H&I), 80
Harden, Neil, Maj., 175–6, 177–9, 181, 182, 184, 185, 186, 188, 191, 193, 194, 195, 197, 199, *see also* photo sections
Hardidge, Frederick, Cfn., 147, *see also* photo sections
Harmer, John, Sgt., *see* photo sections
Harris, Allan, Sgt., *see* photo sections
Hart, Robert, Bdr., 27
Hat Dich 41, 68, 92, 122, 128, 149, 150, 153
Hayes, Terry, 2Lt.: awarded DFC 172; 177
HE *see* rockets, high explosive
Heron, William, 2Lt., 128
Higginbottom, A., Sgt., 35, *see also* photo sections
Hill-Smith, Graeme, Maj.: 148–9, 151, 152, 154, 157; awarded DFC 162, 164–5, 167, *see also* photo sections
Hills, Christopher, Cpl., *see* photo sections
Hills, Robert, Capt., Sioux crash, 160–1, 169, 176, 188
Hoa Long, 41, 65, 68, 110, 141, 171
Hoare, Rockleigh 'Rocky', Sgt.: 188–9; awarded MID 167, *see also* photo sections
Ho Chi Minh, xx–xxii *passim*
Ho Chi Minh Trail, xxi, 68, 85
Hodges, Ronald, Cfn., *see* photo sections
Hodgkinson, Robert, Cfn., 35
Hong Kong, 4, 118
Honner, Bronx, Maj., 132
honours and awards; 65, 74, 81, 83, 90–1, 108, 110, 124, 141, 159, 160, 162, 167, 171–72, 175, 177, 179, 192, 197, *see also* Appendix 2
Horseshoe, *see* fire support bases
Howard, John, Lt., 187, 190
HQ AFV, 39
Hudnott, William, Sgt., 145, 181, 198
Hue, 108
Huey *see* Iroquois helicopters
Hughes, Ronald, Brig., 95, 106, 126, 182
Humphrey, Richard, Cpl., 13, 35
Humphreys, Benjamin (Len), Cpl., 18
Hutchinson, Ross, 2Lt.: 74, 112, awarded MID, 108; crash, 89, 96, 98; *see also* photo sections

Idiens, Les, Sgt., 189, 198
Indochina, xxi
Indonesia: xxii; Indonesian Confrontation, 4
Intelligence: 1ATF difficulties with verification, 81–2; 161 Recce Flight contribution, 82, 115–17; frustration experienced by 161 pilots, 82, 167; sources, 82
Iron Triangle, 20

Index

Iroquois helicopters, 9, 25, 64, 119, 128; RAAF 9 Squadron, 89, 130

Jackson, Owen, Brig., 39, 57–8, 67, 85
Jade *see* forward air control
Jamieson, Michael, Capt., 154
Japan, xxi
Jellie, Alan, 2Lt., Porter crash KIA, 156–7; *see also* photo sections
Jenkins, Daryl, LCpl., 46
Jewell, Jack, Sgt., 48, 76, 144, *see also* photo sections
Jones, James, Cpl., 71, *see also* photo sections
Jordan, James, Cpl., 35
JTC, Canungra, 5

Kangaroo Control (Nui Dat AWCC), 48, 75, 143; functions, 77
Kangaroo Pad, 87, 143
Keating, David, Pte., 70
Kemp, John, Maj., 115
Kennett, Douglas, Sgt.: 63; awarded MID 74
Kerr, Keith, LAC., *see* photo sections
Kimberley, xviii
Kiowa OH-58A LOH: 128; introduction to operational service, 173–4, 181–5; lease from US Army, 173, 181; operational effectiveness, 184–5; operational hazards, 183–4; policy on arming, 173–4, 182; radio relay capability, 184; technical and pilot training, 182
Knight, Richard, Capt., 45–6, 49–50, 74, 88, *see also* photo sections
Korea, xviii
Korean War, xxi, 67, 95
Kruschev, Nikita, President, xxi
Kuching, 4

La Van, 122
Land clearing team, 149
Lang Phuoc Hai, 65
Laos, xxi
Larney, Lloyd, FSgt., 8, 11, 15, 17, 35, *see also* photo sections
Ledan, Brian, Capt., 60
Lennon, Warren, Maj., 54, *see also* photo sections
Lidster, Paul: Cfn., 46–7, 49; Sgt., 100, 141, 145, 170, 180
Light Green, 121, 155
Lindgren, Eric, Cfn., 47
Line Alpha, 43, 52, 56, 65
Line Bravo, 44, 65
Lipscombe, Paul: Capt., 3–4; Maj., 7, 11, 13, 15, 16, 17, 22, 24–5, 26, 28, 30, 31, 45–6, 54–5, 56, 88, 176, 188, *see also* photo sections
Little, Robert, Cpl., 100
logistics: US/Australia Logistics Agreement, 5; difficulties at Bien Hoa, 15-16, 31
Long Binh: 16, 31, 68, 105, 106, 109, 113, 135, 201; rocket attacks, 136

Long Dien, 68, 110, 111, 171
Long Green, 121
Long Khanh Province, 40, 68, 159, 190, 191
Long Hai hills, 40, 41, 65, 68, 100, 111, 121–2, 159, 162, 172, 186, 195
Long Le, District HQ, 41
Long Phuoc: 41; resettlement, 42
Long Son Island, 61
Long Tan: 41, 55; Battle of, 56; resettlement, 42
Luscombe, Bryan, Capt., KIA, xviii
Luscombe Field: 144, 177, 203; construction, 67; establishment of air traffic control facilities, 74–7 *passim*; 143; fire and rescue section, 144; first landing, 67; official opening, 67

M-16, Armalite, automatic rifle, 62, 90
M-60 machine gun: 27, 152; door-mounted, Sioux, 154; fitment to Sioux litters, 153–4
M-73 machine gun: fitment to Sioux, 154
McClymont, Stanley, 2Lt., 127, 148
McFerran, David, 2Lt., 74, 81, 97, *see also* photo sections
McGhie, John, Capt., 185, 190, 195, 197, 198–9, *see also* photo sections
Machin, Leonard, Lt., 161
Machine gun: Browning .50 cal, 152; MG-42 Spandau, 154; *see also* M-60 and M-73
McKay, Gary, 2Lt.: awarded MC 191–2
Mackay, Kenneth, Maj Gen., 39, 46
Mackworth, Digby, Lt., 176, 187, 189, *see also* photo sections
McMahon, Rt Hon Sir William, 191
maintenance *see* aircraft maintenance
Malaya, 4, 118, 148, 176
Malayan Emergency, xxii, 58
Malaysia, xxii, 4
Mao Tse Tung, xxi
Markcrow, Francis, Capt., 151, 153, 164
Matheson, Hector 'Tub', Capt., 88, 124, 176, 183–4, 193, 195, 197, 199, 200, 201, 202, *see also* photo sections
Matthews, John, Pte., 101
May Tao, 40, 68, 90, 128, 164
Mecham, Creagh, 2Lt., 195, 200
medical evacuation, 35
Meehan, Michael, 2Lt., 65, 93–4, *see also* photo sections
Mekong Delta, 185
Menear, Peter, Cpl., 35, *see also* photo sections
Menzies, David, Sgt., *see also* photo sections
Millar, Robert, Capt.: 187; awarded MID 167
Miller, Charles: SSgt., xix; Maj., 170, 180
mine, anti-personnel: M-16, 111; M18A-1 Claymore, 147, 152
minefield, barrier: enemy use of mines, 111; establishment, 86
Mitchell, Felix, Cfn., 47, 48, 72, 101–2, *see also* photo sections
Moffatt, Donald, 2Lt., 116, 120, 122, 127, 129, 150

Moller, Geoffrey, Sgt., *see* photo sections
Monteith, Rowan, Capt., 177–8, 183, 185, 186, 190, 194, 195, 198, 199
morale: 182; infantry ops, 139; mail delays,17; Possum Mail, 78; recreational activities, 142–43; pilots, 179; RAAF-Army personnel relationships,14–15
Moore, S., Pte., 98–9
Muller, W., Pte., 70
Murray, Alan, Cfn., *see* photo

Nelson, Walter, Cpl., 179, *see also* photo sections
New, Ronald, Sgt., *see also* photo sections
New Zealand: 127; Army: 161 Battery, 155; farewell of Victor Coy by 161 Recce Flight, 93; pilots posted to 161 Recce Flight, 123, 124, 151–5, 170, 196–7, Victor Coy RNZIR: 88, 160; Whisky Coy, RNZIR, 160
Ngo Dinh Diem, President, xx–xxi
Nichol, Howard, WO2., *see* photo sections
Nicklin, Gary, Cfn., *see* photo sections
Nolan, Peter, Sgt., *see* photo sections
Normanton, xix
North Vietnam, xx, xxi, xxii, 128
North Vietnamese Army (NVA): xxi, xxii, 41, 113–14; 33rd Regiment, 191; 1/33rd Regt, 140
Nui Dat: *throughout*; map of Task Force base, 69; SAS Hill, 143; selection and establishment of task force area, 40; perimeter defences, 151–2; withdrawal of Australian forces, 195–7
Nui Dinh(s), 40, 53, 59, 67, 113, 159, 160
Nui Le, 191
Nui Nghe, 52
Nui Thi Vai(s), 8, 40, 58, 59, 67, 147, 195

O'Brien, Capt P., crash 98; 106, 112, 116, 123
OCS, Portsea, Victoria, 3
OH-13 helicopter, 24–5,
Okinawa, 24
O'Malley, Capt., 97
O'Neill, Keith., Lt Col., 159
Operations: *Abilene*, 31–2; *Ainslie*, 92; *Ashgrove Tram*, 111; *Atherton*, 92, 159; *Ballarat*, 92; *Blaxland*, 113; *Bondi*, 153; *Bravo*, 65; *Bribie*, 65–6; *Brisbane*, 53, 55; *Cairns*, 92; *Caloundra*, 65; *Camden*, 149–50; *Canberra*, 59; *Capitol*, 130; *Capricorn*, 160; *Clayton*, 111; *Coburg*, 105–9, 110 *passim*; *Concrete 1*, 160, 161–2; *Concrete 2*, 160; *Cooktown Orchid*, 111; *Crimp*, 29; *Cung Chung*, 171–2, 177; *Dandenong*, 111; *Elwood*, 122; *Enoggera*, 44, 52; *Federal*, 136; *Finschafen*, 159; *Forrest*, 94; *Goodwood II*, 132; *Hammer*, 140; *Hammersley*, 159; *Hawkesbury*, 128; *Hayman*, 61; *Hermit Park*, 191; *Hobart*, 55; *Hump*, 26; *Ingham*, 61–2; *Iron Fox*, 184; *Ivanhoe*, 191–2; *Kenmore*, 94; *Keperra*,159; *King's Cross*, 153; *Kingston*, 152; *Lavarack*, 152; *Marsden*, 153; *New Life*, 26–8 *passim*; *North Ward*, 191; *Oakleigh*, 111; *Overlander*, 136; *Overlord*, 190–1; *Paddington*, 90; *Phoi Hop*, 162, 177; *Pinnaroo*, 111; *Platypus*, 122; *Portsea*, 86; *Queanbeyan*, 54, 59, 61; *Renmark*, 65–6, 111; *Road Runner*, 128; *Ross*, 153; *Santa Fe*, 94; *Sydney 1*, 52; *Sydney 2*, 52; *Tamborine*, 65; *Tiger Balm*, 132; *Toan Thang I*, 113–15, 118; map 114; *Vaucluse*, 59
operational areas (AO): Columbus, 107; Surfers, 113, 117; Tuggerah, 128
Otago, Mervyn 'Darky', Sgt., 35
Otter aircraft, 30, 128
OTU, Scheyville, 116, 123–4, 192

pacification: doctrine, 57–8; ops in Phuoc Tuy, 85, 126, 128, 136–57 *passim*, 158-60 *passim*, 174
Partridge, Thomas, 2Lt., 162
patrols: 161 Recce Flight personnel, 146–8
Patterson, Donald, Cpl., 35
Payne, David, Sgt., *see* photo sections
Peacock, Kevin, Lt., 74, *see also* photo sections
'people sniffer' *see* Automatic Personnel Detector
Perth, xviii
Phillips, Terence, WO2., *see* photo sections
Phu Loi, 97, 166, 180
Phuoc Tuy Province: *throughout*; description, 40–1; map, 33; pilot's view, 67–8
Pike, Geoffrey, Cfn., 72, *see also* photo sections
Pilatus Porter fixed wing aircraft: 142; air photography, 156; Beta approach technique, 164; fitment of rocket pods, 156, 164; illumination (flare) missions, 156, 163; psyops, 163–4; replacing Cessna 180, 155, 158; specifications and capabilities, 155–6
Pinkham, Neville, Capt., 22, 30, 55, *see also* photo sections
Pleiku, 185
Porter *see* Pilatus Porter
Possum: *throughout*; call sign for 161 Recce Flight pilots, 9
Power, Ian Maj., 81
Preece, Alec, Lt Col., 32–4 *passim*
psychological warfare operations (psyops): assistance with cordon and search ops, 107, 111, 122; at Bien Hoa, 24; 'Chieu Hoi' program, 93; fitment of voice broadcasting equipment to Cessna and Sioux aircraft, 92–3; fitment to Porter, 163–4; leaflet dropping, 94;
Purvis, John, Lt., 5, 6,17

QANTAS, 200
qualified flying instructor (QFI), xix, 4, 148, 182
Quee, Brian, WO2., 98
Queensland, 3, 5

RA Svy Corps, xviii
RAAF *see* Royal Australian Air Force
RAA, 3
RAASC, 3; 5 Coy, 45

radio rebroadcast (relay): description and 161 Recce Flight capability, 53–4, 176; Kiowa ops, 184; Porter ops, 156
RAEME, xix, 5, 13, 46, 71, 124
Rankin, John, Pte., 70
Rawlings, John, Cpl., 16
Ready Reaction Force, 1 ATF: 178; deployment to Binh Ba, 140
Reardon, Brian, Sgt., 189, 193, *see also* photo sections
Republic of Vietnam, xxi
Reynolds, Michael, Lt., 183, 195, 198, *see also* photo sections
Reynolds, Owen, Cfn.,13
Rich, Rob, 2Lt., 53, *see also* photo sections
Richards, William, Spr., 144
Roberts, Philip, Capt., 74, 77, 106, *see also* photo sections
Robinson, Peter, Capt., 70–1, 96, 97, 100, 141, 149, *see also* photo sections
rockets, 2.75-inch folding fin, white phosphorous target marking and high explosive: fitment to Cessna aircraft, 54–5; introduction of 7-pod launchers, 99–100; on Porter aircraft, 164
Rogers, Peter, 2Lt.: 119, 123, 128., 130, 132, 133; awarded DFC, 141, 147; Rogers' Rangers, 147
Routes (Phuoc Tuy): *2*: 41, 42, 52, 68, 191; *15*: 41, 42, 59, 67, 128, *23:* 41, 86; *44:* 41
Royal Air Force: Central Flying School, xix, 4, 118
Royal Australian Air Force (RAAF): xviii, xx, 5; 9 Sqn, 40, 54, 63, 96, 105, 130, 164, 172; 35 Sqn, 40, 194; Air Movements Section, Nui Dat, 141; Basic Flying Training School, Pt Cook, Victoria, xix; Bushranger gunships, 149, 150; Directorate of Air Force Safety, 115; operational and technical oversight of Australian Army Aviation flying operations, xix–xx; 54–5, 173–4; operational constraints, 190–1; Support Command, 31; Transport Flight Vietnam, 14; Wallaby Airlines (35 Sqn), 141
Royal Australian Navy (RAN): xix, xx, 148; Fleet Air Arm, 148; HMAS *Sydney*, 6–7, 8, 45, 74, 155, 189, 195, 201; MV *Jeparit*, 17
RMC, Duntroon, 91
Rung Sat, 40, 61, 67, 194
Ruttley, J., Pte., 70
Ryan, John 'Skeeta', Sgt., 89, 95

Saigon, xxii, 6, 16, 40, 59, 105, 108, 113, 118, 120, 128, 135, 201
Salmon, Victor, 2Lt., 55, 63, 81, *see also* photo sections
SAS: 39, 44, 112, 152, 198; high jinks with 161 Recce Flight, 111–12; involvement with 161 Recce Flight (recce, insertion), 128, 184; intelligence pre-Long Tan, 55; preparation for patrols, 83, 147; SAS Hill, 143; 'tractor job', 82, 112

Scafe, Owen, WO2., 6, 27
Schafer, Richard, Cpl., 79, *see also* photo sections
Scott, Colin, 2Lt.: 62, 81; awarded DFC 90–1; *see also* photo sections
Scott, Dennis, Cfn., 143
Scott, Keith, WO., 141–2
Scott, Peter, Lt Col., 177
Second Indochina War, xxi
Second World War, xx, xxi, xxii, 25, 95, 121, 154
Shallcross, George, Maj., 63
Shannon, Wayne, WO2., 185, *see also* photo sections
Sherman, Allan, Cpl., *see* photo sections
signals intelligence (sigint) *see* airborne radio direction finding
Sims, Derek, WO2., 188–9
Singapore, 45, 123
Sinnott, Ian, 2Lt., 179, 191
Sioux helicopter: *throughout*; arming of aircraft, 153–4; conversion training of American pilots by Captain Bevan Smith, 25
Skinner, Barry, Cfn., 142, 147
Slocombe, William, Lt Col., 3, *see also* photo sections
Slope 30, 92
SME, xviii
Smith, Alfred, WO2., 145
Smith, Bevan: Sgt., xviii; Capt., 5, 8–9, 22, 25, 28–9, 30, 32–5 *passim*, medevac 35, *see also* photo sections
Smith, Robert, Capt., 164
Smith, Charles, Cpl., 18
Smith, Eric, Lt Col., 111
Smith, Malcolm, 2Lt.: 155; awarded DFC 159
Smythe, Christopher, Cfn., 101
Solomon, John, Sgt., *see* photo sections
Song Rai, 40
Sonneveld, John, 2Lt.: 178, 183, 184; awarded DFC 192
South Vietnam, xviii, xx, xxi, xxii
Southeast Asia, 95
Spoor, Peter, 2Lt., 108, 127, 153
Standard Operating Procedures (SOPs): crashed aircraft, 136; initial 161 Recce Flight, 5; 9 Sqn, RAAF, 190–1
starlight scope, 62, 147
Steel, Grant, Lt.: 178, 195; awarded DFC 197; crash 196–7
Stevens, Philip, 2Lt.: 133; awarded MID 139
Stein, John, 5
Subic Bay, 6
Suez, xxii, 94
Sullivan, Brian, Sig., 77
Sundowner Club, 100
Suoi Chau Pha, Battle of, 92
Suoi Nhac, 190
Supple, Robert, Capt., 60
Swain, Michael, FSgt., 74, *see also* photo sections
Swartz, The Hon. Reginald, *see* photo sections

Sycamore helicopter, 148
Sydney, xviii

Tan Son Nhut, 16, 123, 165, 200
TAOR *see* tactical area of responsibility
tactical area of responsibility: 39, 128; extension of 1 ATF TAOR, 94, 121
target marking *see* rockets
Tasmania, 4
Tet, (Lunar New Year festival): 100; 161 Recce Flight on Operation *Coburg*, 105–9 *passim*; 1968 Offensive, 105, 121, 126, 136, 139, 148, 153; deployment of task force units, 106; effect on communist and US-led forces, 110; launch by opposing forces, 108; in Phuoc Tuy, 109–10; Second General Offensive, May 1968, 113, 126 *see also* fire support bases Coral and Balmoral
Thorp, Ralph, Cpl., 13, 35, *see also* photo sections
Thrush, Kevin, Cfn., *see* photo sections
Thua Tich, 41, 68, 152
Tidd, Donald, Flg Off., 15
Tiger armed reconnaissance helicopter, 203
Timmins, Charles 'Peter', Sgt., 49
Tizzard, Steve, D.Lt., 79, 127, *see also* photo sections
Tolson, J., Gen., 154
Trick, Donald, 2Lt., 75, *see also* photo sections, *see also* Dennis, Donald
Triplett, Thomas, 2Lt., 200

U-2 high altitude surveillance aircraft, 10
UK Army Air Corps: xviii, xix, 4; 656 Squadron, 4
United Nations, 203
United States of America: xviii, xxii, 85, 94; background to involvement in South Vietnam, xxi–xxii *passim*
United States Army: 1st Inf Div, HQ 25, 32; 1RAR op con 20; 1/83rd Arty Coy, Nui Dat, 70; 3rd Fd Hosp, Saigon, 59; 3/17 Air Cav, 173, 187–88; 9th Inf Div, Bearcat, 86, 118; 11th Armd Cav, Black Horse, 86; 54th Avn Coy, Phu Loi, 97; 54th Avn Coy, Vung Tau, 63, 128; 82nd Avn Bn, 25; 93rd Evac Hospital, Bien Hoa, 35; 173rd Airborne Bde (Separate), xxii, 9, 10, 11, 20, 24, 42, 78; 199th Lt Inf Div, 107; 334 Assault Helicopter Coy, 108; Avn Centre, Fort Rucker, Alabama, xix, 119, 176; Avn Centre, Pentagon, 119; avn spt, 24–5, 32; D/16 Cavalry, 11, 17–18; HQ II Field Force, Long Binh, 39, 106; Radio Research Unit, 11, 78
US Air Force, 9
US Army Aviation, xviii, 111
US Marine Corps, xxii
US Military Assistance Command Vietnam (MACV), xxii, 39

Vallance, Robert, Sig., 135–6
Viet Cong: xxi–xxii, 24, 27, 52, 65, 92, 110, 111, 155, 171; 5VC Div, 90, 92; 274 MF Regt, 32, Binh Ba Guerilla Unit, 140; 68, 86, 90, 149–50, 153; 275 MF Regt, 32, 68, 90; ambushes, 28, 32; C25 Coy, 122; D445 Bn (Provincial Mobile Force), 42, 55, 61, 86, 109, 152, 159, 162; D800 MF Bn, 26; forces in Phuoc Tuy, 41–2; Q726 MF Regt, 26
Vincent, Donald, Maj Gen.: 78, 105; pilot training, 135
Vinh Thanh, 122
visual reconnaissance (VR): throughout; development of techniques, 62, 80–1; introduction of top cover technique, 127–8; mentoring, 127, 148–9; night VR with Porter flare drops, 187; scope of task, 23
Vo Dat, 27
von Muenchhausen, Holger, Lt., 8–9, 22, 25, 27, 35, *see also* photo sections
VR *see* visual reconnaissance
Vung Tau, 6, 7, 8–9, 14, 15, 35, 115, 128, 131, 164, 180; Back Beach area, 45–6, 50, 54, Special Zone, 40

War Zone D, 24, 26, 30
Washington D.C., 118, 119, 176
Watson, Philip, Sgt., 201
Weaver, Blair, 2Lt., crash, 96; 98, *see also* photo sections
Webster, Michael, Capt., 45–6, 50, 70, *see also* photo sections
Western Australia, xviii, 124
Westmoreland, William, Gen., 39, 58, 126
Weyand, Frederick, Lt Gen., 109
White, A., Capt., 65
white phosphorus (WP) *see* rockets
Whitehead, Maj., 121
Williamson, Brig Gen (US), 24
Willis, Rex, Cfn., 35, 47, 48
Wilson, Eardley, Cpl., 35, *see also* photo sections
Womal, Cpl., KIA 61
Wood, Harold, LAC., 35, 49
Wood, Laurence, Cpl., 179, *see also* photo sections
Wools-Cobb, Stuart, Sgt., 48, *see also* photo sections
Wright, Graeme 'Blue', 2Lt., 195, 201
Wright, John, Capt.: awarded MID 62, 64, 67, 81, 88, 97, 99, *see also* photo sections
Wright, William, Cpl., *see* photo sections

Xuyen Moc: 41, 68, 86, 90, 96; civic aid by 161 Flight, 83

Yielding, Robert, Sgt.: awarded MID 167

Young, Robert, SSgt.: awarded MID 83

Zitzlesberger, Robert, Sgt.: awarded MID 179, *see also* photo sections

Printed in Great Britain by
Amazon.co.uk, Ltd.,
Marston Gate.